Fulton J. Sheen

Ph.D., D.D., LITT.D., LL.D.

Agrégé en Philosophie de l'Université de Louvain

and

The Catholic University of America

Originally Published and Copyrighted by

The Bruce Publishing Company of Milwaukee, Wisconsin in 1940

Nihil obstat: H. B. Ries, Censor librorum

Imprimatur: ✠ Samuel A. Stritch, Archiepiscopus Milwaukiensis

The *Nihil obstat* ("Nothing stands in the way") and the *Imprimatur* ("Let it be printed") indicate clearance for publication and the authorization by the bishop where an author lives or where the work is published. The clearing of works for publication does not necessarily imply approval of an author's viewpoint or his or her manner of handling a subject.

In the case of this book, the *Nihil obstat* and the *Imprimatur* apply only to the original work and not to the foreword, annotations, notes, or any other material added to this edition by Economic Justice Media, an imprint of the Center for Economic and Social Justice (CESJ). CESJ takes no position on the faith-based doctrine of any religion. Its analysis and commentary are confined to matters pertaining to the natural law and human reason on which social teachings are necessarily based.

If anyone has a disagreement with CESJ on anything pertaining to its understanding and presentation of the "Just Third Way," we invite that person or persons to present their arguments and evidence in accordance with the rules of civil debate. If competent ecclesiastical authority has questions concerning CESJ's understanding of any matters pertaining to faith and morals as taught by the Catholic Church or any other religion, or believes that CESJ has distorted or misinterpreted these matters in any way, we request the opportunity to enter into dialogue with that authority to clear up any differences or misunderstandings.

Dedicated
To
Mary Immaculate
The Mother
of
Him
Who Restored to Us
The Glorious Liberty of the Children of God

•

Editor's Note

Misspellings and typographical errors in the original text have been corrected without noting. Extended quotes have been offset from the main text to improve legibility. Endnotes at the end of the text were shifted to the end of the chapter. Some sources and individuals could not be identified from the evidence given in the text or readily available sources, and were left uncited. Annotations and additional endnotes are indicated by "[Ed.]" at the end of the note. Additions to the author's notes are indicated by putting the addition in brackets, *e.g.*, "[Addition. — Ed.]." A bibliography and index have been added.

Acknowledgements

CESJ thanks Guy C. Stevenson, Project Manager, who first proposed that CESJ republish works by the late Archbishop Fulton J. Sheen in the public domain, and Jeanna Casey who acted as Assistant Project Manager.

CESJ also thanks Dr. Norman G. Kurland, president of CESJ, and Dawn K. Brohawn, CESJ's Director of Communications, for their suggestions and reviews of the work-in-process, and Rowland L. Brohawn for designing the cover and reviewing the formatting of this edition.

The assistance of the staff at the library at the Catholic University of America who researched the copyright status of the cover photo, and that of the Diocese of Rochester, New York, who found the information in their archives, is greatly appreciated.

CESJ particularly thanks Photographer Louis Fabian Bachrach, for giving his gracious permission to use the photograph of Fulton J. Sheen he took in 1965 for the cover of this book.

Most of all, CESJ would like to thank Fulton Sheen, whose work in the moral basis for expanded capital ownership complements and supports the Just Third Way and its reliance on Louis O. Kelso's and Mortimer J. Adler's three principles of economic justice: Participation, Distribution, and Limitation (Harmony).

Contents

Foreword

It now remains to prove that private property is the economic guarantee of human liberty. The basis of freedom on the inside of man, we know — it is his rational soul. But has freedom any support on the outside of man? We would not have to inquire into the external guarantee of our freedom, if we were purely spiritual. But inasmuch as we are composed of body and soul, matter and spirit, we need some visible and external sign of our invisible and spiritual freedom.

— Fulton J. Sheen, *Freedom Under God*

The theory of the Communists may be summed up in the single sentence: Abolition of private property.

— Karl Marx. *The Communist Manifesto*

WHY DOES THE WORLD need the republication of a "long lost" book on the subject of "capitalism versus communism," even by the renowned Catholic "televangelist," Archbishop Fulton J. Sheen? Hasn't communism been defeated with the dissolution of the Soviet Union, and with China becoming more capitalist as its economy expands? Isn't the world becoming more free and democratic with every passing day?

Why? Because at no time in living memory has there been less true human freedom. Even the idea of freedom has decayed to the point where it is effectively meaningless for most people.

In former ages individuals and groups were enslaved. There was, however, generally a clear legal distinction between those who were free, and those who were unfree.[1] This distinction has been lost. Today the proletarian (propertyless) condition is the norm for most people[2] — and lack of capital ownership is tantamount to slavery.

As Sheen notes in this book in support of his thesis on the necessity of true freedom, "Power follows property,

---

[1] As chattel slavery has been abolished, new forms have developed. See Dr. Kevin Bales, *Disposable People: New Slavery in the Global Economy*. Berkley, California: University of California Press, 2004.

[2] See Goetz Briefs, *The Proletariat: A Challenge to Western Civilization*. New York: McGraw-Hill Book Company, Inc., 1937.

and they who own things to a great extent own persons."[3]
If you own capital, you are free. If you do not own capital,
even if you are legally free, you are to all intents and purposes a slave.[4] As Sheen explains,

> Once you concentrate property in the hands of the few, you
> create slaves; when you decentralize it, you restore liberty.
> The objection of the Church to slavery is not that the
> slaves are poor. Slaves need not all be poor. . . . The Catho-
> lic approach is quite different. It starts with the fact that
> no material thing, not even the whole world, shall be al-
> lowed to interfere with the right of a person to attain his
> ultimate end by the exercise of his free will.[5]

Different religions and philosophies may disagree on
why people should be free. They often differ on the means
by which this can be accomplished. They even argue about
what "freedom" means, as Sheen makes clear in this book.
The goal itself, however, is unquestioned.

The Importance of Private Property

To understand why private property is essential to freedom, we need to know what "property" is. "Property" is
not the thing owned. Property is, rather, the natural right
to be an owner, and the socially determined bundle of
rights that limit and define how an owner may exercise
what is owned within a social context. Property means the
right to control what is owned, and enjoyment of the fruits
of ownership.

---

[3] *Freedom Under God*, 38; cf. "Power naturally and necessarily
follows property." Daniel Webster, Massachusetts Constitutional
Convention of 1820; "[W]hoever has no property all too easily
becomes property." Heinrich A. Rommen, *The Natural Law*. Indianapolis, Indiana: Liberty Fund, Inc., 1998, 208.
[4] "Freedom is not an empty sound; it is not an abstract idea; it is
not a thing that nobody can feel. It means, — and it means nothing else, — the full and quiet enjoyment of your own property. If
you have not this, if this be not well secured to you, you may call
yourself what you will, but you are a slave." William Cobbett, *A
History of the Protestant Reformation in England and Ireland*
(1827), § 456.
[5] *Freedom Under God*, 39.

The universal prohibition against theft (*e.g.*, "Thou shalt not steal") implies that private property is a fundamental human right, however much understanding of it may be distorted. Even Marxist communism unconsciously acknowledges the validity of private property by asserting that "surplus value" is *stolen* from workers and consumers.[6] If the workers and consumers did not have private property in "surplus value," how could it be wrong for the capitalists to take it?

That is why we can say no one should be denied the right to own, and what is owned is, in human terms, *owned* individually or jointly "against" everyone else. What someone owns ordinarily cannot be taken without the free consent of the owner(s). As John Locke commented, "what property have I in that, which another may by right take, when he pleases, to himself?"[7]

No one, however, may have absolute or unlimited *use* (exercise) of what is owned. Nor is it expedient that everything be privately owned. For example, while in theory there is nothing that cannot be privately owned, in practice most people would agree that atomic weapons (if they should even exist at all) are not appropriate for private ownership.

Thus, in any discussion of private property, it is critical to realize that while the right to own is inalienable and inherent in each human person, no one can *use* what is owned to harm others or society (the common good) as a whole. Neither can anyone's right to be an owner, or what is owned, be used in any way that inhibits or prevents others from becoming owners or using what they own. This is a matter of prudence, social necessity, and plain common sense.

Sheen and Private Property

That is the legal case for the importance of private property. We have to keep in mind, however, that the title

---

[6] Marx did not invent the term "surplus value," but he developed it in Chapter 8 of *Das Kapital* (1867).

[7] John Locke, *Second Treatise on Government*, § 140.

of this book is "Freedom Under *God*." Sheen's purpose was not to present a treatise or contract delineating humanity's legal rights and duties in human society. Our constitutions, bills of rights, and legal systems are intended to serve that purpose.[8]

Rather, Sheen's purpose was to examine humanity's *moral* responsibilities. In this book, Sheen makes the *moral* case for the importance of private property and its critical role as the prop for true freedom. Even then, he acknowledges the primacy of rights such as life, liberty, and property in human affairs: "[M]an has certain inalienable rights which no one can take away — not even the State."[9]

Moral obligations are "not enforced by human law."[10] They are, instead, something that most people would agree are consistent with basic principles of "right" and "wrong." In Sheen's view, such moral obligations govern our relations with our fellows guided or directed not by human authority under justice, but (for people of faith) by divine authority, under charity.

That is not to say that human laws should not be moral. It does mean that not everything that is moral must or should be enforced by human law backed up with the coercive power of the State. As Aquinas explained,

> Human government is derived from the Divine government, and should imitate it. Now although God is all-powerful and supremely good, nevertheless He allows certain evils to take place in the universe, which He might prevent, lest, without them, greater goods might be forfeited, or greater evils ensue. Accordingly in human government also, those who are in authority, rightly tolerate cer-

---

[8] See William W. Crosskey, *Politics and the Constitution in the History of the United States*. Chicago, Illinois: University of Chicago Press, 1953, for an in-depth analysis of what happens when special interests are able to subvert the original intent of the lawmakers and control the law for their own purposes.
[9] *Freedom Under God*, 74.
[10] Leo XIII, *Rerum Novarum* ("On Capital and Labor"), 1891, § 22.

tain evils, lest certain goods be lost, or certain greater evils be incurred.[11]

There is a very great evil that can "ensue" when someone tries to criminalize everything he or she regards as immoral. That is the possibility that the one making the judgment might be mistaken as to the objective evil of something, and the degree of harm criminalization has the potential to cause. Making everything that is considered immoral also illegal would unnecessarily take away the liberty essential to our full development as human persons.

This is a special danger with respect to laws based on religious beliefs. However true religious beliefs may be, they are necessarily regarded as opinions by the State and society at large — even if everyone in that society holds the same religious beliefs. Freedom of conscience otherwise ceases to have any meaning.[12]

For example, a Jew or a Muslim may regard eating pork as immoral, where a Christian sees nothing wrong in it, while a Buddhist or Hindu might regard all three as unenlightened for eating meat at all. Should the State then prohibit the production, sale and consumption of all animal products? Obviously not.

Similarly, can we legislate against greed, envy, pride, gluttony, or any of the other "seven deadly sins," and force people to be generous, content with their lot, humble, or ascetic? Sheen certainly disagrees. As he explains,

> The asceticism of Communism leaves nothing to free choice; everything is imposed by force. They rend everyone else's garments, sprinkle ashes on everyone else's head, chastise everyone else's body and turn the nation into a vast madhouse where everyone has the vows without ever taking them. . . . The masses all had to take the "vows" of the leaders whether they wanted to or not. . . . Confronted with the problem of abuse they destroyed the use, and face to face with the fact of selfishness they took away everyone else's liberty. Like some vegetarians who would deny meat to anyone else, Communism forces its views down everyone

---

[11] Thomas Aquinas, *Summa Theologica*, IIa IIae q. 10, a. 11.
[12] Cf. *The Catechism of the Catholic Church*, § 1743.

else's throats, an expedient which proves profitable only to the unascetic Red leaders of the new asceticism.[13]

Human law based on justice guarantees our freedom under duly constituted human authority. Divine law based on justice and charity guarantees our freedom under God.[14] Until we understand the difference, we cannot understand Sheen's purpose or even meaning in *Freedom Under God*. To take one example, in Chapter 5 Sheen declares, "though man has a natural right to private property, this right is not absolute."[15]

What? This statement, on the surface, is as contradictory as "everything I say is a lie," "greed is good," or "everyone is equal, but some are more equal than others"! It doesn't make any sense. Natural rights are, *by definition*, absolute rights. Sheen states this explicitly: "inalienable rights which no one can take away — not even the State." As Pope Leo XIII explained,

> [M]an alone among the animal creation is endowed with reason — it must be within his right to possess things not merely for temporary and momentary use, as other living things do, but to have and to hold them in stable and permanent possession; he must have not only things that perish in the use, but those also which, though they have been reduced into use, continue for further use in after time.[16]

Private property is part of human nature, and human nature in Jewish, Christian and Islamic belief is created by a perfect, that is, unchanging and unchangeable God, an Absolute Source. The idea that human nature can be changed is the principal error of socialism; Sheen quotes the Communist Program (the italics are his), "[t]he mass awakening of communist consciousness, the cause of socialism itself, calls for a *mass change of human nature*."[17]

Sheen's apparent contradiction is resolved, however, when we read further. As he explains,

---

[13] *Freedom Under God*, 204-205.
[14] Leo XIII, *Graves de Communi Re* ("On Christian Democracy"), 1901, §§ 6-7, 13, 16.
[15] *Freedom Under God*, 51.
[16] *Rerum Novarum*, § 6.
[17] *Freedom Under God*, 61.

> Only God has an absolute right. The principle of unlimited, unqualified ownership of money, material, and economic goods is wrong and inadmissible. Man is only the steward of wealth — not its Creator.[18]

Even this, however, is unclear, at least to non-theologians — which is most of us. First off, we have to realize that Sheen is using "create" in its theological meaning. When we speak of God as a Creator in theology, it is in the sense of "first cause." Nothing could exist had not some First Cause or Absolute Source brought it into being or "created" it out of nothing.

Human beings obviously create wealth, as Sheen himself states quite clearly a number of times.[19] We do not, of course, create it out of nothing; we are not Creators (First Causes), but creators. We craft artifacts using what God has provided us to create something uniquely our own. In human terms, we own what we produce, and we own it exclusively.

What about this "stewardship" issue, however? That, too, is easily answered. As Sheen points out, the State cannot justly make laws forcing us to "do right" with what we own, especially against our will. After all, is forced charity really charitable? Is coerced virtue truly virtuous?

Of course not. As Sheen notes, "If Crucified Truth were turned into coercive truth, all Christianity would have failed."[20] The same applies to other religions. A revealed religious truth that relies on compulsion to implement and sustain it contradicts the essence of faith itself as a *willingness* to believe.

That is why the popes put the whole issue of "stewardship" under *charity*, not *justice*. Our lack of charity is something for which we answer to God (assuming we believe in Him), *not* to man. As Leo XIII explained,

> [W]hen what necessity demands has been supplied, and one's standing fairly taken thought for, it becomes a duty to give to the indigent out of what remains over. . . . It is a

[18] *Ibid.*, 51.
[19] *Ibid.*, 31, 38-39, 49, 59, 71, 73, 94-120, 189.
[20] *Ibid.*, 212.

duty, not of justice (save in extreme cases), but of Christian charity — a duty not enforced by human law. But the laws and judgments of men must yield place to the laws and judgments of Christ the true God, who in many ways urges on His followers the practice of almsgiving. . . . Whoever has received from the divine bounty a large share of temporal blessings, whether they be external and material, or gifts of the mind, has received them for the purpose of using them for the perfecting of his own nature, and, at the same time, that he may employ them, as the steward of God's providence, for the benefit of others.[21]

The apparent paradox is thus resolved. It is obvious that Sheen is speaking of humanity's *moral* responsibilities under charity and justice enforced by God, not *legal* rights and duties under justice alone enforced by the State. Natural rights — the rights to be an owner, to be alive, to be free, and so on — remain always and everywhere inviolable (absolute) in our relations with other human beings and society at large.

That does not mean we may abuse or misuse our rights to harm others in any way. As Sheen explains, "The right itself must not be curtailed, but only the abuse."[22] The *utendi et abutendi* ("use and abuse") of Roman law[23] refers not to what we may do to others with what we own, but what we may do to or with what we own — the right of disposal. Thus, as Leo XIII noted, "it is not man's own rights which are here in question, but the rights of God, the most sacred and inviolable of rights."[24]

As far as human law is concerned, our right *to be* an owner, our right *to* private property, is absolute and inalienable. The right to be an owner is built into human nature as created by God. The sole exception to the right to property and rights of property is what Leo XIII called "extreme cases."[25] To meet an emergency, duly constituted

---

[21] *Rerum Novarum*, § 22; cf. John XIII, *Mater et Magistra* ("On Christianity and Social Progress"), 1961, §§ 119-120.

[22] *Freedom Under God*, 169.

[23] *Ibid.*, 56, note 21.

[24] *Rerum Novarum*, § 40.

[25] *Ibid.* §§ 119-120.

authority may redistribute a measure of wealth. Redistribution for any other purpose is an abuse of the State's power to tax.[26]

The Slavery of Past Savings[27]

There is, however, a problem that surfaces with respect to recognizing and protecting every human being's right to be an owner, especially of labor-displacing capital (*e.g.*, robots, intellectual technology), which increasingly creates the bulk of the world's wealth. Most of the world accepts without question the disproved assumption that the only way to finance new capital formation is to refrain from consuming all that you produce. In this way, savings can be accumulated for investment. In other words, you must presumably first produce something and refrain from consuming it before you can produce anything for consumption.

If we respect human law, this fallacy (or, at least, incomplete truth) of past savings as the *only* source of financing for new capital restricts all ownership to those who already own and who can afford to refrain from consuming all they produce. The alternative within this framework — humanly speaking — is to change the definition of private property, and put the State in the place of God, with the power to change the definitions of natural rights; "re-edit the dictionary," as the past savings economist John Maynard Keynes put it.[28]

Given the assumption of the absolute necessity of past savings to finance new capital, then, we are faced with

---

[26] Dr. Harold G. Moulton, *The New Philosophy of Public Debt.* Washington, DC: The Brookings Institution, 1943,71-73; cf. *Rerum Novarum*, § 47, Pius XI, *Quadragesimo Anno* ("On the Restructuring of the Social Order"), 1931, § 49.

[27] See the subtitle of Louis O. Kelso and Mortimer J. Adler, *The New Capitalists.* New York: Random House, 1961: "A Proposal to Free Economic Growth from the Slavery of Savings"; "past" savings is understood.

[28] John Maynard Keynes, *A Treatise on Money, Volume I: The Pure Theory of Money.* New York: Harcourt, Brace and Company, 1930, 4.

two alternatives. Neither of these is either realistic or acceptable, but (depending on your orientation) is more or less plausible. We then have a third alternative that does not appear to be practicable.

The alternatives are capitalism, socialism ("Communism"), and what Sheen called "diffused possession" ("Catholicism"), and others "social Christianity."[29] We can, however, more accurately describe a just "diffused possession" as "the Just Third Way." Because justice is based on universal moral values promoted by all major religions, Sheen perhaps should have characterized it as *catholic*, rather than "Catholicism." As Sheen explains,

> There are three possible solutions of the problem of property. One is to put all the eggs into a few baskets, which is capitalism; the other is to make an omelet out of them so that nobody owns, which is Communism; the other is to distribute the eggs in as many baskets as possible, which is the solution of the Catholic Church. Or to characterize them differently: selfish possession (Capitalism); personal dispossession with collective selfishness (Communism); diffused possession (Catholicism).[30]

From Social Christianity to Christian Socialism[31]

Trying to reconcile the demand that the right to private property be regarded as "sacred and inviolable"[32] under human law based on justice, and yet not absolute under divine law based on charity, however, the social Christian paints him- or herself into a corner. Bound by the assumption that past savings are the *only* source of financing for new capital, social Christians can only hope and pray for a change of heart on the part of the wealthy, and urge the poor to resist the blandishments of socialism.[33]

---

[29] Leo XIII expressed a preference for the term "Christian Democracy" over "Social Christianity," which too easily becomes "Christian socialism." See *Graves de Communi Re*, §§ 4-5, 10; Cf. *Quadragesimo Anno*, § 120.

[30] *Freedom Under God*, 33.

[31] *Graves de Communi Re*, §§ 2, 4, 6, 10.

[32] *Rerum Novarum*, § 46.

[33] Cf. *Rerum Novarum*, §§ 25, 61.

Unfortunately, if we wait for the wealthy to have a change of heart before things can get better for the poor, we shall all be waiting a very long time. Added to that is the fact that socialism, as Orestes Brownson pointed out, is so *very* attractive to the poor and their champions that it has the potential to "deceive the very elect, so that no flesh should be saved."[34]

Within the barriers imposed by reliance on past savings as the only source of financing for new capital formation, the rich can more or less honestly claim that, were they deprived of their wealth, little or no new capital would be financed. Few if any jobs would be created. The rich can also claim that, if their savings finance new capital formation, simple justice dictates that they own the new capital for which they have paid.

Out of frustration, social reformers and activists try to justify on the basis of bad faith what cannot be justified on the basis of sound reason. Seeing that the traditional understanding of private property seems to be standing in the way of implementing something they accept on faith as God's Will, they change the definition of private property from a natural right inherent in every human being, to something granted by the State as an expedient. They become socialists and abolish private property.[35]

If liberty (freedom of association/contract) gets in the way, then liberty, too, must be abolished. The so-called "logic of gift"[36] based on wild emotion and false charity must replace God's gift of logic based on calm reason and

---

[34] Orestes Brownson, "Socialism and the Church," *Brownson's Quarterly Review*, January, 1849.

[35] "The theory of the Communists may be summed up in the single sentence: Abolition of private property." Karl Mark and Friedrich Engels, *The Communist Manifesto*. London: Penguin Books, 1967, 96; cf. *Rerum Novarum*, § 15.

[36] See Michael Naughton, *The Logic of Gift: Rethinking Business as a Community of Persons*. Milwaukee, Wisconsin: Marquette University Press, 2012.

true justice.[37] This abolishes not only freedom under God, but under anything else.

In all of this the reformers and activists claim to be enforcing God's law. They conveniently ignore the fact that Christians have been carefully instructed to "render unto Caesar the things which are Caesar's, and unto God the things that are God's."[38] Based on their private interpretation of something they accept on faith as God's Will, their opinion overrides merely human ordinances based on reason, that is, knowledge.[39] They try to render unto God that which belongs to Caesar, or set up Caesar in the place of God.

This, however, is precisely what Leo XIII warned them not to do.[40] In their desire to take revenge for what they see as the crimes of the wealthy and privileged against the poor, they forget that they themselves are not God. They turn social Christianity into Christian socialism, and then into fascist socialism or communism in a vain effort to make their ideal systems work.

The Just Third Way[41]

Fortunately there is a way out of the slavery of past savings, and one that we think Sheen would immediately have appreciated. We believe that the problem is, in large measure, the result of the evolution of a social, monetary, tax, and financial system that operates for the benefit of a few, and to the detriment of the many. This flawed system creates barriers to economic opportunity (primarily ownership of capital) out of outdated methods of finance and

---

[37] See Fulton J. Sheen, *God and Intelligence in Modern Philosophy: A Critical Study in the Light of the Philosophy of Saint Thomas*. London: Longmans, Green, and Co., Ltd, 1925.

[38] Matt. 22:21.

[39] Presumably based on reason; *lex ratio v. lex voluntas*. See Rommen, *The Natural Law, op. cit.*, 36.

[40] Leo XIII, *Immortale Dei* ("On the Christian Constitution of States"), 1885, § 48; *Rerum Novarum*, §§ 7, 30.

[41] See Norman G. Kurland, Dawn K. Brohawn, and Michael D. Greaney, *Capital Homesteading for Every Citizen*. Arlington, Virginia: Economic Justice Media, 2004.

money creation as well as a failure or refusal to understand the results of advancing technology.

To be precise, the principal reason for the rapid growth of moral relativism in the world today, and the cause of the shift from social Christianity to Christian socialism, is that the system as it developed failed to include the essential triad of principles of economic justice. Louis O. Kelso, inventor of the Employee Stock Ownership Plan (ESOP), and the Aristotelian philosopher Mortimer J. Adler first articulated the basis of three interdependent principles that, like the legs of a tripod, combine to form a mutually supportive, interconnected and logical system for sustaining a just, balanced, and free economic system. Kelso and Adler described these principles in Chapter 5 of their best-selling collaboration, *The Capitalist Manifesto*.[42] As we describe and explain them,

1. Participative Justice. This is how one makes "input" to the economic process in order to make a living. It requires equal opportunity in gaining access to private property in productive assets as well as equality of opportunity to engage in productive work. Participative justice does not guarantee equal results, but requires that every person be guaranteed by society's institutions the equal human right to make a productive contribution to the economy, both through one's labor (as a worker) and through one's productive capital (as an owner). Thus, this principle rejects monopolies, special privileges, and other exclusionary social barriers to economic self-reliance and personal freedom.

2. Distributive Justice. This is the out-take principle described in legal terms as the form of justice "which should govern the distribution of rewards and punishments. It assigns to each person the rewards which his or her personal merit or services deserve, or the proper punishment for his crimes."[43]

---

[42] Kelso and Adler, *The Capitalist Manifesto, op. cit.*
[43] "Justice," *Black's Law Dictionary*. St. Paul, Minnesota: West Publishing Company, 1951.

Distributive justice is based on the exchange or market value of one's economic contributions — that all people have a right to receive a proportionate, market-determined share of the value of the marketable goods and services they produce with their labor contributions, their capital contributions, or both. In contrast to a controlled or command economy, this respects human dignity by making each economic "vote" count.

This understanding of distributive justice based on inputs must be clearly differentiated from definitions that base distribution on need. Sheen makes this clear when critiquing the Marxist dictum, "From each according to his capacity, to each according to his needs."[44] Distribution on need is a valid principle for *charity*, a moral responsibility, but not for *justice*, which (of course) is also a moral responsibility.

Charity does have its proper role, however. As Pope John Paul I stated in a talk given during a "general audience" during his brief pontificate, "Charity is the soul of justice."[45] Nevertheless, as Augustine of Hippo observed, "Charity is no substitute for justice withheld." Charity should never be regarded as a *substitute* for justice, but as the *fulfillment* of justice. As Moses Maimonides explained,

> The greatest level [of charity], above which there is no greater, is to support [your fellow man] by endowing him with a gift or loan, or entering into a partnership with him, or finding employment for him, in order to strengthen his hand until he need no longer be dependent upon others.[46]

3. Harmonic Justice. This is the feedback principle, also known as "social justice," that rebalances participative justice and distributive justice when the system violates either essential principle. Harmonic justice includes a concept of limitation that discourages personal greed

---

[44] *Freedom Under God*, 65. This is more usually rendered, "From each according to his abilities, to each according to his needs," as Marx expressed it in his *Critique of the Gotha Program* (1875).
[45] John Paul I, General Audience, Wednesday, September 6, 1978.
[46] Mishneh Torah, Laws of Charity, 10:7-14.

and prevents social monopolies. Social justice holds that every person has a personal responsibility to organize with others to correct their organizations, institutions, laws and the social order itself at every level whenever the principles of participative justice or distributive justice are violated or not operating properly.[47]

The Roots of the Problem

Thus, as Sheen hints, we can trace the moral decay of society and the decline of civilization to the growing economic displacement of ordinary people resulting from the failure to adhere to the principles of economic justice. The primary cause of this failure is ownership and control by a tiny elite of labor-displacing physical and social technologies and natural resources. This imposes on propertyless people throughout the world "a yoke little better than that of slavery itself."[48]

The displacement of most people from capital ownership prevents or inhibits their full participation in economic activity or even, as with actual slavery, the whole of social life. The existence of artificial financial and legal barriers to equal ownership opportunities prevents or inhibits most people in the world from acquiring and developing virtue through the exercise of humanity's natural rights to life, liberty, and property.

Many people are cut off from the "economic common good." This economic common good is composed, in part, of democratic access to money and credit for productive purposes, the rights to and of private property, access to free market competition, and the sanctity of contract (free association/liberty).

The economic common good should be circumscribed (as Pope John Paul II reminded us) "within a strong [albeit limited] juridical framework which places it at the service

---

[47] See the foreword to the CESJ edition of Father William J. Ferree's pamphlet, *Introduction to Social Justice* (1948), http://www.cesj.org/publications/ferree/introtosocialjustice.pdf, accessed July 15, 2013.
[48] *Rerum Novarum*, § 3.

of human freedom in its totality, and which sees it as a particular aspect of that freedom, the core of which is ethical and religious."[49] Most important, ownership of capital must be democratically distributed (*not* redistributed) throughout society as the chief support for both individual freedom and institutional integrity.

We can summarize these "four pillars of an economically just society" as:

1. A limited economic role for the State, confining the State to enforcing contracts, setting standards, and protecting property rights of everyone, as well as lifting all economic and legal barriers to universal ownership participation as a fundamental human right. This is consistent with Paragraph 17(1) of the "Universal Declaration of Human Rights": "Everyone has the right to own property alone as well as in association with others."

2. Free and open markets within an understandable and fair system of laws as the most objective and democratic means for determining just prices, just wages and just profits (*i.e.*, the "bottom line" or residual after meeting all costs for producing marketable goods and services),

3. Restoration of the rights of private property, especially in corporate equity and other forms of business organization, including the right of corporate owners to receive their proportional share of profits, and share in the governance of an enterprise, and

4. Widespread capital ownership, individually or in free association with others.

The question then arises, if the rich have a virtual monopoly on existing accumulations of savings, how are the non-rich to become owners of the capital they need so desperately?

The answer is to shift the financing of new capital from *past* savings (the present value of past reductions in consumption), to *future* savings (the present value of future increases in production). Future savings can be accessed,

---

[49] John Paul II, *Centesimus Annus* ("On the Hundredth Anniversary of *Rerum Novarum*"), 1991, § 42.

at it would refrain from the secular order. Religion
e a circumscribed area of life, insulated from all
t with the secular, and any attempt on the part of
n to inject ethical and moral consideration into
ss was looked upon as meddling, as if the virtue of
were something to be preached in a pulpit on Sun-
t not to be practiced in a factory on Monday. The
vas willing to admit that religion could tell man
is final end, but it refused to allow religion to tell
right means to attain that end.

on came to stand in the same relation to world af-
God did to Newton's astronomy. As Newton
the universe under law, Newtonians assumed
was no longer necessary to account for the order
mony of the spheres, as if the discovery of a law
y with the necessity of the Lawgiver. Newton
God into his universe to account for two irregu-
hich he could not fit into his law; namely, why
xed stars did not fall and why certain orbs re-
different orbits did not collide. God thus be-
andy explanation to account for irregularities
nce could not yet describe, a dignified cosmic
oing about mending the leaks in a Newtonian
In like manner God was permitted to take care
gularities of the political and economic universe,
H His believers could do ambulance work for the
lependents, and defectives which the political
nic order could not yet absorb. Later on with
nd science even these social irregularities
pear and religion would no more be needed. In
ligion was relegated to a place of retreat from
catacomb into which men might go for a rest
er they had washed their hands of business.
lmost think that the man who went to church
t than the man who went to work, or that
litical and economic creature had escaped in
lous way the fall of man. The result of this
religion and public affairs was to drive reli-
osition of increasing irrelevance to public af-
bother the Church, why should the Church

when past savings cannot, by entering into a contract — a
promise to be redeemed at some future date.

In a response to the Keynesian New Deal, Dr. Harold G.
Moulton, president of the Brookings Institution in Washington, DC, from 1928 to 1952, described in *The Formation of Capital*[50] (1935) how future savings can be accessed through the expansion of commercial bank credit.

Moulton's work provided the basis for Kelso and Adler's
second collaboration, *The New Capitalists* (1961), showing
how universal access to capital ownership could be financed with *future* savings, freeing economic growth from
the "slavery" of *past* savings.[51]

Significantly, contract ("exchange"), an application of
both private property and freedom of association, is central to equality of opportunity for all members of society
("social Christianity"[52]), and thus to Sheen's purpose in
writing *Freedom Under God*.

If we reflect for a moment, we see that, "contract" and
"exchange" being virtual synonyms, and "money" being
"the medium of exchange," true freedom can only exist, as
Sheen explains, within a system in which private property is respected and widespread.

Contract is thus central to what Sheen calls "the problem of property,"[53] *i.e.*, who shall own. A contract can be
offered for the purchase of new capital. This is because all
money is a contract, just as (in a sense) all contracts are
money. As such, money consists of *offer*, *acceptance*, and
consideration, "consideration" being the inducement to
enter into a contract, that is, the thing of value being exchanged.[54] "Money," in fact, is anything that can be ac-

---

[50] Harold G. Moulton, *The Formation of Capital*. Washington,
DC: The Brookings Institution, 1935, 75-84.
[51] Kelso and Adler, *The New Capitalists, op. cit.*
[52] *Quadragesimo Anno*, § 87.
[53] *Freedom Under God*, 33, 61.
[54] "Consideration," *Black's Law Dictionary, op. cit.*

cepted in settlement of a debt, *i.e.*, "everything that can be transferred in commerce."[55]

When the capital purchased with these contracts we call money is put to work producing marketable goods and services, and a profit is realized from the sale of what is produced, part of the profits can be used to redeem the promise — the contract — by means of which the capital was purchased. In this way the capital pays for itself out of its own future earnings. Using this method of finance, people without capital can become owners of capital without taking anything from anybody else.

The issue of collateral can also be handled in a way that makes it possible for every otherwise qualified borrower to obtain capital credit. Instead of using traditional accumulated wealth (by definition a monopoly of those who are already rich) to secure a loan, Kelso and Adler proposed using capital credit insurance and reinsurance, with the "risk premium" already charged on all loans used as the premium on an insurance contract.

In this way it is possible for "as many as possible of the people to become owners"[56] without violating the rights of existing owners as the capitalists fear, or redefining human nature to exclude private ownership as a natural right, as the socialists demand. With widespread private property in capital to guarantee everyone's "freedom under God," everyone can achieve the highest freedom "by acting within the law of [our] being and choosing between good things in order to attain the fullest enrichment and flowering of [our] personality."[57]

— Michael D. Greaney, Editor

---

[55] "Money," *Black's Law Dictionary, op. cit.*; cf. Louis O. Kelso and Patricia Hetter, *Two-Factor Theory: The Economics of Reality*. New York: Random House, 1967, 54.
[56] *Rerum Novarum*, § 46.
[57] *Freedom Under God*, 29.

---

1. The Relevance (

WHAT IS THE RELATION betwee
fairs? To this question two di
given in the past century, bot
Religion is *irrelevant* to public
ical to public affairs.

1. The age of Liberalism bel
serve both God and Mammon
a kind of sentimental luxury
himself if he so desired, but
rate compartment from the
Six days a week were given
day a week was to be given
man wished to "go to chur
under no circumstance m
with him on Monday mor
"private" matter; business
considered good form to "
at a dinner party, though
politics or even his cons
nomics were fields in wl
judge of what was righ
the part of the Church
ern these domains was
trusion. Religion was s
clothes, but was not an
hearing.

A mental attitude
demptive act of Calv
cance for the social
portant suburb of th
economics did not
why should religion
Religious liberty w

ing th
becam
contad
religio
busine
justice
day, b
world
about
him the

Relig
fairs as
brought
that God
and har
did awa
dragged
larities
certain f
volving i
came a
which sci
plumber
universe.
of the irre
i.e., He an
poor, the
and econo
progress
would disa
this way re
the world;
but only af
One would
was differe
man as a p
some miracu
separation o
gion into a p
fairs. "I don'

bother me" became the fallacious catchword to justify the divorce of two things which were meant to be as inseparable as head and body.

2. This mental attitude of the irrelevance of religion to public affairs led to the second and more contemporary period when religion is considered *inimical* to public affairs. The transition is rather natural, for to say religion is irrelevant to the social order, is by that very fact to allow irreligion to pre-empt the social order. To leave religion out of public affairs is not like leaving blue out of a crazy quilt; it is like plucking eyes out of the head. Blindness is the consequence of the doctrine that the eyes are irrelevant to life; quarreling is the consequence of the doctrine that mutual love is irrelevant to the relations of husband and wife; violence, disorder, bloodshed are the consequence of the doctrine that *justice* is irrelevant to the economic order. In like manner, leaving religion out of the social order is not a negation of something indifferent; it is a privation of something necessary. To leave justice, love, charity, human rights, and duties, all of which belong to religion, out of the secular order is like leaving the soul out of the body. To leave the soul out of the body is not to have a soulless body but dissolution; to leave religion out of society is not to have a secular civilization but chaos. History proves that a society which ignores religion never becomes just an irreligious society; it becomes antireligious. Life is but the sum of forces which resist death, and once the resistance to those opposing forces ends, decay sets in. In like manner the very second religion is denied relevance to the political and economic order, antireligion take them over. The secular order never lives in a vacuum; it is never even neutral; if the citizens of any state abandon religion and their duty to render to God the things that are God's, Caesar will immediately claim that even God derives His authority from Caesar. Every cheap propagandist from Moscow and Berlin is then permitted to preach his atheism and his racism, while the man of God who preaches justice and charity is regarded as an impractical intruder. Class hatred is the Dead Sea fruit[2] of the irrelevance of charity; dishonesty in politics is the

sad heritage of the irrelevance of justice; Communism in national life is the result of the irrelevance of redemption and brotherly love.

The world makes a great mistake in thinking that it can leave religion out of its pattern of national behavior and be the same world as before. This would be true if religion were only an accident of the social order like horse racing and not the sum of virtues which condition justice and peace. The empty house is, in the end, the ruined house and the a-religious society is in the end the anti-religious society. A religion that does not interfere with the secular order will discover that the secular order will not refrain from interfering with it, just as a mother who will not refrain from correcting her disobedient children will soon have her children correcting her.

The world which twenty years ago agreed that religion was unrelated to economics and politics is today a world that persecutes religion. It is not so much that violence, atheism, racism follow a decline of religion like a spanking follows an act of disobedience, it is rather that they are inseparable, like a decaying lily and a bad odor, or the sowing and the harvest. If a farmer does not plant wheat he will not have a barren field in the fall; he will have weeds. Let men grow careless about whether their souls belong to God or to Caesar and before they know it Caesar owns them body and soul. This is totalitarianism, or the State-theory that the total or whole of man belongs to the State. Such a regime must necessarily persecute religion, for to possess man it has to dispossess religion which asserts that man has rights independent of the State. In theory, a totalitarian philosophy which denies the value of a human person apart from its inclusion in the race or the class, is necessarily anti-religious. Totalitarianism has to be if it is to survive, for it can never possess the whole man until it dispossess the Church which says the whole man does not belong to the State. The Church stands in the way of such absorption of man into the totality and for that reason is persecuted. Once the State includes the religious under the political then every religious activity on the part of the Church is regarded as political interfer-

ence. Totalitarianism is wrong not because it has a dictator, but because the dictator dictates even to the soul of
man by making the person a means to an end, man an
economic aspect of the State, or a drop of blood in the
body politic, or a worker in a State-factory. The more the
Church insists on its claim to the soul of man, the more it
will be persecuted; that is why it has been called "reactionary" in Mexico; "anti-revolutionary" in Russia; "political" in Germany; "counterrevolutionary" in Barcelona.
Caesar will always crucify Christ when Caesar believes
himself to be God.

What has taken place in the modern world is but a rep-
etition of what happened in the beginning of the Christian
era. First the Son of God is ignored as irrelevant to the
world, and then He is persecuted.

At first, He was considered as irrelevant to the world
He came to save. "He came unto His own and His own
received Him not."[3] He was not openly rejected; He was
only ignored. There was no active violence against Him as
His Mother went from door to door in the village of Beth-
lehem. There was simply "no room." After all, what relation has religion to economics, and what relation has God
to the world? Men were then too busy with their little
cash boxes and their ledgers and their taxes to bother
with the Creator, just as now they are too busy with their
business and their politics. He can come into the world, if
He wants to, but let Him find His own place. There is no
room here. In order the better to signify that man had
rejected his Maker, He is forced out of the city into the
hills, away from the inns, out to the stables, away from
humans among the beasts. And as one looks down on that
Infant who was crowded out of the earth He had made,
and literally pushed out of the city of His fathers, lying on
a bed of straw between an ox and an ass, one cannot help
but see in those beasts the symbol of human rejection.
"There was no room in the inn."

Religion, we said before, is first ignored, then persecuted.
Indifference to religion is the beginning of hatred of religion. So it was with Christ. At His Birth men paid no at-
tention to Him; they just slammed the doors in the face of

His Mother. Within two years they are hunting Him down as a criminal. At first they are indifferent as to where He is born; now they are intolerant about His being born at all. At first, they merely do not want Him in their inns; now they do not want Him on their earth. At first, He is so irrelevant to their lives they leave Him to their irrelevant beasts; now He is considered inimical to their lives and more dangerous than beasts. They will now not even leave Him in their stables as Russia will not leave Him in its tabernacles. The order goes out from Herod that every male child under two years of age must be slaughtered. No king can be supreme if this new Infant King also lays claim to kingship. Herod cannot totally own man if this Child calls Himself man's King. He who first despised the Child now fears the Child. The shepherd's cave now becomes the outlaw's den as Herod sends forth his soldiers darting like hawks in pursuit of an Infant that has only learned to walk. Irreligion has pre-empted the palace vacated by religion; persecution followed indifference; the slaughter of the innocents came in the wake of the birthday of the Innocent. Indifference to Christ does not and cannot end in Christ-lessness; it ends in anti-Christ.

It was that way in the beginning; it is that way now, and it shall be so until the end; Europe has been taught to clench its fists and to spit whenever His name is mentioned; they cannot leave Him alone. They are not just men without religion; they are men against religion; they are not cold to God; they are on fire with Godlessness.

Where do they get their energy for such hate? Where such enthusiasm for atheism? Where such an apostolate for anti-Christ; where so many swords for pillage of the things of God and murder of the women of God? Where did Russia get its spark to set up in Valencia for the first time in the history of the Western World a definitely anti-God regime? It got it from the reality of God. Men do not enthuse about ghosts. Men do not go out to do battle against figments of the imagination nor the dead. But they do hate the living. In rejecting Him they are testifying to Him. No one hates Caesar, or Napoleon or Genghis Khan. Why not? Because hate dies when the object hated perishes. Men no longer clinch fists over a Bismarck or stand guard over the tomb of a Nelson. But they do still clench fists over Christ. They say He is dead, but they set up watch over His "tomb." They say He is helpless now as a Babe, but Herod still sends out soldiers to kill the harmless Babe.

The truth is, they hate because they believe — not with the living faith of the redeemed, but with the faith of the damned. There would never be vaccination unless there were germs; there would never be Prohibition unless there were something to prohibit, and there would never be atheism unless there was someone to "atheate." Their hatred is but their vain attempt to despise. They hate only because they were meant to love.

The amazing thing is that just in those nations where He has been most rejected, has man been most defeated. In just the proportion that He is persecuted man is persecuted; as the world rejects Him who said man is of worth, man begins to lose all worth. The moment the world loses Him who loved man enough to die for him, man himself ceases to be a thing of any value; the hour it forgets the price that once was paid for a human soul, the soul begins to be a tool of the State. This defeat of man in Russia, Germany, Mexico, and to some extent in Italy where man has no rights except those which the State grants, becomes all the more striking because it comes at a time when man has everything which should make for successful living. Never before has man had so much Power, and never before has that Power been so amassed for the destruction of human life; never before has there been so much education and never before so little coming to the knowledge of the Truth; never before has there been so much wealth and never before so much poverty; never before did we have so much food, and never before so many hungry men. Man is surrounded by luxuries and convenience of which previous generations had never dreamed, yet he was never so frustrated, never so miserable, never so uncertain of the future. He has everything, yet he has nothing, because he has forgotten one thing — his own worth, his own intrinsic value, his own high des-

tiny. Only Someone who paid the price can tell him how
much he is worth. Having lost the price tag of Redemption, marked "Infinite Value," it is easy for dictators to
think that he has no value at all, to believe that he is only
a drop of blood in the blood stream of the race, another
soldier in an army, and another cog in the Great Proletarian Tractor.

Man needs to be rediscovered, not the animal man of
whom we know so much, but the *rational* man of whom
we know so little. That discovery is conditioned upon
knowing Him according to whose image and likeness man
was made, for only when God is relevant does man begin
to be free.

Endnotes

---

[1] The Phoenician god of wealth. [Ed.]
[2] Something that, to all appearances, is beautiful and full of
promise, but turns out to be illusion. [Ed.]
[3] John 1:11.

2. False Liberties

THE TWO MOST ABUSED WORDS in the modern world are *love* and *liberty*. For our generation love generally means sex, and liberty means the right to make a speech. We are here concerned only with liberty in its two erroneous forms, one which is dying and the other of which is being born. The vanishing error of a decaying social order is liberty of indifference; the rising error which belongs to the new Slave State is liberty of necessity.

Liberty of Indifference

Liberty of indifference is so called because it is indifferent to truth, morality, justice, and the social good. As such it has dominated the world for several centuries, invariably defining itself as the right of the individual to say, do, or think anything he pleases. Assuming that there is no absolute standard of right and wrong, it sets up the individual as the supreme authority and regards all regulation of liberty as unwarranted and unjustified restriction. Evidently such a view understands liberty in terms of the physical rather than the moral, or as an absence of constraint rather than as a right to choose the good. We are all familiar with its various false manifestations in philosophy, religion, education, politics, and economics. In philosophy, it contended that there was no such thing as Truth "with a capital T"; truth is purely ambulatory — we make it as we go. Truth is merely a point of view for each man is his own measure of what is true and what is good. Naturally, such a system produces as many philosophies as there are heads. In order that the world might be made safe for so many conflicting points of view, broad-mindedness was cultivated as the most desirable of all virtues. The man who still believed in truth was often called narrow, while he who cared not to distinguish it from error was praised for his breadth. In religion, liberty

9

of indifference held that it makes no difference what you believe; one religion is just as good as another, which in the end meant one is just as bad as another. In education, it held that all discipline is a restriction of liberty and an unjustified attack upon the individual's right to what was ingloriously labeled "self-expression." In the political order it assumed that the State has a merely negative function; namely, to protect individual rights. Morality was regarded as a question of arithmetic and right and wrong were determined by counting votes, quite forgetful that right is right if nobody is right and wrong is wrong if everybody is wrong. In the economic order it argued that if individuals are left free to run their business as they please without any social interference on the part of the government, the maximum good of all will result. Hence, any attempt on the part of the State to regulate the use of private property was called an invasion and a violation of constitutional rights.

Such were the various manifestations of the false liberty of indifference which has also been called liberalism or the economics of *laissez faire* which meant *laissez moi faire*. The evils of such a false concept were twofold: *social* and *economic*. *Socially*, it produced a civilization made up of a series of cross currents of egotism one at variance with another. The world began to take on the aspect of a "free-for-all" which was dignified by calling it "the struggle for existence." No one was interested in the common good, but only in his own tiny little self, which meant that every man was his own god in the pantheon of other little gods. *Economically*, liberty of indifference resulted in tremendous inequalities of wealth in which property and credit were concentrated in the hands of the few, while the great vast majority of citizens were reduced to the state of wage earners with little or no material security for the future. Once in possession of wealth such liberty could mean only one thing: the right of the rich to be richer and the poor to be poorer. Leaving each economic individual free to do whatever he pleased resulted in a gross maldistribution of wealth. Sixty-five percent of families in the United States received less than $1,500 a year in

1935-36; 48 out of every 100 families had less than $1,000 a year. The top tenth of America's families had 18 times the income of the bottom tenth, while the bottom tenth of the total family income supported 62 times as many families as the top tenth. Fifteen out of every 100 families needed keep[1] to live. Half the farm families were below the $1,000 line and three fourths were below the $1,500 line.

Reaction

Something had to be done to counteract individual selfishness and economic inequalities; some way or other men had to be lifted out of their individual desires and made to look to the good of all; some remedy had to be found to bend economic forces to the common good, to equalize inequalities, and to restore to consciences a sense of the functional character of wealth for the common good. But how make man realize he is his brother's keeper? How train a man to see that liberty does not mean indifference to the good of all citizens? Religion could have done it for only religion has the power to inculcate *charity* and *justice* without which no society can endure. Unity of a social and economic kind would thus have been restored to society freely from within. But since religion was rejected as a solution, partially because minds had lost the love of truth, there was one way left and that was to *force* them to live for the general welfare, *i.e.*, to seize wealth and power in order to equalize the inequalities. Thus were the dictatorships of Fascism, Nazism, and Communism born in Europe. If the sheep will not of themselves run together into the unity of the sheepfold, then send dogs barking at their heels. If individuals will not be responsive to their God-given consciences prompting them to recognize their social responsibilities, then dictators will force them to do it. The unity thus achieved came not from the inside through religion, but from the outside through force.

Dictatorships, Fascist, Nazi, and Communist, represent the swing of the pendulum from a concept of society where the individual was supreme to the equally absurd society where the State is supreme. The active violence associated with Fascism, Nazism, and Communism is but the reaction or perhaps even the harvest of the passive violence of a liberalism which allowed the strong to devour the weak. Of course, no dictator could ever succeed in winning the masses unless he promised them liberty. He would use force, act like a tyrant, blot out all opposition, and purge minorities, but he was always careful to do it in the sacred name of liberty. So it was that the term *liberty* began to take on a new meaning.

Liberty of Necessity

No longer would liberty be identified with indifference, but with necessity. As Frederick Engels the Communist defined it: "Liberty is necessity." For example, a stone is free when it obeys the law of gravitation and falls to the ground when released from the hand. Man is free according to this view, because he knows that he must act according to determined laws. When a man knows what he must do, and does it, then he is free. So, too, the dictators say, a man is free so long as he obeys the will of the dictator who always identified himself with the common good. Thus a citizen in Russia has freedom of speech, and freedom of press only on the condition that he use them to support Stalin; otherwise, he is a "wrecker"; the only freedom he has is the freedom of martyrdom. In Germany, Italy, and Russia there are no political minorities. The government is identified with a party and freedom to vote means freedom to approve the will of the dictator. In theory there is no reason why a dictatorship should invade the sanctuary of the soul; in practice, however, most of them do not confine themselves to politics and economics; they become dictators of conscience as well, as Germany and Russia so well prove. The new dictatorships assume that you can deal with human life as you deal with economic goods and that the soul of man is susceptible to the same regulation as farming or industry. In practice, this means strengthening of the O.G.P.U.,[2] Cheka,[3] and police organizations to ferret out those who think differently. The new liberty in the end then, instead of doing away with chaos, organizes it superficially; it succeeds in getting an external unity thorough the army, though rarely an internal unity through acquiescence. That is why the dictatorships of the world are not inaugurating a new order; they are merely transitions to a new order which it is our duty to create.

Our generation is witnessing, whether it knows it or not, the death and birth of two radically false concepts of liberty. A liberty of indifference which gave the individual the right to ignore society, and a liberty of necessity which gives the State the right to ignore the individual by absorbing him into the race, the nation, and the class and by destroying freedom of choice. The first kind of liberty resulted in license, the second sells us into slavery; the first was indifferent to truth; the second identifies truth with the decrees of a dictator; the first promised individual wealth at the cost of the common good, the second promises social wealth at the cost of personal liberty; the first forgot society, the second forgets man. Liberty of indifference is the sin of a decaying Liberalism; liberty of necessity is the sin of a rising State absolutism. Liberty of indifference acted on society very much like a bomb placed under a house. Once the explosion took place every brick, every beam, every piece of glass, every board was free to do whatever it pleased without regard for the wellbeing of the house itself. Liberty of necessity on the contrary, acts on society like a wine press. Each grape on the vine when thrown into a vat with thousands of other grapes loses its own identify; its existence is now inseparable from the wine. In the first example, liberty of indifference wrecked society by defining freedom as individual license which ignored the social-good; in the second example, liberty of necessity wrecks humanity by defining freedom as necessity which gives the dictator the right to squeeze all the personality out of a man so that he dare not think, will, or feel apart from the mass or the class or the race to which he belongs.

Leo XIII as far back as June 20, 1888, warned us concerning the consequences of the false concepts of liberty. "The true liberty of human society does not consist in every man doing what he pleases, for this would simply end in turmoil and confusion, and bring on the overthrow of the State. . . . Likewise, liberty does not consist in the power of those in authority to lay unreasonable and capricious commands upon their subjects, which would be equally criminal and which would lead to ruin of the commonwealth"[4]

These two false concepts of liberty played a role in the death of our Blessed Lord. It is almost true to say that He was crucified in the name of false liberty. Liberty of indifference or broad-mindedness crucified Him in the individualism of Pilate. Liberty of necessity or the new intolerance crucified Him in the name of the masses. After a night spent in suffering when He was blindfolded, struck, and given a mock crown of thorns and a reed as a scepter, our Lord was led before Pilate. In answer to a question our Lord tells Pilate that His Kingdom is not of this world and then adds: "For this purpose I have been born, and for this purpose I have come into the world — to bear witness to the Truth. Everyone who is of the Truth hears My Voice."[5] Pilate long ago had surrendered the belief in absolute truth and goodness; what men call right and wrong was to him only a "point of view." There was no such thing as universally applicable truth; and the better to bring home his belief in the relativity of truth he sneers a question: "What is Truth?," and turns his back on Truth without waiting for the answer.

Within an hour Pilate's indifference ran its due course as he brought out Christ and Barabbas on his sunlit portico and bade the mob choose between the two: "Which one do you wish me to discharge for you — Barabbas, or Jesus, who is called Christ?"[6] Here was false broad-mindedness in its last and logical stage: indifferent to Christ and Barabbas, right and wrong, truth and error, virtue and vice. It was another way of saying liberty is indifference, and indifferent to truth on that day meant what it has meant every hour since — the crucifixion of Truth. Start with the false assumption that democracy means liberty to be indifferent to truth and to virtue, and democracy will end as it did that day, by crucifying both.

The mob does not always choose what is right; truth is not what the majority wants. Liberty does not mean the right to choose the robber rather than the Savior or to be so broadminded as to nail Justice to a tree. Once such false liberty sees the consequences of its indifference it will strive to wash its hands of guilty blood as Pilate did on that day as he dipped his hands in water; and with the drops glittering as jewels in the sunlight, shouted: "I am innocent of the blood of this man."[7] But water does not cleanse such guilt; not all the waters in the seven seas could wash the blood incarnadined from his hands. So it is to this very hour we say: "suffered under Pontius Pilate."[8]

Pilate could hardly believe his ears when they called for the release of Barabbas, and as their thunderous cries surged against the marble balustrade of his fortress, he asked another question: "What shall I do with your King, Christ?" But they answered: "If thou release this Man thou art no friend of Caesar's. Anyone setting himself up as a king is opposing Caesar."[9]

It was now the turn of the new liberty of necessity and new intolerance to send Him to death. Liberty of indifference had done its work as the majority cast votes for the death of truth; liberty of necessity has still its own dirty work to do. Translated into action it means that there is no God above Caesar, no rights above the government, no freedom of conscience beyond the party, no liberty of speech beyond the ruler. It meant just that on Good Friday, as the masses appealed to their dictator whom they hated more than the serpents, and protested their love of Caesar against Christ. "If Christ will not obey Caesar and give up this nonsense of saying: 'Render unto Caesar the things that are Caesar's and to God the things that are God's' then let Him go down to death. Caesar is the only King; the Dictator is the only law; the party is the only government. Even God derives His rights from Caesar. Either make Him submit or send Him to the cross." For freedom, they thought, is obedience to the will of the dictator.

And to the Cross He went, crucified by a decaying liberty of liberalism which is indifferent to truth, and a demoralizing liberty of dictatorship which identifies Truth with Caesar.

Calvary of that day is the picture of the modern world. The crisis of that day as that of our own day is the crisis of liberty. A Christ was crucified on Good Friday by false liberty, so man is crucified today. The modern world has not had freedom in several hundred years and if it follows the new definition of liberty, it will not have it for a few hundred more. Liberalism and capitalism which were indifferent to morality and truth did not give us liberty but only the excuse to be individually selfish. Dictatorship, totalitarian States, Fascism, and Communism do not give us liberty, but only the right to be collectively selfish. The first bred economic slaves, and the second breeds political slaves. Both are lovers of their own kind of liberty, and no man is a lover of liberty unless he is desirous of others having it as well as himself. Liberalism and capitalism, because they were indifferent to truth, make it impossible for a democracy to defend itself against Fascism or Communism or Nazism, for if there is no truth, then there is nothing to defend.

Liberty is more than an economic phenomenon as a decomposing democracy claims; it is more than a political phenomenon as a tyrannical dictatorship claims; liberty is more than an aristocracy of wealth as capitalism claims; and more than an aristocracy of privilege as Communism claims; liberty does not mean the separation of right from responsibilities as liberalism said; nor does it mean the separation of responsibility from rights as Communism says. Liberty is not free thought as Liberalism believes, nor is it dictated thought as dictatorships believe. Liberty is not the right to choose between Barabbas and Christ as broad-mindedness proclaims; nor is it the right to say that there is no God but Caesar as the new intolerance proclaims.

We have no liberty in our modern world, but we must recover it or perish. We will not find it by reacting to Liberalism, nor by revolting into dictatorships, for it is in neither. It can be recovered only by going back to a Truth which is neither majority made nor minority dictated, a Truth which is inseparable from the purpose of man; namely, union with his final end, who is God. As man corresponds in his thinking and in his actions with that Purpose, he is free because he is true. Is it asking too much of the modern world to do that? Must our modern civilization like the Christ be first crucified by a liberty of indifference and a liberty of necessity before it can rise again? The answer to that question is in the hands of God. But this we do know — if we love the Truth, the "Truth will make us free."[10]

Endnotes

[1] Basic maintenance. [Ed.]

[2] "Obedinennoe Gossudarstvennoe Politicheskoe Upravleniye." The State secret police organization in the U.S.S.R. from 1923 to 1934. [Ed.]

[3] Russian, *Cheká, Vecheká,* from the names of the initial letters of Vserossíĭskaya chrezvycháĭnaya Kommíssiya (po bor'bé s kontrarevolyútsieĭ, spekulyátsieĭ i sabotázhem): "All-Russian Extraordinary Commission (for the Struggle against Counterrevolution, Speculation and Sabotage)." The State secret police organization in the U.S.S.R. from 1917 to 1922. [Ed.]

[4] Leo XIII, *Libertas Praestantissimum* ("On the Nature of Human Liberty"), 1888, § 10.

[5] John 18:37.

[6] Matt. 27:17.

[7] Matt. 27:24.

[8] The full phrase from the Christian Creed is *Crucifixus etsiam pro nobis sub Pontio Pilato, passus, et sepultus est*: "And was crucified for us under Pontius Pilate, suffered, and was interred." [Ed.]

[9] John 19:20.

[10] John 8:32.

3. True Liberty

IN ORDER TO UNDERSTAND what freedom really is, it is important to avoid the two extreme positions of which we spoke in the last chapter. One extreme error is that of liberalism for which liberty means the right to say, think, or do anything the individual pleases. Fourth of July orations, political campaigns, the harangues of capitalists and labor organizers, certain graduation addresses, and radicals all sound the clarion call to this kind of liberty. There is one thing common to them all — they all talked as if freedom in this world were an end instead of a means. They pleaded for freedom, but none of them told us why they wanted to be free. They insisted on *being free from* something, but they forgot that *freedom from something* implies *freedom for something*. Freedom from rheumatism is intelligible only because I want to be free to walk. Forget the purpose of freedom, and freedom is absurd. The modern world has been talking about a freedom which forgot why it wanted to be free. It made willing more important than the object willed. This is wrong, because no one wants to be free just to be free, but to be free in order to fulfill a purpose or attain a goal. We want the windshield of our auto to be free from dust in order that we may drive safely. Unfortunately, too many in their pleas for liberty wanted a richer, fuller, and more abundant liberty without ever deciding what they wanted to do with it. Because they forgot the purpose of life, they invented the idea of progress, which is change without purpose. They confused a step forward with a step in the right direction. Instead of working toward an ideal, they *changed the ideal and called it progress*, forgetting that they can never know whether or not they are making progress unless they have a fixed point. In this sense Chesterton was right when he said "there is one thing that never makes any progress. That is the idea of progress."[1]

Such a false freedom created minds who were more interested in the search for truth, than the truth itself; they sought not to find, but to have the thrill of seeking; they knocked not to have the door of truth opened, but to listen to the sound of their knuckles; they asked not to receive the purpose of life, but to hear the tones of their own voices. They loved to talk about the glorious quest for truth, but they were very careful to avoid discovering it. The search for truth carries but few responsibilities and may often be veneered with priggish insincerity, but its discovery is a burden and a challenge which few were willing to face. Herein is the first defect of our decaying liberty — we forgot *why* we wanted to be free. Until we answer that question, our talk about liberty is but "sounding brass and tinkling cymbal."[2]

The other extreme error we have to avoid, is the false liberty of Fascism, Nazism, and Soviet Fascism or Communism which says that liberty means obedience to the will of a Dictator. Dictators saw that man had to have some ideal or purpose outside himself, but instead of making this purpose the development of human personality, they imposed as a goal, race as in Nazism, the State as in Fascism, and the class as in Communism. A totality thus took the place of personality. This idea is right in insisting that freedom has a purpose, but it is wrong in dictating the wrong purpose; namely, the omnipotent State. Dictatorship is right in giving a goal, but it is wrong in imposing an earthly one instead of a heavenly one, an economic end instead of a spiritual one, a Caesar instead of God. In the end this means the destruction of freedom of choice of all the citizens of the State, *e.g.*, the freedom of speech, the freedom of conscience, freedom of press and assembly. The citizens in Russia and Germany have much the same kind of freedom as two men fighting in a jail. One said to the other: "I want you to know that I have just as much right in the jail as you have." This new kind of freedom is very much like the freedom of cuckoos in cuckoo clocks. When the time comes for the people to vote 100 percent behind the Dictator, the mechanism of an army, terror, propaganda, and fear of purges, set the electorate in action, as the mechanism sets the cuckoo in action at the appointed hour.

Such a concept of freedom is wrong also because it places freedom in the collectivity instead of in man and identifies freedom with what men *do*, instead of with what man *is*. *Freedom* then becomes the attribute of the State instead of man;[3] on this theory it is the composite which is free, not the components. Each person is like a cog in a machine whose function is wholly determined by the state engineer or the dictator. A man in Russia or Germany, for example, has no more freedom of choice than a piston in an engine. He is free so long as he acts as a piston, but if he asserts that man is more than a piston and is free to choose not to be a piston in the engine of the State, he is purged as a "wrecker." The term *wrecker* is significant, for the very fact that a human being is called a "wrecker" is in itself an admission that the State is only a machine and not a moral body made up of human beings each endowed with inalienable rights, the most precious of which is freedom.

Two errors then must be avoided: one which forgets the purpose of freedom, the other which claims that liberty resides only in the collectivity, but not in man. If we avoid these two extreme positions of a dying Liberalism and a growing Dictatorship, we come to the more positive and correct idea of liberty, which avoids the two above errors: Liberty is not the right to do whatever I please, nor is liberty the necessity of doing whatever the dictator dictates; rather liberty is the right to do what I ought. In these three words: "please," "must," and "ought" are given the choices facing the modern world. Of the three we choose "ought."

That little word *ought* signifies that man is free. Fire *must* be hot, ice *must* be cold, but a man ought to be good. "Ought" implies morality, *i.e.*, a moral power distinct from a physical power. Freedom is not the power to do anything you please, so often expressed by the modern youth as: "I can do it if I want to, can't I? Who will stop me?" Certainly you *can* do anything if you please or want to. You can rob your neighbor, you can beat your wife, you can stuff mattresses with old razor blades, and you can shoot your neighbor's chickens with a machine gun, but you *ought* not to do these things because ought implies morality, rights, and duties.

Freedom then is a moral power rather than a physical power, an "ought" instead of a "can." Furthermore, "ought" is intrinsically related to purpose. When I say, "I ought to eat my dinner," there is an unmistakable relation between eating and health, *i.e.*, the purpose of eating is to conserve my health. When I say: "I ought to study" the word *ought* involves the purpose of study; namely, the acquisition of knowledge. There are thousands of little "oughts" in every life, each one of which is inseparable from a goal or an end or a purpose, for example, "I ought to pay my bills," "I ought to be kind." Reason is constantly setting up little targets of "oughts" or purposes and the will like an arrow tries to hit the mark. Underlying all little "oughts" of life, there is one supreme ought; namely, I ought to attain the end for which I was made. Behind all purposes is one great purpose, which is given in answer to the question: "Why do I exist?" That is a question very few ever ask themselves. They would not have a ten-cent gadget in their homes for five minutes without knowing its purpose, but they will go through life without knowing why they are living. Until we answer that question there is no question worth answering; and the way we answer it determines our character in this world and our destiny in the next.

Why was I made? What ought I to do with my life? Suppose we stopped a number of men on the streets and put to them this question, what answer would we receive? One would probably say: "In order to raise a family"; another, "in order to get rich"; another, "in order to be educated." But these are only partial answers. The obvious answer is: Man wants to be happy, and raising a family, accumulating a fortune, or being educated, are to him ways of realizing that happiness. Fundamentally, he wants life, he wants truth, he wants love. He does not want life for only the next thirty-two minutes, but always; he does not want to know the truths of geography alone, but all truth; he does not want a love that dies, but an eternal, beautiful ecstatic Love. Hence the ridiculousness of modern marriages with their divorces: "I will love you for two years and six months." Earth does not give such happiness, for when he has raised his family, he hates to leave it; when he has piles of his dollars, he wants a larger pile; and when he has become educated, he begins to feel proud of what he knows and thus lapses into the most abysmal ignorance. Since the happiness of eternal Life, Truth, and Love cannot be realized here below, it follows that their attainment is beyond this life, for if there were no food there would be no stomach; if there were no things to see, there would be no eyes; and if there were no Perfect Life, Truth, and Love there would be no mind or will or heart craving and striving for them. Reason thus suggests the purpose of man which is identical with the answer of Revelation. The best way of finding out why a thing was made is to go to its maker. "Why did God make you?" and the Maker gives the answer: "God made me to know Him, to love Him, to serve Him in this world, and to be eternally happy with Him in the next."[4]

Since the "ought" of man is the perfecting of his personality in its highest reaches by eternal union with the Perfect Life, Truth, and Love which is God, it follows that freedom has something to do with the choosing of the means to realize that purpose, or to reject it altogether. Thus a man may choose to save his soul by being an honest lawyer, rather than an honest doctor, or he may choose not to save his soul at all.

But which is the greater kind of freedom? To do what I *ought*; namely, obey my conscience and save my soul, or to do *whatever I please*, whether it be right or wrong. Both are aspects of freedom, for man is a saint by the same will by which he might become a devil. The problem is: Which is the higher form of freedom? Certainly, doing what we *ought* is a higher kind of freedom than doing what we *please*, because the former ends in the perfect development of our personality and the latter ends in its enslavement. For example, a man *ought* to be temperate and not overindulge in intoxicating liquors. Suppose, however, he says: "I am free, and that means no taboos, outworn moralities nor Puritanical restrictions; I will therefore drink as much as I please." After a while, that man finds himself enslaved to liquor; instead of doing what he pleases, he takes liquor not to give himself pleasure but to avoid the displeasure of not having it. Having done evil, his will is still free to *choose* what is good, but he is not free *to do it*. All powers of resistance have been broken down, as his freedom ends in slavery. The mistake he made, is the mistake the modern world is making; namely, thinking that liberty means independence of law, and that breaking the commandments of God is a form of "self-expression." What we must get into our heads as citizens, as parents of children, and as educators, is that freedom does not mean lawlessness. On the contrary, freedom is conditioned upon obedience to law. There is no such thing as freedom *from* law; there is only freedom *within* law, whether that law be scientific, natural, human, or divine. For example, an aviator is free to fly only on condition that he submit himself to the law of gravitation, *i.e.*, he must act *within* the law, and not outside it. Just try to be self-expressive and jump off the Empire State Building, and you will find that within a minute you have lost all freedom — even to live. Try and be broadminded and draw a triangle with four sides as a proof that you can do anything you please, and you will discover that you are no longer free to draw a triangle. Forget the purpose of a razor and use it for opening tomato cans, and you destroy the razor because you forgot its purpose. Be a broad-minded artist ignoring the nature of things and draw a giraffe with a short neck, you find you are not free to draw a giraffe.

So it is with the moral law; we are most free when we obey purpose or the law for which we were made; namely, the unfolding and development of our personality by eternal happiness with God. We are free to ignore the moral law, to drink, to steal, to be adulterous, to shake our fists in violent hate, just as we are free to ignore the law of gravitation, but each time we ignore it, we either diminish or destroy our liberty. Real freedom then is attained not by acting outside the law, but inside it. As long as I obey traffic laws I am free to drive, but when I say liberty means the right to do what I please, and I drive through red traffic lights, I soon discover that I am no longer free to drive. So it is with the moral law. God has implanted in human nature, and in His Church, those laws which enable us to realize the purpose of life and attain the highest goal of our personality. These laws are not like dams impeding progress; they are like levees preventing the waters of selfishness and concupiscence from flooding the countryside. If I obey, or do what *I ought*, I am free. If I disobey them, or do what *I please*, I am acting against the best interest of my nature. Every time I sin, I am to that extent less a man, just as an engine used in violation of the maker's instructions is less an engine. Sinning, which is a contempt of purpose and the law of life, is not the proof of freedom, it is the beginning of slavery, for as our Lord has put it "everyone who commits sin is the slave of sin."[5]

Freedom is not merely a constitutional right, nor natural right, nor human right, nor social right; it is above all things else a spiritual right. One of the reasons why democracy finds it so difficult to set limits upon what a man may say, or do, or think is because it forgets the purpose of man. Liberalism and dictatorships must each realize its error. Democracy must be made to see that freedom must never mean freedom for oneself and slavery for others, nor that the strong are free to assert their rights, and the weak are free to be defenseless. Dictatorships must be made to see that freedom is not in the State, nor the collectivity, nor the race, nor the class — it is in man, enshrined in every person, tabernacled in every soul as a gift of God, and no State can take it away. Our liberal freedom had created monstrous economic injustices; the dictatorship freedom has recreated slavery. Each loved liberty in his own sphere; the Liberal in his own selfish ego and the dictatorship in its collective ego. Liberalism was not the birth of liberty; dictatorship is not its discovery. Freedom had its roots in man's spiritual nature before there was a Liberal, a Democrat, a Fascist, or a Soviet Fascist or Communist. Freedom did not arise out of any social organization, or any constitution, or any party, but out of the soul of man. Nazis, Fascists, and Soviet Fascists or Communists flatter themselves that they are restoring liberty to man by handing him over to the collectivity; Liberals flatter themselves that they are preserving liberty because they give greater satisfaction to material appetites. How confused and muddled is the world's thinking is proved by the fact that Stalin can justify a purge of the innocent, and a Union Square orator can justify overthrow of the American Government in the name of Liberty. It is about time the Liberals and Dictators stopped talking about giving liberty to man, and realize that man gives them their liberty. Then let man in his turn realize that the roots of his freedom are in his purpose as a creature made to the image and likeness of God. We have gone on the assumption too long that if we were free, we would discover the Truth. Our Blessed Lord has put it the other way around: "The Truth will make you free."[6] This means that real liberation comes from the knowledge of the purpose and destiny of man. Our indifference to truth has resulted in our loss of the passion for Truth. The result is that today there are very few ideals for which a man would die, or even suffer sacrifice. Our false broadmindedness, if we only knew it, is born of our loss of faith and certitude. As we forget the purpose of life, we lose the dynamism to attain it; as we lose the basic certainties of life, we also lose the energy to strive for them. Because we have lost our passion for truth, justice, and righteousness, a lethargy and an apathy have so seized our civilization that we find it difficult to defend even the ordinary loyalties of life. We have no strong passion for great causes, no great hatred of evil, but only half-drawn swords and one-fisted battles; we have thrown away our maps of life and know not which way to turn. It is horrible to contemplate, but there is probably not enough love of truth in the world to start a crusade.

This loss of enthusiasm for the good has had the sorry consequences of permitting evil and irreligion to spread like a pestilence. Many men love truth less than others hate it. This is a grave danger for democracy. Hatred is rapidly becoming a stronger force than love, or truth or justice or righteousness. There is, for example, a greater hatred of capitalism by certain groups in our country, than there is among those very groups a love of social justice. There is a greater hatred of labor unions among certain groups in our country than there is love for a downtrodden fellow man. This growth of hatred is dangerous for any civilization; it has now reached a point that in order to spread it, hypocrisy ceases to be a sin and becomes a virtue. Because we have forgotten the reason for living, there are those who say: "Only a class has a right to live." Because we have forgotten truth, there are those who say that: "Only error shall be spread." Because we have forgotten justice, there are those who say that: "Only violence shall rule." Because we have forgotten man, there are those who say "Only the State shall endure."

All ideologies of Fascism, Nazism, and Communism seek to confine the purpose of man within the phenomenal limits of blood or a party. By forcing man to surrender to their final authority, they cut man off absolutely from the very ends to which he had become already indifferent through irreligion. The world-man as a result has thrown dust in his own eyes and then had his eyes plucked out so that he no longer can find the gate which leads back home. He was told religion was an opium and eternal purpose only theological folklore and that if he dispossessed himself of its obligations and worries, he could make a paradise of this world. Foolishly man did this, but instead of finding his material life enriched, discovers that it becomes more precarious each day, without the consolations of hoping for anything beyond the grave of a tomorrow. Having lost the purpose of life he now has left only purposes which are so many loose ends he can never piece together.

There is no way to stop this betrayal of liberty than by Christianity preaching the purpose of man; namely, the social, economic, and political unfolding of his personality in this world and his spiritual efflorescence in the next. God could save us from our chaos and our slavery by force, but that would be the destruction of liberty. God awaits man's free and unforced response to His call, that is why His last farewell to the world was from the power-lessness of the Cross where only His eyes could summon us to the sweet purpose of life. He even bore with the greatest wrongdoers for the sake of freedom. Such free-dom is not a freedom which is indifferent to truth, nor tolerant to untruth, but a freedom which believes in truth so sacred that it is worth a death on a Cross. Faith in the truth of Calvary is faith in the freedom of man. Only un-der that Cross does man realize that freedom is not in liberation from truth, not in violent subjection to it, but in the loving embrace of a soul that has realized its purpose and cries out from the depths of a heart aflame with truth: "I am Thine O God! Help me whom Thou hast made."[7]

Endnotes

[1] This appears to be Sheen's paraphrase of a passage from Ches-terton's *Orthodoxy* (1908), which reads, "It is true that a man (a silly man) might make change itself his object or ideal. But as an ideal, change itself becomes unchangeable. If the change-worshipper wishes to estimate his own progress, he must be sternly loyal to the ideal of change; he must not begin to flirt gaily with the ideal of monotony. Progress itself cannot pro-gress." Significantly, the quote is from Chapter 3, "The Suicide of Thought," the theme of Sheen's first book, *God and Intelli-gence* (1925), to which Chesterton wrote the introduction. [Ed.]
[2] 1 Corinthians 13:1-2.
[3] That is, the false belief that rights come from the State and are not inherent in the human person. [Ed.]
[4] "Question 6" of the Baltimore Catechism. [Ed.]
[5] John 8:34.
[6] John 8:34.
[7] Psalm 119.

4. The Economic Guarantee of Human Liberty[1]

FREEDOM IS ROOTED IN THE SPIRIT. Only rational and spiritual creatures are free. Stones and sealing wax, carnations and cows are not free but determined by inherent laws or instincts. Man alone is self-determining. Because possessed of reason he can set up his own goals and purposes and choose the means to attain them. His highest freedom is achieved by acting within the law of his being and choosing between good things in order to attain the fullest enrichment and flowering of his personality in God.[2]

Such has been the development of the idea of freedom up to this point. It now remains to prove that private property is the economic guarantee of human liberty.[3] The basis of freedom on the inside of man, we know — it is his rational soul. But has freedom any support on the outside of man? We would not have to inquire into the external guarantee of our freedom, if we were purely spiritual. But inasmuch as we are composed of body and soul, matter and spirit, we need some visible and external sign of our invisible and spiritual freedom. Our Blessed Lord in instituting the sacraments so recognized man's need of the sensible that He chose to pour His invisible grace into our souls in a visible way by using the material as a channel for the spiritual. We know, for example, that original sin is being washed away in Baptism by its external sign which is water. We know we are receiving Divine Life as the supreme nourishment of our souls, through the external sign of bread. We know we are being strengthened in our spiritual life so as to resist the onslaughts of evil, by the external sign of oil and the blow on the cheek.

Even in the natural order, do we not resort to signs and symbols as external expressions of our internal sentiments, *e.g.*, the handshake implies more than it manifests? Now, if man is free because he has a spiritual soul, must there not be an external sign for that inner freedom, *viz.*, something he can call his own on the *outside*, as he calls his soul his own on the *inside*? Freedom means responsibility or mastery of one's own acts, but how can this inner responsibility be better shown externally than by owning some material thing over which one can exercise control? Just as an artist is most free to express his spiritual ideas when he owns the canvas, the brush, and the paints; just as the sculptor is most free to leave the impress of his ideal on marble on condition that he owns the marble, so, too, man is most free on the inside when he owns something on the outside to which he can give the imprint of his personality. Man will know he *is* responsible, only by having responsibility. How manifest this inner responsibility externally except by giving him something over which he can exercise control? If he had nothing for which he could be responsible, he would not be free both inside and out. But give him something which man can make according to his own image and likeness, as God made man to His own image and likeness, and he will be economically free. That thing is *private property*. That is why we say private property is the *economic* guarantee of his liberty as the soul is his spiritual guarantee — the proof that he is free on the outside as well as on the inside; the guarantee that he is the source of responsibility not only as regards what he is, but also what he has.[4]

The right to private property is therefore grounded on the nature of man. The State does not give us the right to it, as the Mexican and the Russian constitutions contend. Man has the right prior to any State and the State cannot destroy the right without destroying the nature of man. This point needs to be stressed. How the right of property flows from the human person can be easily shown. What makes a man a man, or a person? For one thing, it is the power to reflect and say: "I am." That simple statement means, "I am my own and nobody else's." "I am responsible to myself." In order to express the uniqueness of self, every free man has a name — a *proper* name; something which distinguishes him as incommunicable, *sui juris*,[5] and possessed with the quality of "no-one-else-ness."

But because man can say "I am," he also has a right to say, "I have." Of the two the first is manifestly more important, for when I die what "I have" I leave behind; what "I am" I take with me. I can dispossess myself of my possessions, but I cannot dispossess me of myself entirely. That endures to determine my eternal destiny.

"I have," we said, is an extension of our being. Because there is something *proper* about what "I am," I have a right to impress that uniqueness upon what I have; thus it is that which is "proper" to me, becomes "property," something[6] that is one's own and over which one can exercise control. Because I am a person, I have a right to those things which are necessary for the preservation of my personality. But my personality is made up of body and mind. Because I have a body, I have a right to the food and shelter which is necessary for my physical life; no one denies that eating and drinking is the assimilation of the outside world to myself — a kind of "having" to sustain my "being." But since I have a soul with its reason and its will, I have a right to assimilate that part of the outside world which is necessary to the maintenance of my freedom. I must, in other words, *have* something as my own so that I may be independent of others. What the assimilation of food and drink is to my organic life, that the appropriation of property analogically is to my spiritual life — the guarantee of its preservation.

The right to property flows directly from my personality, and the more intimately things are associated with my person, the more personal is my right to them; the more they receive the impress of my rational nature, the more they are my own. That is why writings which are the immediate creation of a mind, and why children, which are the immediate products of a body are so very much man's own. That is why the State will protect an author by copyright laws, and why the State recognizes that the right of education belongs to the parents rather than to the State itself. Man's right to have, then, follows from his right to be himself or to his own life.[7]

Personality thus becomes a center around which there are a number of zones of property, some very close, some very remote; in the proximate zones of property come our body, food, clothing, habitation, literary products, artistic products of one's own brain and hands, *etc.* In the outer zones are the superfluities and luxuries of life. The right to own property, therefore, does not apply equally to all things; rather the right to property varies in direct ratio with proximity or remoteness to personality; the closer things are to our person, the more profound the right of having; the nearer things are to our inner responsibility, the stronger our right to ownership, as the nearer we get to fire the greater the heat. That is why a millionaire's right to his second million, is not at all the same kind of right as that of a poor worker to some share in the profits, management, or ownership of the industry where he labors; that, too, is why a man's right to a yacht is not as primary as a man's right to a living wage.[8] The capitalist who invokes the right to property against the State taxing his superfluous wealth for the sake of the needy, is not appealing to the same basic right as that to which the farmer appeals in claiming his cows are his own. Because property is the extension of personal responsibility, it also follows that five shares of stock in a billion-dollar corporation is not the same kind of property nor is title to it as sacred as the widow's right to five bushels of potatoes in her back yard. In other words, the right to property is not absolute and inviolable. The right to it increases with its relatedness to personality; the right decreases with its unrelatedness to it.[9]

There is too much loose talk in the modern world about property, in which it is assumed that because we have the right to property, therefore that right is unbounded and applies with equal force to all things. The rich man's claim to his summer home is not as basic as the laborer's right to his *only* home. A starving man has a right to enough food to preserve his life,[10] but not necessarily and absolutely a right to enough food to sell; in like manner, the rich man's right to necessities of his state in life is not the same kind of right as to his superfluities.[11]

Presently, we are concerned with property in relation to freedom. Because the ownership of external things is the sign of freedom, the Church has made the wide distribution of private property the cornerstone of her social program. There are three possible solutions of the problem of property. One is to put all the eggs into a few baskets, which is capitalism; the other is to make an omelet out of them so that nobody owns, which is Communism; the other is to distribute the eggs in as many baskets as possible, which is the solution of the Catholic Church. Or to characterize them differently: selfish possession (Capitalism); personal dispossession with collective selfishness (Communism); diffused possession (Catholicism).

The present economic ills are due to the fact that the few own too much and the many own too little. As the Church puts it: "the immense number of propertyless wage earners on the one hand, and the superabundant riches of the fortunate few on the other, is an unanswerable argument that the earthly good so abundantly produced in this age of industrialism, are far from being rightly distributed and equitably shared among the various classes of men."[12] Recognizing the same evil which Socialism and Communism recognized, the Church goes on to elaborate her program. "Every effort must be made, at least in the future . . . that the working men may by thrift *increase their possessions* and by their prudent management of the same, be enabled to bear the family burden with greater ease and security, being free from the hand-to-mouth uncertainty which is the lot of the proletariat. Thus they will not only be in a position to support life's changing fortunes, but will also have the reassuring confidence that when their lives are ended, some little provision will remain for those whom they have left behind."[13] . . . "Wealth which is constantly being augmented by social and economic progress, must be so distributed among the various individual and classes of society, that the common good of all . . . be thereby promoted."[14]

It may be asked: Why is the Church so insistent on the wider distribution of private property? Because private property is the economic guarantee of human liberty. Because to renounce property is to bind yourself to another person or thing. If I renounce my right to private property, I bind myself either (1) to the State or collectivity, which is Communism, or (2) to my fellow man, which is generally Capitalism, or (3) to God, which is the vow of poverty. Under the latter consecration, the man who renounces all possesses all, for there is nothing left to desire. For practical purposes we can ignore the vow of poverty. Because the abolition of property is the beginning of slavery, the Church is opposed to Capitalism which concentrates property in the hands of the few, and to Communism which confiscates it all in the name of the collectivity. Being profoundly interested in the liberty of man, the Church takes the practical step of suggestion that which will make him free; namely, give him something he can call his own.

We are confronted with two incompatible factors; we must either restore property or destroy freedom. The dictatorship of the proletariat is not the solution of our inequalities, for the history of Russia with its daily bloodlettings proves that dictatorship of the proletariat in practice means dictatorship *over* the proletariat. Communists are only fooling themselves by attacking productive property. They attack it, not because they believe property is intrinsically wrong, but because they believe property has been filched from them by Capitalism. There is a strong element of envy in the Communist attack on private property. It really hates property owners because it admires them; it hates Capitalism, because it wants to become capitalistic itself, as this story illustrates: a Communist was one day explaining to a farmer that everything would be equally shared. "Does that mean," said the farmer, "that if you have four cows, I get two?" "Yes," answered the Communist. "And if you have twenty chickens, I get ten?" "Yes." "And if you have ten horses, I get five?" "No!," said the Communist, "You know I have ten horses." If Communists would honestly analyze their emotions, they would discover that what they are really after is the Christian solution, *viz.*, the doing away with the proletariat as the preponderant element in society, for as long as the proletarian lives at the will of another, he is not free, whether he lives by the wages of the capitalists or by the sufferance of Red Leaders.

It is the position of the Church that wider distribution of private ownership is necessary in order to protect and safeguard human liberty. This does not mean that everyone should own private property, but that enough should own to give a tone to society.[15] By this method the Church aspires to introduce democracy into the economic order as it is supposed to exist in the political order. Industrial democracy does not mean that labor will take over the control and management of the industry as the Reds insist, nor does it mean that labor will be regarded as merchandise, as Capitalism claims; but it does mean a rebirth of decent human relations, which will give the worker in the industry the same opportunities for expressing his needs, his desires, and his rights that he has as a citizen in a political democracy. Political freedom will thus expand into economic freedom, so that corresponding to his vote as a responsible citizen; there will be, as the Holy Father puts it, "some share in the profits, management or ownership of industry"[16] as a responsible partner in industry. Capitalism wants to keep industry as it is; Communism wants to "break up" Capitalism and give us the slavery of Russia; the Church wants to "break down" Capitalism so that there will be more owners and sharers of productive wealth as the economic guarantee of their human and political liberty.

America has not yet begun, and probably has not even tried to understand the position of the Catholic Church on this question.[17] In pleading for property the Church is pleading for liberty, for there is no greater thrill of freedom and liberation in all the world than slamming the door of your home, entering into it to sit down even upon a broken chair as a throne where you can survey the empire that is yours.

A few centuries ago the Church had to go out to do battle with Calvinistic determinism which declared that a man was sentenced to heaven or hell irrespective of his merits. In order to refute that error the Church had to

defend the liberty of a man to be a saint. The Church today goes out on new battlefields, not to defend the freedom of a man to be a saint, but the freedom of a man to be
a man — the right to be independent of those who now
own him because they own that upon which he works. The
Church which once struggled for independence from that
theological *fiat* of an arbitrary sovereign will, now struggles to free man from the economic *fiat* of arbitrary Capitalism.

By pleading for economic democracy through a wider
distribution of the management, profits, and ownership of
industry the Church is hearkening back to the true American position of property as the economic basis of liberty
and the surest guarantee against human tyranny.[18]
America set out to be a country of well-distributed property as the sociological foundation of liberty and to that
sound Americanism the Church bids us return.

Few have better stated this truth than Nicholas Roosevelt in his work *A New Birth of Freedom.*

> The advocates of the redistribution of property are con-
> vinced that society still rests on the family and that the
> family still centers around the hearth — even if this be on-
> ly a gas range or a radiator. They know that economic and
> spiritual values attach to the ownership of a home. No
> trailer, no tenement, no rented farm, can ever mean as
> much as the home that is owned. Better a shack on a lot
> that belongs than a place for which rent is paid. Ownership
> of a home stimulates all the constructive forces in man's
> moral nature. It furnishes the roots without which no fami-
> ly can attain its full spiritual development. It supplies a
> form of financial and mental security that no mere rented
> house can ever give. When a family ceases to own the home
> it lives in, when it no longer has a plot of land, however
> small, where a few vegetable and flowers can be grown,
> when its members are no longer attached to a bit of soil
> that they can call their own, it is on the verge of social deg-
> radation. The propertyless throughout the ages have been
> the depressed — and the oppressed. They have ever been
> at the mercy of the rich and the powerful.
>
> Conversely, men of property have been free. The ownership
> of property has implied, from the earliest days, a degree of

economic independence. In the history of Europe those who did not own land were little more than slaves — always excepting the craftsmen and merchants of the towns. Property was a means to an independent livelihood. He who owned land was freed from the necessity of working for someone else. The ownership of land thus early became identified with personal freedom. In fact the term 'freeman' long applied only to men of property. They had more rights and powers than the propertyless — and more responsibilities. Having a stake in the country they were naturally the preservers of order, the conservators of tradition, the upholders of law, the 'sound men' of the community. In contrast, families without property, men and women without a stake in the land, those who are mere subsistence wage earners or submarginal tenants, never have had, and cannot be expected to have, the same interest in the community as the propertied class.[19]

Is America presently tending in the direction of a wider diffusion of private property or not? In other words, is America tending in the direction of freedom? The answer must be, unfortunately, in the negative. Neither Capital nor Labor seems to be concerned about the restoration of freedom through a wider distribution of property. Capitalism is not, for except in a very few instances where there has been some distribution to the workers, it is concerned only with the maintenance of its *status quo* and the reduction of taxes. It is thinking only of entering into more or less temporary arrangements with labor so as to guarantee economic peace during the period of the contract.

Neither is labor tending in the direction of liberty. Practically all the demands of labor today are tending in the direction of wage-hour, legislation, betterment of working conditions, and the right to organize — all of which are good, necessary, and indispensable. They must be encouraged and not discouraged. But these demands indicate that labor today is stressing the means rather than the end. They prove that labor is thinking in terms of that which will satisfy man's material appetite rather than that which will satisfy his dignity as a human being. Labor is thinking more about material security than about liberty or independence. Independence can come only from that which guarantees it; namely, private property.

By private property here, we do not mean principally consumable goods such as a rented house, food, clothing, an automobile, but rather *productive wealth, e.g.,* his own farm, cooperative enterprises or a share in the management, profits or ownership of industry. It would seem today that labor is satisfied with only created wealth; not creative wealth; with consumptive wealth, not productive wealth. While labor must insist upon its rights and upon short hours, just wages, good working conditions, and the right to its own unions, it must at the same time not forget that its real peace and prosperity lie beyond any of these things. For when they are all cared for, man is still not independent. So long as a laborer receives his salary from an employer who pays him, so long as he is dependent upon an organization for a continuation of his just working conditions, he is not independent, though he may be well fed. Liberty means the liberation of personality from the tyranny of the herd. Labor must remember that it is possible to have a country of well-fed slaves. A nation of dependent citizens is not the kind of nation we set out to be. It is not enough for the labor to be *politically* free, it must also be *economically* free. Unless there is a wider plea for that independence which comes from the *ownership of private property,* labor will degenerate into economic slavery and will have no other security for continued material prosperity than the threat of a revolution. The ideal is not to make the workers dependent on industry but to make them to some extent independent of it. This means that labor must not forget that it cannot stand on its own, unless it has something it owns. Communism wants the continuation of the proletariat, the Church wants the elimination of the proletariat through the restoration of the person, free on the inside because he has a soul, and free on the outside because he has something to prove it.

Power follows property, and they who own things to a great extent own persons.[20] That is why in Russia, since all the productive property is in the hands of a few selfish opportunists, the citizens may go to the polls, but they may never exercise their freedom. So too under a highly capitalistic system, the laborers may vote for the president of their country, but they have nothing to say about the industry where they work. Once you concentrate property in the hands of the few, you create slaves; when you decentralize it, you restore liberty. The objection of the Church to slavery is not that the slaves are poor. Slaves need not all be poor. Some are very rich in Russia, as some were very rich in Rome and comfortable on the Southern plantations. No! The Catholic approach is quite different. It starts with the fact that no material thing, not even the whole world, shall be allowed to interfere with the right of a person to attain his ultimate end by the exercise of his free will. Why is the Church opposed to low wages? Because low wages make it impossible to have an automobile and a 16-tube radio and an electric kitchen? No! But because unless he has the necessities of a decent, normal, comfortable existence he is not independent enough to save his soul.

Let labor forget its cheap champions who are urging only the distribution of created wealth instead of the redistribution of creative wealth. Instead of alleviating economic discontents these comfortable Reds add to its cause, not by restoring productive ownership to persons, but by denying its perpetuity to all.

Let labor think well before making material security rather than liberty its goal. A man can sell his body into slavery, but only at the price of his soul. Even the best of material rewards is but a tawdry exchange for liberty. Let labor think less than about what Capitalism will give, and think more about what Capitalism will share. Let property be concentrated in the hands of the few and you will work on their terms, as is the case in Russia where not even the right to strike is permitted. Labor's dignity is not in transferring its role from that of taxpayers to tax receivers, but in owning something that is taxable because [they are[21]] free citizens of a free country. What shall it profit a man if he get his closed shop but loses his soul? Surrender ownership of productive property to a few capitalists or a few dictators and you will get your mess of porridge[22] with a ticket to a theater thrown in free, but it will only be to keep you quiet. You will go to work in bigger and bigger factories, and you may carry bigger and bigger dinner pails, and you may bring home bigger and bigger checks but you will still be slaves. It has taken a hundred years to correct the abuses of Liberalism, but if we give way to those who ask us to think only in the terms of the satisfaction of our lower appetites, and not in terms of the opportunity for freedom, we will have lost the thrill of freedom, and then we will have to buy it back as Christ bought us back, with blood and sacrifice. Neither be fooled by those who identify liberty with plenty, or who say as an English writer puts it: liberty means "enough playing fields, enough and cheap enough transports to the country, enough and cheap enough cinemas, theatre seats and the like."[23]

It is pure nonsense to say that freedom consists in obedience to the will of any man, or that if a Dictator supplies all the material needs of a people, therefore the people are free. It is false to identify liberty with material abundance, for such freedom is the freedom of cows in clover, boys in jam factories, crows in cornfields, and the president of the Society of Militant Atheists in a sanctuary. Freedom does not consist in the abundance of material things that a man possesses. If such is the essence of freedom, then there is no difference between a cat full of canaries and a Red Leader full of caviar. Both are free because they are full. Such a view confuses liberty with comfort, willing with having. Liberty does not come from a full stomach, it comes from the spirit, that is, the right of a man to choose the good, whether his stomach be full or empty. Slaves who are treated well by their masters have all the material comforts, but they are not free to think themselves freemen. What good will material comforts do, if a man cannot be free to deny that the State is omnipotent? What good are all the cinema tickets in the world, if you have not the right to obey God according to the dictates of your conscience? Even if a State could be erected in which there would be no unemployment, no poverty, and an abundance of transportation to the country and playing fields, the citizens would still be unhappy, for with all that wealth they would still want to buy something which the State would not sell them because it did not have it on the market to sell; namely the right to be free.[24]

If we had to choose, it would be better to choose poverty rather than slavery, but since we are still freemen, we can choose the free way out. Our charter of freedom is contained in a song taught us by the most beautiful and pure soul that ever trod this earth of ours — the peaceful woman who was the Mother of Christ. Before He was born, she sang a hymn called the *Magnificat* in which she predicted the great Christian revolution of her Son Christ: "*Deposuit potentes de sede, et exaltavit humiles.*"[25] First, let the mighty be removed from their seats, not by violence and force, but by *justice, charity,* and *truth.* That is already being accomplished. But the more difficult and supreme task awaits us still; namely, exalting the humble to the status of freemen who can call their souls their own because they believe in God, and who can call property their own because they believe in liberty.

Endnotes

---

[1] As noted in the foreword, Sheen discusses private property (and, by extension, all natural rights, such as life and liberty) as they exist under charity and justice, that is, God's law that cannot be enforced by human authority, not man's law under justice alone (albeit inspired and fulfilled by charity) that must be enforced by human authority. See Leo XIII, *Rerum Novarum* ("On Capital and Labor"), 1891, § 22. [Ed.]

[2] Cf. "Only man, the human person, and not society in any form is endowed with reason and a morally free will." Pius XI, *Divini Redemptoris* ("On Atheistic Communism"), 1937, § 29. [Ed.]

[3] There is a technical difference between the terms *freedom* and *liberty.* Freedom is spiritual and is rooted in the soul. Liberty is external and implies a removal of hindrances or restraints so that a person may act freely. No modern writer has more clearly expressed this difference than Ross Hoffman. "Between the words *liberty* and *freedom,* as used in the essay, there is an important difference. Liberty denotes that set of conditions or circumstances wherein a person may act from choice, as it pleases that person — the sphere of unconstrained action, in which one

meets with no external compulsions or prohibitions. Freedom, on
the other hand, is a subjective conception. It designates a consciousness in us of what we are, an inner illumination of our
nature whereby we know ourselves as moral agents, able to dis-
cern right and wrong and to exercise the power of moral choice.
In this sense no man is free who does not know himself as being
possessed of free will. Our Lord, it will be remembered, did not
say the truth would set us at liberty, but that it would make us
free. For liberty may be conferred from without, as a slave is
emancipated or a prisoner discharged, but freedom can be had
only by men who know what kind of creatures God fashioned
them to be.

"Now the reason for making this distinction of word meanings
should, I think, be readily obvious. For it is this: there must not
be any suggestion here that property ownership, which can secure men against tyranny in the State, is a generative cause of
the self-knowledge which is freedom. The roots of freedom are in
the spiritual order, not in the social-economic system; and it
would be quite erroneous to fancy that any restoration of diffused property ownership could of itself effect the return of the
spirit of freedom which was the mark of our society in its Christian past. That spirit will return when our religion returns;
nothing else can bring it back. Indeed, any belief that such a
result could issue merely from a rearranged property system
would imply acceptance of one of the characteristic falsehoods of
positivist and Marxian sociology." — Ross Hoffman, *Tradition
and Progress*. Milwaukee, Wisconsin: Bruce Publishing Company, 1938, 103, 104.

[4] The right to private property is founded on the dignity of human personality and not upon the grant of a State. The State
may confirm the natural right, but it in no sense creates it. Because personality is the foundation of private property, it follows
that animals have no rights to property because they lack a rational soul. The more complete presentation of this idea has
been given by Leo XIII in his Encyclical *Rerum Novarum*. "For
every man has by nature the right to possess property as his
own. This is one of the chief points of distinction between man
and the animal creation, for the brute has no power of self-
direction, but is governed by two main instincts, which keep his
powers on the alert, impel him to develop them in a fitting manner, and stimulate and determine him to action without any
power of choice. One of these instincts is self-preservation, the
other propagation of the species. Both can attain their purpose

by means of things which lie within range; beyond their verge
the brute creation cannot go, for they are moved to action by
their senses only, and in the special direction which these sug-
gest. But with man it is wholly different. He possesses, on the
one hand, the full perfection of the animal being, and hence enjoys, at least as much as the rest of the animal kind, the fruition
of things material. But, animal nature, however perfect, is far
from representing the human being in its completeness, and is
in truth but humanity's humble handmaid, made to serve and to
obey. It is the mind or reason, which is the predominant element
in us who are human creatures; it is this which renders a human being human, and distinguished him essentially and gener-
ically from the brute. And on this very account — that man
alone among the animal creation is endowed with reason — it
must be within his right to possess things not merely for temporary and momentary use, as other living things do, but to have
and to hold them in stable and permanent possession; he must
have not only things that perish in the use of them, but those
also which, though they have been reduced to use, remain his
own for further use.

"This becomes still more clearly evident if man's nature be considered a little more deeply. For man, fathoming by his faculty
of reason matters without number, and linking the future with
the present, becoming, furthermore, by taking enlightened fore-
thought, master of his own acts, guides his ways under the eternal law and the power of God, whose providence governs all
things. Wherefore it is in his power to exercise his choice not
only as to matters that regard his present welfare, but also
about those which he deems may be for his advantage in time
yet to come. Hence man not only can possess the fruits of the
earth, but also the very soil, inasmuch as from the produce of
the earth he has to lay by provision for the future. Man's needs
do not die out, but recur; although satisfied today they demand
fresh supplies for tomorrow. Nature accordingly owes to man a
storehouse that shall never fail, affording the daily supply for
his daily wants. And this he finds solely in the inexhaustible
fertility of the earth.

"Neither do we, at this stage, need to bring into action the interference of the State. Man precedes the State, and possesses, pri-
or to the formation of any State, the right of providing for the
sustenance of his body. To affirm that God has given the earth
for the use and enjoyment of the whole human race is not to deny that private property is lawful. For God has granted the

earth to mankind in general, not in the sense that all without
distinction can deal with it as they like, but rather that no part
of it has been assigned to anyone in particular, and that the limits of private possession have been left to be fixed by man's own
industry, and by the laws of individual races. Moreover, the
earth, even though apportioned among private owners, ceases
not thereby to minister to the needs of all, inasmuch as there is
no one who does not sustain life from what the land produces.
Those who do not possess the soil, contribute their labor; hence
it may be truly said that all human subsistence is derived either
from labor on one's own land, or from some toil, some calling
which is paid for either in the produce of the land itself, or in
that which is exchanged for what the land brings forth." — *Rerum Novarum* §§ 7-8.

[5] "Of one's own right"; someone who has all the rights to which a
freeman is entitled. [Ed.]

[6] Sheen's reference to property as the thing owned corroborates
the fact that he is referring primarily to "use" (exercise) not "access" (the inalienable, natural right, like life and liberty, to be
an owner every human being has). "Property" is not the thing
owned, but the right to be an owner (the right *to* property) and
the socially determined bundle of rights that limit and define
what may be owned and how it may be used (the rights *of* property). [Ed.]

[7] It is not contended that the right to property is absolutely the
same as the right to life, for the individual life has a right to
self-preservation by the natural law, but God did not earmark
property for any particular person. "And to say that God has
given the earth for the use and enjoyment of the universal human race is not to deny that there can be private property. For
God has granted the earth to mankind in general; not in the
sense that all without distinction can deal with it as they please,
but rather that no part of it has been assigned to anyone in particular and that the limits of private possession have been left to
be fixed by man's own industry and the laws of individual people." — *Rerum Novarum* § 8.

[8] More accurately, the right to the means to generate a living
income. Even Monsignor John A. Ryan, in his book, *A Living
Wage* acknowledges that the right to a living *wage* is a "secondary right" derived from the "primary right" to own capital as the
primary means to generate a living *income*. (John A. Ryan, *A
Living Wage: Its Ethical and Economic Aspects*. New York:
Grosset and Dunlap, Publishers, 1906, 67-80.) [Ed.]

[9] This passage makes it clear that Sheen is discussing property in the context of God's law, that is, charity. As Leo XIII explained, "[I]t is not man's own rights which are here in question, but the rights of God, the most sacred and inviolable of rights." (*Rerum Novarum*, § 40.) The case is different when we discuss the application of *human* law based on *justice*. Sheen would otherwise be directly contradicting Leo XIII, who went on to explain that, as far as the relations of one person to another are concerned, "We have seen that this great labor question cannot be solved save by assuming as a principle that private ownership must be held sacred and inviolable." (*Rerum Novarum*, § 46.) [Ed.]

[10] There may be certain conditions, though difficult to find realized in our complex civilization, where stealing is justified. But stealing would not be justified if the right to private property were absolute. Now what are the conditions that would justify stealing? First, there would have to be extreme need for preserving the good of a higher order than the property which was taken, *e.g.*, your life. Secondly, all legitimate means of satisfying that need should have been exhausted, and thirdly, one should not take more than that which is absolutely needed.

[Sheen's analysis is incomplete. Theft — stealing — is *never* justified, even in charity. As Aquinas explains, however, when someone or his or her dependents is *in extremis*, that is, someone will die or become permanently disabled unless the want is relieved, whatever is sufficient to relieve the want, *but no more*, to which another has nominal title becomes in a sense common property and may be taken without incurring moral guilt. There are, of course, conditions attached, as Sheen notes. One, the need must truly be extreme; it must not be a question of mere expedience or convenience, but of dire necessity. Two, all other recourse, including begging and pleading, must have been exhausted. Three, the one whose goods are taken must not thereby be forced into want; it must be a genuine surplus. Four, when the emergency is over, reparation must be made, if possible. Finally, although the one who takes the goods does not incur *moral* guilt, he or she may be guilty of breaking human law, and would thereby be subject to appropriate punishment in order that a bad example not be given to others, encouraging them to break the law for lesser cause. — Ed.]

[11] Cf. "[N]o one is commanded to distribute to others that which is required for his own needs and those of his household; nor even to give away what is reasonably required to keep up becom-

ingly his condition in life, 'for no one ought to live other than becomingly.' But, when what necessity demands has been supplied, and one's standing fairly taken thought for, it becomes a duty to give to the indigent out of what remains over. 'Of that which remaineth, give alms.' It is a duty, not of justice (save in extreme cases), but of Christian charity — a duty not enforced by human law." *Rerum Novarum*, § 22. [Ed.]

[12] Pius XI, *Quadragesimo Anno* ("On the Restructuring of the Social Order"), 1931, § 60.

[13] *Ibid.*, § 61.

[14] *Ibid.*, § 58.

[15] Cf. Hilaire Belloc, *An Essay on the Restoration of Property.* New York: Sheed and Ward, 1936. [Ed.]

[16] *Quadragesimo Anno,* § 65.

[17] This is not entirely correct. In the early 20th century, Judge Peter Stenger Grosscup of the United States Court of Appeals for the Seventh Circuit wrote a series of articles warning of the dangers of concentrated ownership of capital, while Frederick Jackson Turner's "frontier thesis" made widespread ownership of land the foundation of a democratic political order. [Ed.]

[18] "Liberty is closely connected with property; this is true philosophically, not only in our bills of rights. It is common theory that the idea of property follows immediately from the idea of person. It is philosophically a necessary consequence of it. The right to property is simply an enlargement of the person, and the right of liberty is realized in the right of property. Therefore the institution of property, the *suum* as related to things, is presupposed by the legal order. The bills of rights do not create it, even as they are not competent to destroy it. The institution of property is like a dowry of the personality." Heinrich A. Rommen, *The State in Catholic Thought.* St. Louis, Missouri: B. Herder Book Company, 1947, 188. Cf. Frederick Jackson Turner's belief that the end of free land under Abraham Lincoln's 1862 Homestead Act meant the end of democracy. CESJ's "Capital Homestead Act" proposal would open up equal access to the means of acquiring and possessing private property in industrial and commercial capital, as well as landed capital. See *Capital Homesteading for Every Citizen* (2004). [Ed.]

[19] Nicholas Roosevelt, *A New Birth of Freedom.* New York: Charles Scribner's Sons, 1938, 50, 51.

[20] "In ownership lies the guaranty not only of security of the material conditions of existence, but also of the specifically human perfection, greater personal freedom. To state the matter negatively; whoever has no property all too easily becomes property,

a mere means in the hands of one who possesses a superabundance of property." Heinrich A. Rommen, *The Natural Law*. Indianapolis, Indiana: Liberty Fund, Inc., 1998, 208; Cf. CESJ's slogan, "Own or Be Owned." [Ed.]

[21] The words "they are" were omitted in the original. [Ed.]

[22] The reference is to Esau, who sold his birthright to Jacob for a bowl of boiled grain. Gen. 25:29-34. [Ed.]

[23] John Strachey, *The Theory and Practice of Socialism*. New York: Random House, 1936.

[24] Cf. "Under full Communism there would be no unemployment, just as there is no unemployment in a prison. Under full Communism there would be no distress or poverty, save where the masters of the nation chose to starve men or give them insufficient clothing, or in any other way oppress them. Communism worked honestly by officials devoid of human frailties and devoted to nothing but the good of its slaves, would have certain manifest material advantages as compared with a proletarian wage-system where millions live in semi-starvation, and many millions more in permanent dread thereof. But even if it were administered thus Communism would only produce its benefits through imposing slavery." Hilaire Belloc, "The Modern Phase," *The Great Heresies*. New York: Sheed and Ward, 1937. [Ed.]

[25] "He has brought down the mighty from their thrones and exalted the humble." Luke 1:52-62. [Ed.]

5. Communism, Capitalism, and Liberty

MOST LEGISLATIVE PROGRAMS, political slogans, and radical catchwords of our times are concerned with the satisfaction of material wants. The Communist catchword is "jobs"; the politician's slogan is "work"; the legislator's promise is "material security." Add to this the sad fact that millions of citizens, whose bodies and souls have been ravaged by a materialist civilization, have reached a point where they are willing to sacrifice the last crumb of liberty for a piece of the cake of security. Reformers have not understood their cry. Because men make demands for security, our reformers have neglected to inquire what they really want. A starving man asks for bread, when he really wants life. "The body is more than the raiment, and life is more than the food."[1] The unemployed, the socially disinherited, the poor broken earthenware of humanity ask for "work," but what they really want is independence. The normal man does not want to be fed either by a social agency or a state; he wants to be able to feed himself. In other words, he wants liberty. But, as we said in the last chapter, there is only one solid economic foundation for individual liberty and that is a wider distribution of property.

Property is here understood primarily as productive property, such as land, or a share in the profits, management or ownership of industry.[2] Property does not mean a distribution of created wealth such as bread, circuses,[3] and jobs, but a redistribution of creative wealth; not rations handed out by an agency or an employer, but a shared ownership of productive goods. Liberty to be real, concrete, and practicable must have a foundation in the economic order; namely, independence. As Ross Hoffman puts it so well:

Indeed when these people of the Left use the word *liberty* they do so loosely, not meaning the condition in which human beings may act from independent choice, and in matters of the highest human importance, but meaning rather an increase of leisure and consumable goods for the masses. The real crime which industrial capitalism has done against liberty; namely, the destruction of its economic basis in diffused property ownership, they do not seem to resent at all. They talk of higher wages and shorter hours, of nationalizing this and that instrument of production, of various forms of social insurance, of better housing provided by the State, of increased social services — yes, of 'the more abundant life' — but they do not talk much of liberty, unless it be to use that noble word in the sense of the political right to agitate publicly for these servile ends. For the truth is that the objective of nearly all this collectivist striving is not a liberty suitable to men of free will, but a smoothly operating economic mechanism for the satisfaction of unlimited material appetites.

To such a pass has come the great movement for human liberty begun a century and a half ago. The effort to restore the Republic (that public thing which is distinguished from the private thing, and also from the royal thing) gradually becomes an effort to create the Soviet, which may be defined as what results when the public thing swallows all private things; when it strips men of all but their status of citizenship and then degrades that status; when it standardizes and isolates men, defenseless before public power; when it transforms a hierarchical federation of personal, family, and group autonomies into a single mass community. How great has been our fall from the old republican idealism! The liberals of an earlier day who fought and shed blood for liberty, knowing what it is and why men should have it, and affirming a creed of natural rights upon which no power could trample lawfully — these liberals have passed away. An in their wake have come their epigones, men of a different creed or of no creed at all, men who commonly equate liberalism with the most unprincipled kind of sociological adventuring.[4]

Without property, the saint may achieve spiritual liberty, but within the present social order it is impossible for anyone short of a saint to achieve it without property. The regrettable thing is that few men in our country today are interested in the restoration of liberty, except the liberty understood as license or leisure. One cannot force real independence on men any more than one can force Bolshevik dependence. They must love liberty and then they will strive for it; otherwise the State and the employers will keep on tossing bigger and bigger pieces of security to keep them quiet,[5] as one might toss meat to a caged lion. The great mass of this country must once more awaken in themselves the spirit of independence which gave birth to America, or they will have to do and think and live the way men who feed them dictate they shall. Unfortunately, the property instinct, liberty, and independence are not strong in our national life simply because men have lost their sense of responsibility, for liberty and responsibility are inseparable. It is the point of these chapters to re-enkindle a love of liberty in the hearts of the disinherited, by inspiring them to ask for more than bread, not as greedy men, but as human persons, *i.e.*, a restoration of property as the economic basis of family integrity, the guarantee of economic independence, the foundation for liberty of conscience, and the legitimate expression of a citizen of the United States of America.

But suppose we did convince the masses to plead for liberty rather than security, what would be the objection on the part of those who concentrate in their hands the productive property of the country? What would Capitalism say? We know the answer: "My right to property is absolute. Being a natural as well as a civil right I refuse to admit that anyone may tell me how to use it. From my right to it follows the right to use it as I please."

Is that true? Has a man a right to own property? Yes. Private ownership is the natural right of man, and to exercise that right, especially as members of society, is not only lawful but absolutely necessary.[6] "The abolition of private ownership would prove to be, not beneficial, but grievously harmful."[7],[8]

But though man has a natural right to private property, this right is not absolute. Only God has an absolute right. The principle of unlimited, unqualified ownership of money, material, and economic goods is wrong and inadmissible. Man is only the steward of wealth — not its Creator.

At the very beginning of the discussion of property the Church makes an extremely important distinction between the "right" to property and its "use." "The right to property must be distinguished from its use. . . . It is idle to contend that the right of ownership and its proper use are bounded by the same limits."[9] Property has a double aspect: individual and social;[10] the *right* to property is *personal*, but the use or the *function* of property is *social*. It is not quite right to think of property as being divided only into "mine" and "thine." The Church reminds us that there is also such a thing as "our property," because in certain circumstances the "right of others" weighs upon my right; in case of extreme misery it may become an "individual right." For example, the right to life is higher than the right to property, hence if a rich man refuses bread to a man dying of starvation, and he had no other way of obtaining bread, the dying man has a right to take what is necessary to preserve his life, and this would not be stealing. He could not do so if the right to property were absolute and unconditioned by its use.[11] Normally, the "social function" of property, however, is determined by those who have the care of society.[12]

How sane and fundamental is this distinction between right and use can be seen by reducing it to the concrete. For example, you may own as private property the carpets on your floor, but a city ordinance forbids you to shake them out your apartment windows, because your right to property is *socially conditioned*, that is, by the use you make of it in relationship to your fellow man. You may have a right to your own automobile as private property, but you may not use it to drive on sidewalks. You may own a wine cellar, but you may not use it to put yourself and your neighbors in a state of intoxication; you may own a piece of property, but you may not build a bar upon it directly adjoining a school. The question then of how one uses one's possessions is not inseparable and unrelated to one's right to them. The right to own may be personal, but the right is to some extent conditioned by the use. The basic idea is that we may not so exercise our rights as to injure or interfere with the common good, and if we be

Christians, we must always make use of our rights in such a way as to aid our brother in Christ in coming to his full spiritual stature as a member of the Mystical Body of Christ.

Suppose the right to property is abused; does the abuse immediately destroy the right? Suppose an employer is not paying a living wage; does that mean that the employees may dispossess him of his industry? No! "The misuse or even the non-use of ownership does not destroy or forfeit the right itself."[13] This is a principle which aids in the solution of the sit-down strikes. Because a man drives an automobile over a flower garden, he does not forfeit his right to an automobile; but he does condition his right. So it is with property; if industry abuses its rights of property, the State may justly limit or interfere with that right in the interests of the common good. "The right to property is not absolutely rigid. . . . To define in detail the duties (to the common good) when the need occurs and when the natural law does not do so, is the function of the government. Provided that the natural law and the divine law be observed, public authority, in view of the common good, may specify more accurately what is licit and what is illicit for property owners in the use of their possessions. Moreover Leo XIII has wisely taught that,

> . . . the defining of private possession has been left by God to man's own industry and to the laws of individual peoples. . . . Most helpful therefore, and worthy of all praise are the efforts of those, who, in a spirit of harmony and with due regard for the traditions of the Church, seek to determine the precise nature of their duties and to define the boundaries imposed by the requirements of social life upon the right of ownership itself and upon its use. On the contrary, it is a grievous error so to weaken the individual character of ownership as to destroy it. . . . However when civil authority adjusts ownership to meet the needs of the public good, it acts not as an enemy, but as the friend of private owners; for thus it effectively prevents the possession of private property, intended by Nature's Author in His Wisdom for sustaining human life, from creating intolerable burdens and so rushing to its own destruction. It does not therefore abolish but protects private ownership,

and far from weakening the right of private property, it
gives it new strength.[14]

Capitalism

Once the distinction between the right to property and
its use is understood, it is quite easy to detect the two
basic economic errors of the present day, Capitalism[15] and
Communism.[16] Capitalism insists on the right to property
but forgets its social use; Communism insists on the social
use but forgets the personal rights; the Church insists on
the personal right conditioned by the common good.
"There is therefore a double danger to be assiduously
avoided. On the one hand, if the social and public aspect
of ownership be denied or minimized we fall into Individualism, as it is called or something akin to it; on the other
hand, the rejection or diminution of its private and individual character necessarily leads one into Collectivism,
or at least compels one to adopt its tenets."[17] Capitalism
says: "This is mine for me"; Communism says: "This is
ours for us, but I, the dictator, tell you how much is
yours." Catholicism says: "This is mine for us." Capitalism
is private persons swallowing social purpose; Communism
is social purpose swallowing private persons; Catholicism
is private persons living for social purposes.

The best expression of Liberalism and Capitalism is: "I
have a right to this property; therefore I can do with it
what I want, and I want no State nor Church nor Labor
organization telling me how to use it." This is, as we have
seen, not true, for "it is one thing to have a right to the
possession of money, and another thing to have a right to
use the money as one pleases."[18] The right to use is neither the right to abuse nor the right to ignore the common
good. The personal right to property requires some justification. A man is responsible for his property not to himself alone, *but also to his neighbor and to God.* There is no
record in the Gospel that Dives[19] ever did anything dishonest, nor that he ever underpaid a servant; he dined
and feasted lavishly every day and clothed himself in soft
garments, which most Americans would call the right of
any man. But Dives lost his soul because he refused to
recognize the social responsibility of his wealth by sharing

his superfluities with the poor beggar at his door. He did not fail because he had no right to his property, but because he failed to use it as he ought. Property rights therefore are limited by the use in the exercise of both Justice and Charity. A man must use his possessions in harmony with its twofold character: personal, as regards its right and social, as regards its function.

The fallacy of Liberalism and Capitalism is that they assume that if a man has a legal title to property he can do with it whatever he pleases. They even go a step farther and claim that the only reason a Government exists is to protect their legal titles to property. Liberalism and Capitalism must be reminded that there is something more than a deed required. To the legal title there must be added the moral title that the property has been used to social advantages and for the common good. Liberalism thinks only of the right of ownership, but never of its function. The Church reminds it that a legal right to property is not the same as a moral right. A policeman has a legal right to carry a gun, but that does not give him the moral right to use it to shoot children. The mayor of the city has a legal right to his office, but not a moral right to use it to the detriment of the common good. There is entirely too much insistence today on the purely contractual basis of ownership, with the result that we have built up a superficial order, in which the employer speaks of his right to property, and the employee speaks of his right to a job, and neither remembers that a civilization and culture are built on the word *duty*.

In vain does Liberalism appeal to the great progress the world has made since the days of the Industrial Revolution to justify itself; in vain does it flatter itself that it is the cause of enriched living, new gadgets, the more abundant life and a press-buttoned existence. These higher standards of life are not due to our break with the Christian concept of property; rather, they are benefits of machinery functioning in an age which breathes the moral discipline and the economic freedom of the past. Now that the Christian legacies are disappearing, Liberalism has proven that it cannot give us even the necessities of life.

The flotsam and jetsam of a shipwrecked Christian unity floating about the world acted like oxygen on Liberalism and Capitalism — it gave them the appearance of life. With the advent of a purely pagan civilization which Liberalism has created, machine civilization dies of auto-intoxication. The muddle we are in today is nothing but the concrete proof of the fallacy of power without responsibility, rights without duties, privileges without moral obligations.

Private property has lost much of the connotation it traditionally and rightfully possessed. St. Thomas following the Christian tradition and quoting verbatim St. Basil describes it as *potestas procurandi et dispensandi* or the power of administration and distribution.[20] As a *power* it is more than a right: it is a right and also a function, a right for oneself and a function to fulfill for the common good. For Roman law[21] and for Liberalism, property is not a *potestas* but a *jus*: *jus utendi et abutendi*, the right to use and abuse. According to its original and true signification, property was inseparable from responsibility, because it was a personal right inseparable from social obligations. Under Liberalism and monopolistic Capitalism the right to property became divorced from responsibility and its social function. *The present tendency is to equate property with source of revenue instead of with revenue and responsibility.*[22] This distinction is concretely presented by Herbert Agar in his *Land of the Free*:

> If I own a farm or a machine-shop or a cross-roads store or a Gloucester fishing-boat, I have both responsibility and control. My success or failure will depend in large part on my ability, my character, and my reputation among my neighbors. In bad times I can at least make a fight to save myself. I may lose the fight, but in any case I am not quite helplessly subject to the whims of anonymous finance. That is the sort of ownership which has a moral effect on the owner. That is the sort of private property which can be defended on moral grounds. But if I own ten shares of New York Central Stock, I have no control, no responsibility; there is no moral element in such ownership; I might just as well own a lottery ticket. If my luck is good, I make money; if my luck is bad, I don't. In neither case does it

make any difference whether I am a good man or a knave, an industrious man or a lout.

Certain enterprises in the modern world (and they are not so numerous as many people think) have to be on so huge a scale that either widely diffused corporate ownership or state ownership is indicated. But we warp our minds and make our basic problems insoluble if we confuse real ownership, the form of private property which makes freedom and self-government possible, with this attenuated, irresponsible, lottery-ticket type of ownership. 'Property,' in other words, is used in three different senses. It is used to mean personal possessions, such as radios and hats; it is used to mean lottery tickets, such as my hypothetical ten shares of New York Central stock; it is used to mean responsible ownership of some part of the means of production. It is only in the last sense that private property makes for independence, makes for character, makes for the free society that America set out to be. And in this last sense, this real sense, private property is disappearing from American life.[23]

There is little responsibility in monopolistic Capitalism because ownership is so dispersed through stocks that it is difficult to fix responsibility.[24] Those who manage the corporation say they do not own, and they who own say they do not manage. It is extremely difficult under such an arrangement to fix the blame for injustices; the directors blame the stockholders and the stockholders blame the directors. If I own a car I am responsible for its misdeeds. But if ten thousand people had a share in its ownership, the responsibility declines proportionately.[25] Furthermore, the ease with which wealth is shifted by the transfer of titles, makes it not only irresponsible through anonymity, but irresponsible through fluidity. It is hard to find who has your nickel when twenty men are passing it quickly one to another. The loss of connection between the personal and the physical is the negation of responsibility. Corporation law has made the corporation a moral person, but it has not imposed on it the obligations of a person. The result is that what is today called property is not property in the traditional sense of the term, for property implies *ownership* and *control*.[26]

Property which once meant control and responsibility now means to a great extent an *interest* in the enterprise of the one who owns some stock without any control over it, and a power over the enterprise on the part of the one who manages it but without any duty. The two attributes of property, ownership, and control, now belong to two distinct groups of individuals: the stock owner or the risk-taker on the one hand, and the directors or controllers on the other. The owner of a horse is responsible for the horse but the owner of a thousand shares of stock has no such responsibility toward his corporation. How many who own shares in corporations ever become concerned about the living wage of the employees? How many ever thought of any responsibility except their returns? The man who owns a few shares may still dispose of them; to this extent he has private property. But the penny postal card he returns to the corporation giving someone else the power of voting shows how minimal and insignificant is his control over the corporation. His stock is really only a token representing some ill-protected rights, some frustrated hopes, and dim expectations.[27]

It is evident then that when the modern man whose fortune is invested in stocks talks about his private property, he is not invoking the same kind of right his ancestors talked about. Then ownership and control were identified; now they are divorced.[28] Those who actively manage do not own, and those who own do not actively manage. That is why it is so difficult to fix responsibility for economic injustice. Since the divorce of ownership and management in big business which has destroyed the essence of private property, there has also been a distortion of profit distribution. Profits go always to those who *own* the stocks, and none to those who manage or make the profits. Profits go to control, rather than to labor or management. To the defenders of the traditional concept of property this is a half-truth. Profits should flow from management and labor as well as from control. The modern mind has to learn that because a man who owned and controlled his enterprise was entitled to profits, it does not follow when ownership and control are broken up into two groups, that only one should share; namely, owners. Since he has given up some of the attributes of his property; namely, responsibility, should he not give up also some of its fruits? Once the distinction is made between property in the traditional sense and in the modern sense, it follows that there must be a revision of the term *profits* as well. Those who create wealth should have some share in profits as well as the man who clips coupons.

Berle[29] and Means[30] in their study of *The Modern Corporation and Private Property* indicate how much the traditional concept of property has been distorted by the above-mentioned divorce.

> (1) Most fundamental of all, the position of ownership has changed from that of an active to that of a passive agent. In place of actual physical properties over which the owner could exercise direction and for which he was responsible, the owner now holds a piece of paper representing a set of rights and expectations with respect to an enterprise. But over the enterprise and over the physical property — the instruments of production — in which he has an interest, the owner has little control.

> (2) The spiritual values that formerly went with ownership have been separated from it. Physical property capable of being shaped by its owner could bring to him direct satisfaction apart from the income it yielded in more concrete form. It represented an extension of his own personality. With the corporate revolution, this quality has been lost to the property owner much as it has been lost to the worker through the industrial revolution.

> (3) The value of an individual's wealth is coming to depend on forces entirely outside himself and his own efforts. Instead, its value is determined on the one hand by the actions of the individual in command of the enterprise — individuals over whom the typical owner has no control, and on the other hand, by the actions of others in a sensitive and often capricious market. The value is thus subject to the vagaries and manipulations characteristic of the market place.

> (4) The value of an individual's wealth not only fluctuates constantly — the same may be said of most wealth — but it is subject to a constant appraisal. The individual can see the change in the appraised value of his estate from mo-

ment to moment, a fact which may markedly affect both
the expenditure of his income and his enjoyment of that income.

(5) Individual wealth has become extremely liquid through
the organized markets. The individual owner can convert it
into other forms of wealth at a moment's notice and, provided the market machinery is in working order, he may do
so without serious loss due to forced sale.

(6) Wealth is less and less in a form which can be employed
directly by its owner. When wealth is in the form of land,
for instance, it is capable of being used by the owner even
though the value of land in the market is negligible. The
physical quality of such wealth makes possible a subjective
value to the owner quite apart from any market value it
may have. The newer form of wealth is quite incapable of
this direct use. Only through sale in the market can the
owner obtain its direct use. He is thus tied to the market
as never before.

(7) Finally, in the corporate system, the "owner" of industrial wealth is left with a mere symbol of ownership while
the power, and responsibility, and the substance which
have been an integral part of ownership in the past are being transferred to a separate group in whose hand lies control.[31]

Communism

This brings us to the second extreme error concerning
property; namely, Communism. Capitalism speaks only of
the rights of property, and forgets its use, while Communism speaks only of the use of property and forgets
rights. Communism lays the flattering ointment to its Red
head that it is the great enemy of Capitalism. As a matter
of fact Communism takes over all the bad features of Capitalism and ignores its better ones. Both Capitalism and
Communism concentrate property; the first, into the hand
of a few financiers, the second in the hands of a few bureaucrats. Capitalism denies the right of productive ownership to the majority; Communism denies it to all; Capitalism makes the production of material wealth the principal end of man; Communism makes it the unique end of
man; Capitalism makes it difficult to own productive
property as the protection of liberty; Communism makes

it impossible; Capitalism tolerates the right to strike; Communism outlaws it as "wrecking"; Capitalism exercises economic rights over the workers by determining to a great extent the way they will live; Communism exercises not only economic but even juridical rights over the workers, determining not only how they will live, but also how they will die and when they will die.

Communism is right in only one thing, and that is its protests against concentration of wealth in the hands of the few; it is wrong in its reform because it carries that concentration to a point where nobody owns the means of production except the State, though they humbug the workers into believing that they own it. Putting all the productive property into the hands of the collectivity is no solution of the problem of property. Among the many defects of the system, these few might be mentioned:

a) It is difficult to see why our economic and social problems would be any easier to solve after a revolution than before. That a revolution must precede Communism, though never mentioned in the cooing speeches of Stalin's agents over the radio for the sake of creating a democratic front, is nevertheless called for by their Official Program from which I quote:

> Between capitalist society and communist society a period of revolutionary transformation intervenes, during which one changes into the other. . . . Proletarian revolution signifies the forcible invasion of the proletariat into the domain of property. . . . The conquest of power by the proletariat is the violent overthrow of bourgeois power, the destruction of capitalist state apparatus (bourgeois armies, police, bureaucratic hierarchy, the judiciary, parliaments, *etc.*). The mass awakening of communist consciousness, the cause of socialism itself, calls for a *mass change of human nature* which can be achieved only in the course of revolution. Hence revolution is not only necessary because there is no other way of overthrowing the ruling class, but also because in the course of revolution is the *overthrowing* class able to purge itself of the dross of the old society and become capable of dealing with a new society.[32]

To say that we must first have a revolution and a civil war between the classes with all its bloodshed and ruin before we can ever have peace, is just like saying that before we can have health we must have pneumonia, typhoid fever, cancer, and ulcers. When a husband and wife are quarreling it is no solution to say that if you burn their house and purge their children, they will live happily ever after. In a society as complex as our own, the revolution would not be to the advent of Communism, but a return to barbarism. It proved so in Barcelona,[33] in Hungary,[34] and in Russia[35] and would doubtless prove so again. Destruction is rapid; but reconstruction is slow. We could undo in a day what it took centuries to accomplish. The forces of destruction never win for the simple reason that construction has a purpose, but destruction has none. Furthermore, all that revolutions do anyway is transfer booty from one group to another.

There are but a few reformers who advocated a bloody revolution and class hatred who were interested in anything but loot. History proves that those reformers who gave the most revolutionary economic schemes for society were either men who could neither manage their own affairs, such as Fourier[36] and St. Simon,[37] or else were dependent on others for their living, such as Karl Marx the founder of Communism, who from the day he went to England until the day of his death, never earned a single cent as a worker. It is no wonder that his wife said to him: "Karl, if you had only made some capital instead of writing about it we would have been far better off."

b) Communism forgets that there is no magic in the transfer of the title of property from a few Capitalists to a few Red Commissars. Like most violent reformers they reform the wrong thing. The truth of the matter is that the cause of our ills is not in property, but in the person who owns it; hence, there will never be a radical transformation of society unless there is a spiritual regeneration of persons through a rebirth of justice and charity. By outlawing religion, Communism makes this impossible. Thinking that if we transfer the ownership of all property into the hands of a few Red Commissars, we will do away with economic injustice, greed, and exploitation, is just like thinking that if you register an automobile in the

State of Illinois instead of the State of New York, it will never backfire nor run out of gas. The communization of property has not eliminated greed nor injustice for there is still something to be envied; namely, privilege. History has yet to record a single instance where those who gained power by violence ever exercised it without violence, or ever voluntarily relinquished it. Is it not also logical to assume that if wealth is acquired by the injustice of confiscation, that it will not be distributed through the virtue of justice? Bank robbers do not become philanthropists when they acquire their loot, nor have murderers ever been conspicuous either in slum clearance or love of the poor.

c) Communism can give us no assurance that the workers will be greater beneficiaries of State-owned combines than they are under a Capitalist-owned combine. The point is not who owns the property, but who divides the spoils.[38] This is always a problem when administration is distinct from ownership. Putting all property into the hands of the State may do away with private property but it will not do away with lust. It only transfers the lust from ownership to privilege. There is still something to be envied under Communism; namely, who will have the privilege of distributing the booty. The constant butchering of so-called "wreckers" and "Trotskyites"[39] and "public enemies" in Russia proves that it is probably more difficult to find there, than in America, economic eunuchs so devoid of the passion of wealth as to give every man his due. In 1937 one hundred and thirty-two commercial workers were arrested and tried for theft.[40]

Facts bear this out. Workers are no better there than anywhere else; they are worse. Every newspaper correspondent who has ever been to Russia, and their name is legion, with the exception of Walter Duranty, of the *New York Times*,[41] and the Moscow's propagandists for the Stalin three daily newspapers in the United States, have all agreed that the poor on relief in America are far better off than the employed in Russia. Added to the testimony of André Gide,[42] Sir Walter Citrine,[43] William Chamberlin,[44] Harold Denny,[45] the correspondent of the *London Times*,

John D. Littlepage, John T. Whitaker,[46] and dozens of others, there is now to be added the testimony of another American engineer, Edmund J. Lowry, who has just returned to America after eight years of residence in Russia. In a series of syndicated articles he writes:

> Russian workers are not only among the lowest paid in the world but they also are undoubtedly the most heavily taxed.

> There is unquestionably a greater array of direct and indirect imposts in the Soviet Union than in any other country, and hardly a minute goes by for the Russian citizen — with the exception of the top stratum of favored bureaucrats — that he is not exploited by the State, the superemployer owning and managing everything, to an extent which would lead to an immediate revolution in any democratic country.

> The average monthly earnings of the great majority of Russian workers range from 90 to 350 roubles, or from $1.35 to $5.25 a week, measured in purchasing power of 6 cents per rouble. You'd think that's low enough a wage scale and, as I will show, barely sufficient to keep body and soul together, to say nothing of clothing the body.

> But the Russian worker never actually gets his full pay. Every month — Russians are paid on a monthly instead of weekly basis — about 28 percent of his wage is deducted in direct taxes and so-called "loans." These direct levies are over and above the numerous indirect taxes which the government raises at every stage of production and distribution, on the profits of individual plants which otherwise might have gone into higher wages, on the prices of goods which otherwise could be sold at lower prices and every other form of activity.

> Let's take the average unskilled Russian worker who earns 200 roubles a month, or $3 a week, and see how much he actually gets and what he can buy for his money.

> About 56 roubles is deducted from this worker's pay as follows: State loan, supposedly "voluntary," but woe to the man who balks at paying it, 10 percent or 20 roubles; income tax, 3 percent or 6 roubles; educational tax, the same amount; sick benefit tax, 1 percent or 2 roubles; trade union fee, 2 percent or four roubles; special tax for the support of military aviation, 1 percent or 2 roubles; special

levy for Spain, China, or some other cause currently being aided by the Soviets, 8 percent or 16 roubles.[47]

The average monthly wage in large-scale industry was 231 rubles a month. (Incidentally in figuring the average wage Russia counts only 27,000,000 out of a vastly larger number of working people which there must be in a population of 170,000,000.) Although this wage represents a nominal increase of 400 percent over the wages of 1926, during that same period the price of food increased 1,000 percent which means that real wages were considerably less than in 1926.

d) Planned economy of 170,000,000 where all factories, mines, stores, telephones, hotels, railroads, farms, banks, hospitals, laundries, plumbing establishments, nurseries, meat shops, department stores, belong to the State, creates a problem of distribution and consumption which is too great for any planning body in the world. No individual can indulge in private production for profit, for on the Communistic theory that is the basis of exploitation.

Think of the government determining how many pants it would make, how many cows it would butcher, how many shirts it would make, how many razors it would manufacture, how many hats it would make and what size and color they would be, how much each government store would get. Think of all the purging that would be necessary; all the wrecking dairymen who like Kulaks[48] refused to milk cows for the State, all the wrecking farmers who refused to grow State onions; all the pushcart salesmen who insisted on making their own articles to sell them; all the prices which would have to be fixed; all the concentration camps which would have to be found for a man who wants to call his shoe shop his own.

The Collectivist slogan "from each according to his capacity, to each according to his needs"[49] sounds well in theory, but who is going to decide what is each man's capacity and what is each man's needs? The answer is: the bureaucrats. And who determines the bureaucrats? The Dictator. And what is Dictatorship according to Lenin: "Dictatorship is an authority relying directly upon force and not bound by any laws. The revolutionary dictatorship of the proletariat is an authority maintained by means of force over and against the bourgeoisie and not bound by any laws."[50]

e) Collective planning for any complex civilization in which no citizen owns productive property will result in chaos as the facts prove.

(1) All butcher shops belong to the State. The State raises the cattle and pigs and sheep, the State butchers them, dresses them, and sells them. Moscow which is better fed than all the rest of Russia, planned to distribute in 1938, 31 pounds of meat per year to each comrade or 2½ pounds a person per month or 1-1/3 ounces per day which is indeed very little where everyone is a worker.[51]

(2) On May 17, 1937, the People's Commissariat of Light Industry approved a Production Plan for the year of 1938 of 393,000,000 pairs of socks, which if the plan were achieved would allow each citizen a fraction over two pairs per year. The number of shops to supply State-owned food is naturally less than where private enterprise supplies it. In England there is a grocery shop for every 430 persons. In Russia there is one for every 24,400. This accounts for the long lines outside the stores. When one does arrive one finds that very often there are no vegetables.[52]

In the Central Moscow *Univermag* in the spring of 1937, men's ready-made suits were limited to seven sizes; an inspection of 260 shops in the province of Voronezh disclosed that 69 had no sugar, 49 no confectionary, 36 no salt, and 26 no cigarettes.[53] In 1938 according to Tchourakov, the Head of the Restaurant Department "the popular restaurants in the course of the year 1938 existed on famine rations."[54] As regards transportation there is not a sufficient number of auto buses to handle the traffic; of 915 auto buses controlled by the "Mosautobus" only 460 could run.[55] The director of the automotive factory of Podoisk himself said that "There are defects in our motors which endanger the lives of those who use them."[56] Every time a comrade wants his roof fixed he has to get in touch with the State roof mender. Moscow set aside 120,000,000 rubles to repair houses in 1938,[57] but in the previous year with two months of the year left, out of 12,500 houses needing repairs only 1,435 had been fixed "by the State that year."[58] It is interesting to note that if one uses some of the pre-revolutionary artisans to repair the houses the work is better done and in a shorter time than if the State is called in.[59]

The destruction of private property in favor of government ownership does not, as Communism claims, result in greater benefits to the workers. Soviet economists are fond of pointing out that overhead costs in Soviet trade add only 11 percent to the wholesale cost of goods, as against 25 percent in capitalist trade. But in practice this does not mean the advantage accrues to the purchaser. In fact, he loses many advantages under government-owned business: women lose the thrill of "sales" for there is no competition when the State owns everything and Stalin is the salesman behind every counter; there are practically no deliveries of purchase. "Gastronom No. 1" which is the largest provision shop in Moscow delivered only 1.65 percent of its total sales; the regular daily delivery of bread, milk, etc., to private dwellings is unknown; furthermore, there is a decreased selection of goods.

f) Communism forgets that the collective ownership of productive wealth means the destruction of personal interest and initiative, for as Aristotle said: "That which is the care of all is the care of none."[60] The workers in Russia own the factories in the same way we in America own the parks, but how many Americans do you see going out into their parks on Monday morning out of love for their country to pick up the greasy lunch litter of the day before? No man will treat property with care or affection unless it is his own. "You wouldn't do that in your own house" is an expression full of the profoundest understanding of human nature.

Stalin discovered that when he steals the cattle and horses from the peasants they are not going to have the same care for them as before. "In 1928," said Stalin, "the peasants owned 307,000,000 cattle, cows, heifers, sheep, goats, and hogs." And since the enforced collectivization of farm produce in 1938 there were only half that number.[61]

Stalin made some concession to the peasants allowing them now to keep a cow — but not a horse.[62] The revenue of the Russian farmer is only 12 pounds of wheat a day (or half a ruble).[63] The most successful farmers earn 280 rubles a year[64] which was just enough to buy a pair of shoes. *Pravda*,[65] narrates a "miracle" which happened at Kertch in the Crimea. The citizens of that city could never find the necessities of life in the government stores. But one day when they went there were all kinds of fish, fruits, vegetables, and in such abundance that it was not necessary to stand in line to wait for their arrival. This "miracle," for the *Pravda* explains it as such, was soon explained. The Commissar for Commerce stopped at Kertch and he provided everything for his visit so there would be no complaints. The next day everything returned to "normal."

Once the collectivity becomes the sole owner of productive goods of all descriptions, it can do whatever it likes with the individuals. Once you begin taking your jobs, your education, your food, your work, your clothing, and your housing from the State, it will only be a matter of a few visits from the police until you take your thinking from the State, and that is the end of liberty.

This is the basic defect of Communism — the destruction of liberty. Power follows property. Put all productive property in the hands of the State and you take freedom out of the souls of men. Children can be encouraged to betray their parents who criticize Communism. Instead of being ashamed of such want of parental love and the right of a father to dissent with an enslaving government, Mikoyan in the official review *Partiinoie Stroitelstovo*, January 15, 1938, boasts that "such acts are not possible in any capitalistic country, but we have many of them here." To be what corresponds to a Cabinet Minister in the United States is indeed a perilous one. In 1937, 15 ministers (People's Commissars) without counting hundreds in the Federal republics were shot; eleven Ministers of Agriculture in 1937 in the Federal republics, along with Echernov,[66] the Minister of Agriculture of the Soviet Republic, were shot. Two assistants of Litvinoff (Finkelstein)

Kretinsky and Karakhan, have been shot. Four assistants to the Minister of Defense, two Army Marshalls, Under-Secretary of the Navy, Under-Secretary of the Air Minister, and fifty-five generals and admirals met their death in that "land of liberty and democracy" in 1938. It is no wonder all the resolutions of the Communist Party are all passed "unanimously."

If one wants some concrete proofs that there is liberty under Communism (a) try to send to Russia a year's subscription to any American daily newspaper or the *Atlantic Monthly*[67] or *Harper's*[68] or *Time*[69] to one hundred peasants or workers there who are not members of the Communist Party. (b) Offer to pay the fare of Stalin's agents in the United States to Russia, on condition that they abandon their American citizenship and live under a regime such as they would establish in the United States. Not one of them will go. They would rather live in America, which they are seeking to undermine, than in the "Paradise" which their philosophy of class struggle has created. The truth is: They are Communists until they have to live under Communism; then they want to be Americans.[70]

In between these two extremes is the position of the Catholic Church, which against Capitalism affirms the social function and responsibility of wealth, and which against Communism affirms the right to own it personally as the foundation of liberty.

Property, as Chesterton pointed out, is very much like sex and is capable of being abused in the same way.[71] Just as our modern world understands love only in terms of sex, so it understands property only in terms of money, *i.e.*, something which is immediately consumed and gives momentary pleasure. Birth control is the artificial limitation of the fruitfulness of love, as Bolshevism is the artificial strangulation of the fruitfulness of property. From the very beginning, love and property are considered by the modern mind as things only to enjoyed, whereas both were made to assure perpetuity and bear fruit, the pleasure and enjoyment being only incidental. In birth control and Communism man is only a consumer, not a producer. The destruction of family life is therefore one with the destruction of property — a repudiation of the foundation of posterity, security, and liberty. A proof of this thesis is that Russia, which destroyed family life in the name of the "worker," destroyed property in the name of Communism. "The whole system was directed toward encouraging or driving the worker to spend his wages, to have nothing left on the next pay day; to enjoy everything, in short, to shudder at the thought of only one crime, the creative crime of thrift. It was a tame extravagance, a sort of disciplined dissipation, a meek and submissive prodigality. For the moment the slave left off drinking all his wages; the moment he began to hoard or hide any property he would be saving up something which might ultimately purchase his liberty. He might begin to count for something in the State; that is, he might become less of a slave and more of a citizen. But they have Article 131 in their constitution to cover just such an eventuality. The man who stores up productive personal property is called "an enemy of the people."

The correct understanding of love and property both involve the distinction of right and use. In both, the right is personal, *i.e.*, the right to one's body and the right to property (though the first is more primary). But the use of both is social to assure posterity through the family, and to assure liberty through security. The frustration of these social purposes for the mere sake of personal pleasure is wrong.

The divorce of right and use is the beginning of all irresponsibility. The radical who believes that the right to free speech means that he can use it to destroy that right, breaks down democracy, just as the husband and wife who divorce sex and its function, break down the family and as the Capitalist who divorces the right to property and its social responsibility, breaks down our whole economic structure.

The Church in pleading for a restoration of property does not mean that the big industries must be destroyed, so that every man will weave his own rugs, grind his own wheat, or sew his own clothes and raise sheep in his own back yard. This cheap retort to the Church's position as-

of property, not as the right to a thing to do with it whatever you please, but property as ownership bound up with
control as the last and solid bulwark of free men in a free
country.[75]

Monopolistic capitalism is faced with three alternatives:
(1) It will either be taxed out of existence by the government, with the government increasing the dependence of
its citizens through bureaucratic handouts; or (2) it will
involuntarily be dispossessed through class struggle; or
(3) it will voluntarily share control and responsibility with
labor, with a consequent rebirth of the pleasure and pride
of creative work in the restoration of liberty. Property will
thus become the *art* of democracy, or the God-given right
of every human being to shape something according to his
own image, as the potter shapes his clay, the gardener his
garden, and now we may add — as the laborer shapes his
capital.

Capitalism, Communism, and Catholicism find their
parallels in the Gospel story of our Divine Lord: The extreme of Liberalism and monopolistic Capitalism is illustrated in the story of our Lord's visit into the country of
the Gerasens.[76]

There was in that country a young man with an unclean
spirit dwelling in a tomb and he could be bound by no
man, not even by chains. He often broke the chains and
fetters into pieces, and would roam about the mountains
and monuments crying and cutting himself with stones.
Our Blessed Lord approached him and said: "Go out of the
man, thou unclean spirit." The unclean spirits going out of
the young man entered into a herd of swine, and the herd
of about two thousand with great violence was carried
headlong into the sea and stifled there. Seeing this, the
owners of the swine came to our Lord, and saw the young
man beside Him, now relieved from his trouble, well
clothed, and in full possession of his wits. The Gerasens
were not interested in the young man, but only in their
swine. So they therefore bade our Lord leave their shores.
Translating the language of the Gerasens into our modern
industrial language, the answer of Capitalism to Christianity runs as follows: "If you came here to preach the dig-

nity of man and the living wage, and thus cause us loss of
our profits; if you think the restoration of a man to his
manhood is more than property, then leave our shores."
The Gerasens were far more interested in swine than they
were in man; more disturbed about the loss of some of
their material wealth than the restoration of human
rights and dignity. They thus become a symbol of those in
the spirit of Capitalism in our day for whom profits mean
more than human rights.

Another story in the Gospel illustrates Communism or
how man may be enslaved not to wealth or individual selfishness, but also to collective selfishness. In the above
instance, man is less than profit; in this instance he is
less than the collectivity or the State. Shortly before our
Blessed Lord was crucified, Caiphas, the High Priest of
that year, said to the Pharisees that it was expedient that
our Blessed Lord should die rather than that the State or
the nation or the collectivity should be challenged.[77] There
was no question of our Blessed Lord being condemned because He was guilty of any moral injustices toward His
neighbor; it was rather that the nation or the collectivity
reserved the right to itself to crush human personality in
the interests of the collectivity. Never once did it enter
into the head of Caiphas that man has certain inalienable
rights which no one can take away — not even the State.[78]
He was concerned only with the fact that a human person
is of no worth in contrast to the power of a party. Translating this into our modern language the party groups of
Germany and Russia are saying: "Let the righteous die,
but let not the party perish. If any man asserts that he
has freedom of conscience, or the right to preach that religion is worth more than State worship and if any man
insists that he has rights which are independent of the
party — then let him be purged; if any Church asserts
that man has rights and that he is willing to render to
Caesar the things that are Caesar's but insists on render-
ing to God the things that are God's, then let him die, for
there is no God but Caesar." By denying that a good man
has any right to independence of the State, they made

man wholly dependent on the State as the Gerasens made man wholly dependent on property.

Among other causes, economic and political power sent our Lord to the Cross: selfish economic power such as one finds among the Gerasens, and selfish political power one finds in Caiphas. They asked our Lord to come down from the Cross out of mockery to His subjection to that economic and political power. And He refused to come down! Why? Because if He had used His power, He would have destroyed their freedom. He wanted not the obsequious tribute of dependent slaves, but the gracious love that comes from freedom. By such refusal to match Power with power, He kept His freedom — He kept His soul free, and His body free. He kept His soul free; thus He could commend it into the Hands of His Heavenly Father; He kept His body or His property free, therefore He could give it to us. That was the first and a spiritual Declaration of Independence; a God man who kept His soul free gave it back again to God. The second Declaration of Independence written under its inspiration was a political one which proclaimed that man has rights independent of a State. The third Declaration of Independence remains to be written; namely, the economics in which spiritual men will stand on their own because they can call something their own. That is the liberty the Catholic Church proclaims for the worker!

Endnotes

[1] Luke 12:23.

[2] "Capital." [Ed.]

[3] *Iam pridem, ex quo suffragia nulli uendimus, effudit curas; nam qui dabat olim imperium, fasces, legiones, omnia, nunc se continet atque duas tantum res anxius optat, panem et circenses.* "From the days when we sold our vote to no one, the people have abdicated their duty; for the people who used to hand out military command, the civil power, legions — everything — now cares for just two things: bread and circuses." Juvenal, Satire X. [Ed.]

[4] Hoffman, *Tradition and Progress, op. cit.*, 105, 106.

[5] Cf. Goetz Briefs, *The Proletariat: A Challenge to Western Civilization*. New York: McGraw-Hill Book Company, Inc., 1937, 253-267.

[6] *Rerum Novarum*, § 22.

[7] *Quadragesimo Anno*, § 44.

[8] Private ownership is, as we indicated in the preceding chapter, an extension of human personality. The right of inheritance is a proof of it; the one who inherits to some extent continues the person of who willed the property. "For that which is required for the preservation of life and for life's well being, is produced in great abundance by the earth, but not until man has brought it into cultivation and lavished upon it his care and skill. Now, when man thus spends the industry of his mind and the strength of his body in procuring the fruits of nature by that act he makes his own that portion of nature's field which he cultivates — that portion on which he leaves, as it were, the impress of his own personality; and it cannot but be just that he should possess that portion as his own and should have a right to keep it without molestation." — *Rerum Novarum*, § 9.

[9] This distinction is founded on the very nature of things. Leo XIII writes: " 'It is lawful,' says St. Thomas of Aquin, 'for a man to hold private property; and it is also necessary for the carrying on of human life.' But if the question be asked, How must one's words of the same Holy Doctor: 'Man should not consider his out-possessions be used? The Church replies without hesitation in the ward possessions as his own, but as common to all, so as to share them without difficulty when others are in need.' " (*Rerum Novarum*.) The right to property is personal; the use is common. The specification of private property, *i.e.*, who should own this or that piece of property is not in the primary natural law, but in its application. "Community of goods is ascribed to the natural law, not that the natural law dictates that all things should be possessed in common, and that nothing should be possessed as one's own: but because the division of possessions is not according to the natural law, but rather arose from human agreement which belongs to positive law, as stated above (IIa IIae q. 57, aa, 2, 3). Hence the ownership of possessions is not contrary to the natural law, but an addition thereto devised by human reason." (*Summa*, St. Thomas, IIa IIae q. 66 a. 2 ad 1.) Man has a right to use creation because of his natural right to live. But when he uses it, he uses it as an intelligent being. Thus on one level man collaborates with matter which gives him the right called *use*, *e.g.*, the sculptor with his marble. But on another level, man's subjection of matter to his intelligent direction

and purpose gives a right which is called *dominion*, or in the broad sense of the term *ownership*, *e.g.*, when he impresses on the marble the ideal pattern in his mind, *e.g.*, our Blessed Lady. *Use* reflects man's technical mastery over nature; *dominion* reflects his purposive, intelligent mastery. The right to any *particular* piece of private property is not a primary natural right, but an *acquired* right; it depends on some adventitious title such as a gift of purchase.

10 "First let it be made clear beyond all doubt that neither Leo XIII nor those theologians who have taught under the guidance and direction of the Church, have ever denied or called in question the two-fold aspect of ownership, which is individual or social accordingly as it regards individuals or concerns the common good. Their unanimous contention has always been that the right to own private property has been given to man by nature or rather by the Creator Himself, not only in order that individuals may be able to provide for their own needs and those of their families, but also that by means of it, the goods which the Creator has destined for the human race may truly serve this purpose. Now these ends cannot be secured unless some definite and stable order is maintained." — *Quadragesimo Anno*, § 45.

11 As discussed above, Sheen here refers to a moral right, not a civil right. A starving man incurs no moral guilt if, after having exhausted *all* other recourse, he takes enough to preserve his life from the superabundance of another. He may, however, run afoul of human law, and be justly punished for breaking human law, even though he is not morally guilty under God's law. [Ed.]

12 "It follows from the two-fold character of ownership, which We have termed individual and social, that man must take into account in this matter not only his own advantage but also the common good. To define in detail these duties, when the need occurs and when the natural law does not do so, is the function of the government. Provided that the natural and divine law be observed, the public authority, in view of the common good, may specify more accurately what is licit and what is illicit for property owners in the use of their possessions. Moreover, Leo XIII had wisely taught that 'the defining of private possession has been left by God to man's own industry and to the laws of individual peoples.'

"History proves that the rights of ownership, like other elements of social life, are not absolutely rigid, and this doctrine, we ourselves have given utterance to on a previous occasion in the following terms: 'How varied are the forms which the right of property has assumed! First, the primitive form used amongst rude and savage peoples, which still exists in certain localities even in our own day; then, that of the patriarchal age; later came various tyrannical types (we use the word in its classical meaning); finally, the feudal and monarchic system down to the varieties of more recent times' (Cath. Action Cong., 1926). 'It is plain, however, that the State may not discharge this duty in an arbitrary manner. Man's natural right of possessing and transmitting property by inheritance must remain intact and cannot be taken away by the State from man.' (*Rerum Novarum*, § 13) 'For man precedes the state and the domestic household is antecedent, as well in idea as in fact, to the gathering of men into a community'." (*Ibid.*)

Hence the prudent Pontiff had already declared it unlawful for the State to exhaust the means of individuals by crushing taxes and tributes. "The right to possess private property is derived from nature, not from man; and the State has by no means the right to abolish it, but only to control its use and bring it into harmony with the interests of the public good." (*Rerum Novarum*, § 47) — *Quadragesimo Anno*, § 49.

[13] *Quadragesimo Anno*, § 47.

[14] *Ibid.*, § 49.

[15] Capitalism is here understood as: "The accumulation of wealth, immense power and despotic economic power in the hands of the few, so that those few are frequently not the owners, but only the trustees and directors of invested funds, who administer them at their good pleasure. This power becomes particularly irresistible when exercised by those, who, because they hold and control money, are able also to govern credit, and determine its allotment, for that reason supplying, so to speak, the lifeblood to the entire economic body, and grasping, as it were, in their hands the very soul of production, so that no one dare breathe against their will.

"This accumulation of power, the characteristic note of the modern economic order, is a natural result of limitless free competition which permits the survival of those only who are the strongest, which often means those who fight most relentlessly, who pay least heed to the dictates of conscience.

"This concentration of power has led to a threefold struggle for domination. First, there is the struggle for dictatorship in the economic sphere itself, then, the fierce battle to acquire control of the state, so that its resources and authority may be abused in the economic struggles: finally the clash between states them-

selves. This latter arises from two causes: because the nations apply their power and political influence, regardless of circumstances, to promote the economic advantages of their citizens; and because, vice versa, economic forces and economic domination are used to decide political controversies between peoples."
— *Quadragesimo Anno*, §§ 105-108.

[16] ". . .Communism is the only complete and logical working model of Capitalism. The sins are there a system which are everywhere else a sort of repeated blunder. From the first it is admitted, that the whole system was directed toward encouraging or driving the worker to spend his wages; to have nothing left on the next pay day; to enjoy everything and to consume everything and efface everything; in short, to shudder at the thought of only one crime; the creative crime of thrift. It was a tame extravagance; a sort of disciplined dissipation; a meek and submissive prodigality. For the moment the slave left off drinking all his wages, the moment he began to hoard or hide any property, he would be saving up something in the State; that is, he might become less of a slave and more of a citizen. Morally considered, there has been nothing quite so unspeakably mean as this Bolshevist generosity. But it will be noted that exactly the same spirit and tone pervades the manner of dealing with the other matter. Sex also is to come to the slave merely as a pleasure; that it may never be a power. He is to know as little as possible, or at least to think as little as possible, of the pleasure as anything else except a pleasure; to think or know nothing of where it comes or where it will go to, when once the soiled object has passed through his own hands. He is not to trouble about its origin in the purpose of God or its sequel in the posterity of man. In every department he is not a possessor, but only a consumer; even if it be of the first elements of life and fire in so far as they are consumable; he is to have no notion of the sort of Burning Bush that burns and is not consumed. For that bush only grows on the soil, on the real land where human beings can behold it; and the spot on which they stand is holy ground. Thus there is an exact parallel between the two modern moral or immoral, ideas of social reform. The world has forgotten simultaneously that the making of a Farm is something much larger than the making of a profit, or even a product, in the sense of liking the taste of beetroot sugar; and that the founding of a Family is something much larger than sex in the limited sense of current literature; which was anticipated in one bleak and blinding flash in a single line of George Meredith; 'And eat our pot of money on

the grave.' " — G.K. Chesterton, *The Well and the Shallows*.
New York: Sheed and Ward, 1935, 235, 236.

In the problem of property, it is evident that it is the *use* or social function of property, which gives it a moral aspect, simply because it is the basis of the property owner's responsibility to society.

In order to understand this, recall that property has a double value: an exchange value and a use value. Exchange value is its relation to others; namely, what a thing will bring in barter. The use value is in relation to the owner. The laborer with a dozen hens can either sell the eggs for fifty cents a dozen, or he can use them to feed himself and his family. His liberty consists in choosing between selling and using, and the important word here is choosing.

Now it is evident that in monopolistic Capitalism, the only value which a thing has is its *exchange value*. If I had ten shares in a corporation I would have no liberty of choosing between exchanging or using, which the farmer has, who, if the egg market goes down, can use them. It is this emphasis on exchange value, to the utter forgetfulness of use value which has brought on the peculiar modern paradox of starvation amidst plenty. During the days of the famine, Irishmen starved because of a scarcity of potatoes; today Americans are poor because there are so many potatoes we have to dump them into the sea. In other words, we think of having only in terms of exchange value. We have made trade so primary that we think less about coffee as something to drink and more about it as something to sell. The idea of enjoying a thing for oneself has become almost inconceivable. The normal thing is for a man to raise pears in order that he may eat them, and secondarily to sell them. In other words, production exists for consumption, not consumption for production.

It is no answer to retort: "then everyone must raise his own pears" though I could conceive a man being happier at that than raising someone else's cranes. The elementary example is used because one must understand things in their simplicity in order to find a way out of modern duplicity. Liberty resides more in use value than in exchange value. The American system originally was founded on the use value of agriculture because a man who lives on land is less dependent than a man who lives on the market.

Chesterton contends that the exchange is the price and the use is the value. Quoting Oscar Wilde who defined a cynic as a "man who knows the price of everything and the value of nothing" Chesterton adds: "It is extraordinarily true; and the answer to most other things that he said. But it is yet more extraordinary that the modern men who make that mistake most obviously are not the cynics. On the contrary, they are those who call themselves the Optimists; perhaps even those who would call themselves the Idealists; certainly those who regard themselves as the Regular Guys and the Sons of Service and Uplift. It is too often those very people who have spoilt all their good effect, and weakened their considerable good example in work and social contract, but that very error: that things are to be judged by the price and not by the value. And since Price is a crazy and incalculable thing, while Value is an intrinsic and indestructible thing, they have swept us into a society which is no longer solid but fluid, as unfathomable as a sea and as treacherous as quicksand. Whether anything more solid can be built again upon a social philosophy of values, there is now no space to discuss at length here; but I am certain that nothing solid can be built on any other philosophy; certainly not upon the utterly unphilosophical philosophy of blind buying and selling; of bullying people into purchasing what they do not want; of making it badly so that they may break it and imagine they want it again; of keeping rubbish in rapid circulation like a dust-storm in a desert; and pretending that you are teaching men to hope, because you do not leave them one intelligent instant in which to despair." — Chesterton, *The Well and the Shallows, op. cit.,* 230, 231.

[17] *Quadragesimo Anno,* § 46.

[18] *Rerum Novarum,* § 22.

[19] Luke 16:19-31.

[20] More accurately, the power of obtaining (the absolute right *to* property), and the rights of control and disposal (the limited rights *of* property). [Ed.]

[21] Sheen appears to imply that under Roman law an owner could do as he liked to others with what he owned. That is incorrect. Roman law made a clear distinction between ownership of property (title, *dominion* or *proprietas*), and exercise of property (use, *usufruct*). "Use and abuse" refers to what one may do *to* what one owns, not what one may do to others *with* what one owns. See J. A. Crook, *Law and Life of Rome, 90 B.C. - A.D. 212.* Ithaca, New York: Cornell University Press, 1967, 139-178. [Ed.]

[22] Cf. Hilaire Belloc, *The Restoration of Property, op. cit.,* 9-11. [Ed.]

---

23 Herbert Agar, *Land of the Free*. New York: Houghton Mifflin Co., 1935, 66, 67.

24 This is because under current law minority shareholders do not have their full rights of ownership, *e.g.*, receipt of all income attributable to their proportional share of ownership, and why CESJ includes "Restoration of the rights of private property, especially in corporate equity" as a pillar of an economically just society. See *Dodge v. Ford Motor Company* 204 Mich. 459, 170 N.W. 668. (Mich. 1919). [Ed.]

25 This was correct at the time Sheen wrote. Since the 1970s, however, it has become more common for the courts to "pierce the corporate veil" and hold boards of directors personally liable for the acts of the corporation. [Ed.]

26 Cf. "Property in every day life is the right of *control*." Louis O. Kelso, "Karl Marx: the Almost Capitalist," *American Bar Association Journal*, March, 1957. [Ed.]

27 This is why one of the "four pillars of an economically just society" is the restoration of the rights of private property, especially in corporate equity. See the Foreword, xvi. [Ed.]

28 This philosophy was embodied into law with the adoption of a rule or principle of law called "the business judgment rule" that effectively gave total control to the Board of Directors over, *e.g.*, payment of dividends. Shareholders can sue for payment of dividends if they can prove that the corporation does not need the cash for legitimate business purposes. This puts the shareholders in the situation of having to prove a negative (*i.e.*, that the corporation does not need the cash), which is logically impossible. *Dodge v. Ford Motor Company* is one of the first cases to be decided on the basis of the business judgment rule. [Ed.]

29 Adolf Augustus Berle, Jr. (1895-1971), American lawyer and diplomat, and pivotal member of President Franklin Roosevelt's "Brain Trust." Berle was instrumental in inserting a new concept of private property into U.S. law. [Ed.]

30 Gardiner Coit Means (1896-1988), American economist who coined the term "collective capitalism." Cf. Peter F. Drucker's "Pension Plan Socialism." [Ed.]

31 Adolf A. Berle and Gardiner C. Means, *The Modern Corporation and Private Property*. New York: Macmillan and Co., 1940, 66-68.

32 Program, N.Y. edition, 1936, pp.34, 35, 36, and 52.

33 The two major factions in the Spanish Civil War (1936-1939) were the fascists ("Nationalists") and the communists ("Republicans"). [Ed.]

[34] The Hungarian Soviet Republic was established in 1919 but was quickly overthrown in the economic and political chaos following World War I. [Ed.]

[35] The Russian Revolution of 1917. [Ed.]

[36] François Marie Charles Fourier (1772-1837), French utopian socialist.

[37] Claude Henri de Rouvroy, comte de Saint-Simon (Henri de Saint-Simon) (1760-1825), French positivist philosopher and socialist theorist. [Ed.]

[38] This is the point of Henry George's "single tax," by means of which the State would take all income and profits from land ownership, making title irrelevant. Henry George, *Progress and Poverty*. New York: The Schalkenbach Foundation, 1935, 406. [Ed.]

[39] Supporters of Leon Trotsky (1879-1940), leader of the Menshaviks. Trotsky opposed Stalinism. He was deported from the Soviet Union in 1929 and assassinated in Mexico in 1940 at Stalin's orders.

[40] *Pravda*, March 20, 1938; *Iszvestia*, February 3, March 5, May 14, June 15, 1938.

[41] Walter Duranty (1884-1957) was an Anglo-American journalist who was the Moscow Bureau Chief for the *New York Times* from 1922-1936 who won a Pulitzer Prize in 1932 for a series of articles praising the Soviet Union. Duranty is best known for denying widespread famine, most notably in the Ukraine in the early 1930s, and for defending the Stalinist purges of 1938. The Pulitzer Prize committee has consistently refused to revoke Duranty's award on the grounds that Duranty did not engage in deliberate deception, but was merely a dupe of Stalin. [Ed.]

[42] André Paul Guillaume Gide (1869-1951), French novelist and essayist, Nobel Laureate in Literature (1947), noted for his repudiation of communism after visiting the Soviet Union in 1936. [Ed.]

[43] Walter McLennan Citrine, 1st Baron Citrine (1887-1983), English trade unionist strongly opposed to both fascism and communism who opposed the Labour Party's drift to the Left in the 1930s. [Ed.]

[44] William Henry Chamberlin (1897-1969), American historian and journalist who served as the Moscow correspondent for *The Christian Science Monitor* (1922-1934). Originally a Marxist and Soviet sympathizer, he became convinced that communism, socialism and collectivism were in error after seeing the famine in the Ukraine in the 1930s. [Ed.]

[45] Journalist who was groomed by Walter Duranty as his successor. [Ed.]

[46] John Thompson Whitaker (1906-1946), American journalist who is most noted for covering the Spanish Civil War and Fascist Italy under Mussolini until he was expelled. [Ed.]

[47] E. J. Lowry, in *Washington Evening Star*, December 26, 1938.

[48] Prior to 1906, "kulak" was a pejorative for a greedy merchant or village moneylender. After 1906, kulaks were peasants who owned their own farms and, as a class, resisted collectivization in the 1920s and 1930s. Stalin labeled them oppressors and class enemies, targeting them for "liquidation." [Ed.]

[49] Karl Marx, *Critique of the Gotha Program* (1875). [Ed.]

[50] Lenin, *The Proletarian Revolution*, Communist Party Publications, London, p. 15.

[51] *Vetch Moskva*, July 7, 1938; *Izvestia*, March 29, 1938.

[52] *Vetch Moskva*, July 14, 1938; *Izvestia*, July 8, 1938; *Pravda*, February 2, 1938; *Vetch Moskva*, July 14, and 25, 1938.

[53] Soviet Trade Distribution, cf. *Pravda*, May 17, 1938.

[54] *Sovietskaia Torgovlia*, No. 114, 1938.

[55] *Pravda*, January 17 and July 7, 1938; *Pravda*, September 28, 1938.

[56] *Pravda*, April 27, 1938.

[57] *Pravda*, July 11, 1938.

[58] *Vetch Moskva*, December 22, 1937.

[59] *Vetch Moskva*, July 13, 1938.

[60] Aristotle, *The Politics*, 1263a.

[61] *Bolchevik*, No. 7, 1938.

[62] *Izvestia*, February 18, 1935.

[63] *Izvestia*, April 2, 1938.

[64] *Visti*, February 12, 1938.

[65] December 4, 1937.

[66] This may be an error on Sheen's part. The only Soviet Minister of Agriculture named Echernov or Chernov we can identify was Viktor Mikhaylovich Chernov, a.k.a., "Boris Olenin" (1873-1952), who served briefly as Minister of Agriculture in the Socialist Revolutionary government opposed to the Bolsheviks in 1917, before emigrating to Paris in 1920 where he lived until World War II, when he went to the United States, where he contributed anti-communist articles to periodicals. [Ed.]

[67] An American magazine founded in Boston, Massachusetts, in 1857. [Ed.]

[68] The second oldest continuously published monthly magazine in America, founded in June of 1850 in New York City. [Ed.]

[69] An American weekly news magazine founded in 1923 in New York City. [Ed.]

[70] Cf. *Flemming v. Nestor*, 363 U.S. 603 (1960), in which Nestor, a convicted communist, sued for his Social Security benefits on the grounds that he, a communist whose whole theory rested on the abolition of private property, had private property in his account balances. [Ed.]

[71] G. K. Chesterton, "Sex and Property," *The Well and the Shallows, op. cit.*

[72] Contrast this with E. F. Schumacher's treatise, *Small is Beautiful: Economics as if People Mattered* (1973), that many people today consider an expression of authentic Catholic social thought. [Ed.]

[73] Cf. Louis O. Kelso and Mortimer J. Adler's two collaborations, *The Capitalist Manifesto* (New York: Random House, 1958) and *The New Capitalists* (New York: Random House, 1961), which presented a proposal to make workers into owners, but without redistributing existing ownership. This can be done by making capital credit available to the workers based not on past savings, but on future savings, allowing them to buy in to capital expansion of the enterprise, paying for it with their share of the future profits of the company itself. This would be a political dilution, but leave the existing ownership stake of current owners fully intact. The importance of future savings as a source of financing growth is highlighted by the subtitle of *The New Capitalists*: "A Proposal to Free Economic Growth from the Slavery of [Past] Savings." [Ed.]

[74] There is also the effect of "binary growth" noted by Professor Robert H. A. Ashford in his book *Binary Economics: The New Paradigm*. Lanham, Maryland: University Press of America, 1999. As people who formerly owned little or no capital receive capital incomes out of funds that were formerly retained for re-investment in the corporation, demand increases, creating an incentive for increased production and more rapid rates of growth. [Ed.]

[75] Cf. Belloc, *An Essay on the Restoration of Property, op. cit.*; Michael D. Greaney, *The Restoration of Property: A Reexamination of a Natural Right*. Arlington, Virginia: Economic Justice Media, 2012. [Ed.]

[76] Mark 5:1 ff.

[77] John 11:20.

[78] Cf. *Quadragesimo Anno*, § 49. [Ed.]

6. The Dignity of Labor

IN THE DAYS OF PROSPERITY the word most often used is "progress"; in the days of depression the word most often used is "labor." But there is danger that just as during the days of prosperity we forgot the goal and purpose of progress, so too today we may forget the nature and dignity of labor.

Labor is not an isolated thing detached from the rest of life. Economically it is bound up with capital as a co-partner in production; socially, it is bound up with what used to be called contemplation and now is called leisure.[1] Spiritually it is bound up with salvation. History records two errors concerning labor: the error of the Greeks and the error of the moderns. Both are guilty of divorcing that which God had joined together and bade man not put asunder; namely, labor and contemplation. The Greeks despised labor; the moderns despise contemplation. This idea has been most clearly presented by Étienne Borne[2] and François Henry in their book *A Philosophy of Work*[3] to which we record our debt.

According to the Greeks, work was not human, but an irrational necessity foreign to the nature of man. Plato, for example, recognized the beauty of the body apart from the soul, and the beauty of the soul apart from the body, but never the beauty of both simultaneously. He argued that anything which hurts the body such as labor must necessarily hurt the soul. Furthermore, anyone who works for gain is rendered incapable of ever knowing the truth. Aristotle also impugned labor and refused to grant to slaves the virtues of temperance, justice, and courage for the reason that the slaves lacked liberty.[4] Xenophon argued that a man who works with his hands, has no time for friends or for cultivation of the mind or for the State. This supercilious attitude toward labor manifested itself in the legislation of Thebes, decreeing that a man could not be a magistrate until ten years after he had given up business. At Sparta the law forbade any citizen to follow any occupation, which was equivalent to saying that laborers were not citizens.

The result of the Grecian attitude was the creation of two races of men: one the race of slaves, the other the race of the contemplatives of the freemen. In the language of Plato, the republic was made up of two classes of people, sages and warriors. There was never any question of putting them on an equal basis, for he contended, the art of producing is inferior to the art of enjoying. Any dignity which the slave or the laborer possesses is derived from the dignity of his master, and not from himself. In a civilization of that kind the only citizens who mattered were those who had the time and the leisure for contemplation. Working for gain was a mark of inferiority because it rendered a man incapable of ever coming to a knowledge of the truth. In fact, the worker never came into his own until the advent of Christianity when our Blessed Lord liberated the sons of Martha without ceasing at the same time to glorify the sons of Mary.

The other extreme error, that of the modern world, glorifies labor to the detriment of contemplation. The ancients despised the workers; the moderns despise the mystics, or to put it another way, the Greeks exalted the philosopher, the moderns exalt the doer. There are three stages in the development of the modern idea:

(a) The period of the Religious Revolution which despised contemplation and identified a life spent in prayer with laziness. Monasticism being under attack, the only virtues considered worthy of the name were the active virtues. Previously, during the days of Christian unity, work had significance because it prepared for rational repose; now the worker is exalted, not as something positive, but simply because he is not in repose. Under the traditional concept, faith and works were inseparable for "faith without good works is dead." Now justification comes by faith alone; hence work is indifferent to salvation. The great benefactor of civilization is not the philosopher of the Greeks, nor the contemplative of the Christians, but the doer, the worker for "in the beginning was not the Word," but "in the beginning was the Worker."

b) The next stage in the development of the modern idea is the Industrial Revolution, in which the exaltation shifts from that of the "worker" to "work," or from the personal to the mechanical. This was rather a natural transition during the days of machinery, for the industrialist did not need laborers as much as he needed labor, *i.e.*, a kind of robot to stand by the machines to keep them running. When this happened labor began to be a commodity, or a piece of merchandise. The laborer of the Christian civilization who is a person, now becomes a thing — something to be bargained for over the counter like a piece of bric-a-brac or a bag of potatoes.[5] The result was that his wages were no longer determined by his personal rights and dignity, but by the economic law of supply and demand. If there was an abundance of labor, the wage was low; if there was a shortage of labor the wage was high.

c) Man was now ready for his final dehumanization. Divorced from the purpose of his work by the Religious Revolution; divorced from his personality by machinery, there was nothing left to do but let Communism, as always, carry Capitalism to its extreme and thus complete the final degradation of man. Under Communism it is not the "laborer" who is primary; nor is it "labor"; it is "production." The difference between "labor" and "production" is that labor looks to the individual; production looks to the collectivity. Under such a plan, man no longer has any bargaining power; it is the State which dictates how much wages he will receive, wages which are presently so low that Sir Walter Citrine, the President of the Labor Trade Union Congress of England, says that those on relief in America, France, and England are better off than the workers of Russia. Not only are his wages fixed by the Dictator, but he may not strike to receive better wages for the strike is considered treason and the striker is shot as an enemy of the people. To strike under Communism is not just a crime; it is suicide. Furthermore, if a worker refuses to accept the work offered by the State, he is punished by privation of work elsewhere, for the same "boss" is everywhere. Where he may travel is likewise limited for the passports determine where he shall live. Neither may the worker retain for himself any productive property, *i.e.*, own a business of his own as a mark of his liberty and independence. One worker, Kliniova of Stalingrad, was condemned to ten months of hard labor for having sold six pounds of bread. Note that it was not for stealing bread which he probably needed, that he was condemned, but for selling it. Only the State may sell it.

The Communist State, instead of protecting the workers against exploitation, rather protects the State through the exploitation of workers. If we needed any further official confirmation that what Communism defends is not the worker but production, just recall the decision of the Ninth Union Congress of the Soviet Union: "workers organizations have for their principal object the *increase of the output* of labor, the lowering of price as a result of that increased output, and the amelioration of its quality." Not a word about the right of the worker to a living wage.[6] Article 126 of the Soviet Constitution declares that the purpose of workers' organizations is "to strengthen and develop the socialist system." This in plain simple English means man exists for the State, the worker exists for production. Instead of working for a few Capitalists, the State now becomes the supreme Capitalist; the person fades out and becomes a tool-making animal whose sole business it is to pile up more wealth for the State. Man is thus thrust into a frenzy of toil, with no vocation independent of the economic order, with no rights other than those which the State gives him, and with no other interest than to increase production until the day when Russia can overthrow its enemy Capitalism and itself become so Capitalistic that no one may challenge it. Under Communism labor exists for only one purpose — to be exploited by a few opportunists who bombed their way to proletarian thrones and set themselves up as gods to receive the enforced adoration of puppets who once were men and who, by the grace of God and the restoration of freedom, will be men once again.

The Catholic Position

History reveals two major distortions of labor; the ancient error which considered it an ignoble, and the modern error which makes it first a commodity as did Capitalism, and then State property as does Communism. Confining ourselves to our times, we might summarize the development as follows: Capitalism regarded man as a "hand"; the Capitalist spoke of having 500 "hands" in his factory. This "hand" was a "commodity" to be bargained for in view of profit. Communism, later on, out-capitalizes Capitalism by regarding man as a "stomach" or as a living machine not to be bargained with, for he has no bargaining power, but to be fed by the State and not for the sake of profit, but for greater production. The common fundamental error of both is that man exists for work.

The Catholic position is just the contrary: man exists not for work, but work exists for man. Neither profit nor production is the end of man, for if they were, man would be subservient to profit as he is under Capitalism, and subservient to production as he is under Communism. That brings us back again to our starting point: the crisis of our day is the crisis of liberty. Shall man be freed, or shall he continue to be less than profit and production? Our Lord said that one man was worth more than all the world. This means that the right of a single man to a decent, comfortable, normal existence is primary to a 2,500 percent return on an industrial investment, or to the daily output of 250,000 tractors for Soviet farms. This saying is hard, but down deep in our hearts we know it to be true. What have we been doing for decades but using man for production? Because we concentrated on production as our goal, instead of on man, we soon reached our goal when we produced more than we needed. We used man to produce, and now we throw him out on the street because he has produced too much. We taxed people in order to pay for limitation of production and thus made men contribute from their wages to their own impoverishment. If we made production exist for man, instead of man for production, we would not be starving in the midst of plenty. Even the present tendency to birth control the fecundity of the earth or to toss huge quantities of grain into the sea, for the sake of an economic price, when we still have bread lines, is a form of the same fallacy — *viz.*, man exists for the economic not the economic for man.

The Catholic position is that working is to some extent like eating — it is a means to an end, and that end is freedom to develop oneself as a child of God and an heir of the Kingdom of Heaven. As we do not live to eat, so neither do we live to work — we work to live, not only physically as the cows and camels, but spiritually as persons endowed with an intellect and a will who seek the perfection of their personalities in Him for whom they were made.

Work is a condition of developing our personality, because through work man establishes relations with (1) God; (2) his neighbor; and (3) nature. Work is a means to the salvation of our souls, the betterment of society, and the advancement of civilization.

1. First of all, work unites us to God, not only by its ascetic character, it imposes discipline on man by subjugation of his lower passions to order and reason. But more than that, through the intention of the worker the material universe is brought back again to God. St. Paul tells us: "All are yours; you are Christ's and Christ is God's. All are yours"[7]; the rivers, the seas, the birds and beasts, the gold and steel, the earth and the fullness thereof. All belong to man, but as such they are not to be turned to his selfish ends, but to be used as means to lift both him and them to God through Christ. The universe is thus a kind of scaffolding up through which man climbs to the Kingdom of Heaven; it is also a kind of sacrament — a material thing used as a channel of spiritual sanctification. Flowers and trees, metal and machines are dumb and inarticulate. Flowers have no other voice than their perfume, and trees no other speech than the whispering of their leaves. Their mute gaspings need a mind and a voice to lift them out of the materiality and give them utterance before the throne of God.

The man who labors does this; when he goes down into the bowels of the earth and says to the gold: "Praise ye the Lord" and hammers it into a chalice to contain the redemptive wine of Calvary, he has united himself to God in one of the noblest of human prayers. The worker in the automobile factory who adds only a screw to an engine, can if he uses his will, make that act a prayer. If in his own mind, he says: *"Propter te Domine,"*[8] he has made a piece of steel a prayer, and his act will be far richer for his salvation than the carrying of a sick man for miles in the name of science. The Catholic philosophy of life is that not all the best prayers are said on our knees; some of them are said not at work, but by works.[9] And just as the flower of a garden can take an added value when plucked out of love for our mother, so a street cleaned by a worker can take an added value when done out of love for God. The kind of work we do has nothing to do with its value; its value comes from the One in whose Name it is given. A drink of cold water in His Name receives reward a hundredfold. The professor at his desk, the scientist in his laboratory, are not nobler men if they work for a salary and human glory than the bootblack or the delivery boy who do their appointed tasks not just to live, but to live for God.

There are millions of Catholics in the world today who are doing these very things, though no one except probably their confessor knows anything about it; *e.g.*, typists who in their souls breathe the Divine Name of Jesus every time they put a sheet of paper into their typewriter; iron molders who mark with their thumbs on their great ladles the sign of the cross; night watchmen who make their rounds saying their rosary; nuns and nurses and doctors in hospitals who open sick doors to face in each sick bed in human disguise the suffering and bleeding Christ; policemen and firemen who begin their daily rounds of duties by climbing Calvary, offering its mystical renewal in the Mass as a consecration of their whole day to Christ; mothers feeding, nourishing, and watching over their children as future citizens of the Church and members of the family of the Blessed Trinity; and athletes offering an aspiration to the Blessed Mother before their race. So the litany of historical cases might go on, but of them the rest of the world is ignorant, because it has forgotten that work is not an end but first and foremost a means to the salvation of one's soul and the glory of God.

2. Labor is not only the bond uniting man to God; it is also the bond uniting man to man; a kind of school of social service, a base of human solidarity, a testimonial to the insufficiency of man without his neighbor. Work has its social roots in the impotency of man to satisfy his needs alone and without the help of others. In working with others, man ratifies his social dependence and performs an act of natural charity, because he helps create utility for others and thus adds to the happiness of his fellow man. The Catholic view, it will be noted, here adds that labor must always be used, not to dissociate ourselves from our neighbor, but to unite us to him.

Communism is wrong in saying that labor is the basis of class antagonism, or that capital and labor must forever be enemies. This is just as stupid as saying that husband and wife have different functions in life, therefore, they should always be at one another's throats. The labor of the laborer and the labor of the capitalist are bonds uniting them in a common enterprise for the sake of a common end. Capital cannot do without labor and labor cannot do without capital any more than an iron molder can mold without iron.

As Pius XI put it:

Universal experience teaches us that no nation has ever yet risen from want and poverty to a better and loftier station without the unremitting toil of all its citizens, both employers and employed. But it is no less self-evident that these ceaseless labors would have remained ineffective, indeed could never have been attempted, had not God, the Creator of all things, in His goodness bestowed in the first instance the wealth and resource of nature, its treasures and its powers. For what else is work but the application of one's forces of soul and body to these gifts of nature for the development of one's powers by their means? Now, the natural law, or rather, God's will manifested by it, demands that the right order be observed in the application of natural resources to human needs; and this order consists in everything having its proper owner. Hence it follows that unless a man apply his labor to his own property, an alliance must be formed between his toil and his neighbor's property, for each is helpless without the other. This was what Leo XIII had in mind when he wrote: "Capital cannot do without labor, nor labor without capital." It is therefore entirely false to ascribe the results of their combined efforts to either party alone; and it is flagrantly unjust that either should deny the efficacy of the other and seize all the profits.[10]

The greater the material advancement of any country, the more profound should be its spirit of neighborliness. Good roads, telegraph, radio, railways, automobiles, airplanes, ships, are to be conceived as so many new links binding man to his fellow man. The neighbor is no longer down the road; he is within the sound of the human voice, maybe at the other end of the world. Machinery then is not to be decried as materialistic, for it is not of its essence to be that, for that which brings us closer to our fellow man is born of the same stuff as that which brings us to God; namely, toil.

3. Finally, work unites us with nature. It does this by enabling us to prolong the creative work of God and to make each of us in the language of St. Paul *"adjutor Dei."*[11] God, the supreme Artist, has communicated artistic causality to man, so that he can now make things to his image and likeness, as God made him to His Image and likeness. God, who had the Power to make something out of nothing, gives to man the power to make something out of something. Instead of filling the world with ready-made things, God chose to give man the power of designing and tailoring them. He did this through the twofold gift of raw material and intelligence. The marriage of both is, in the improper sense of the term our "creation." Work, looked at from this point of view is just as personal as the act of living. The union of man and nature becomes a fecund union, and from them is generated civilization. Hence the nobler the thoughts and ideas which man impresses on matter, the loftier is civilization. Workers, who use their brains to devise chemical gases for the extinction of their fellow man, are not producing civilization, but chaos. Hence the great importance of the way we

think in relation to civilization. It is absolutely false to
say it makes no difference what you believe or think, but
only how you act, because we act on our beliefs. Nature
too responds to our beliefs. The way we utilize nature is
an indication of our thinking and our sense of values. Is a
civilization better because it has more bathtubs than another civilization which has fewer bathtubs but more
saints? Where our treasure is, there is our heart also.
From the Catholic point of view, that civilization is best in
which man cooperates with nature as the handiwork of
God, as his soul cooperates with grace as the gift of God.
The Divine Plan in nature calls for human completion, as
Divine Grace in man calls for human cooperation. Work
then is the redemption of nature as Christ is the redemption of man, and civilization is the product of both redemptive acts, the completion of the circle by which nature serves man and man serves God.

Application to: (a) Living Wage, (b) Class Struggle, (c) Unemployment.

Since work is the bond uniting us to God, to our fellow
man and to nature, it is easy to understand the Catholic
attitude toward three concrete problems of labor.

1. *Living Wage.*[12] Why does the Church plead for a living wage for an employee, one which must be sufficient to
support him and his family in reasonable comfort? Not
that he may have two automobiles and the luxuries of life,
but that he may be dispensed from economic necessities in
order that his soul may be free to attain the end for which
it was created, both in this world and the next. Such is
the first practical application of the first principle given
above that labor is the bond uniting us to God. Cows are
well fed in order to be milked or butchered; but man is to
be well fed to be a man. And what does it mean to be a
man? To be a man means to be superior in value to anything else. Wages exist for man, not man for wages. Just
as it is difficult for a man to pray when hungry, so it is
difficult for man to perfect himself intellectually and spiritually if he lacks the ordinary comforts of life. Hence the
necessity of a living wage, because, in the language of the
Church, first of all man's "possessions. . . are his spiritual

and mental interests. Life on earth, however good and desirable in itself, is not the final purpose for which man is created; it is only the way and the means to that attainment of truth, and that practice of goodness in which the full life of the soul consists. It is the soul which is made after the image and likeness of God; it is in the soul that sovereignty resides, in virtue of which man is commanded to rule the creatures below him, and to use all the earth and ocean for his profit and advantage. 'Fill the earth and subdue it; and rule over the fishes of the sea and the fowls of the air, and all living creatures which move upon the earth'."[13] That is why the Church in discussing the problem of wages and hours and working conditions avoids two extremes: the extreme of being so concerned with the eternal destiny of the worker as to be disinterested in his temporal welfare — the other extreme of being so interested in the temporal welfare of the worker as to forget his eternal destiny. The Church is concerned with both for the simple reason that work and eternal rest cannot be divorced. Is it not disinterested in the temporal condition of the workingman, but strives to better his condition for the sake of freedom. Material necessities are the conditions of spirituality. As St. Thomas puts it: "Two things are necessary for the wellbeing of man: the first and principle thing consists in acting virtuously; the second is to have a sufficiency of material goods, which is necessary for the exercise of virtue."[14] Economic rights to a decent human existence therefore in the eyes of the Church, are inseparable from eternal ends.

2. *Class Struggle.* Because work unites us to our fellow man the Church is opposed to Communism with its philosophy of violence and class struggle. Work of its nature does not create opposition, but unity, for men who work on the same thing exercise a common function. If then, it is asked why is the Church opposed to class hatred, it is because work is the foundation of neighborliness. That is why the Church asks that the State interfere against both the covetous employers and the violent organizers of labor.

. . . it is essential in these times of covetous greed, to keep
the people within the line of duty; for if all may justly
strive to better their condition, yet neither justice nor the
common good allows anyone to seize that which belongs to
another, or, under the pretext of futile and ridiculous
equality, to lay hands on other peoples fortunes. It is most
true that by far the larger part of the people who work pre-
fer to improve themselves by honest labor rather than by
doing wrong to others. But there are not a few who are im-
bued with bad principles and are anxious for revolutionary
change, and whose great purpose it is to stir up tumult and
bring about a policy of violence. The authority of the State
should intervene to put restraint upon these disturbers, to
save the workmen from their seditious arts, and to protect
lawful owners from spoliation[15]

Because we have forgotten the Christian philosophy of
work as a bond uniting us to God, we have at the same
time forgotten it as a bond uniting us to our fellow man.
The great inventions of printing, radio, and rapid transportation which should have been the bonds of greater
unity, have become the very basis of our discords. As we
all communicate in the truth of the multiplication table,
and as Catholics we communicate in the Truth of the
same Creed without a shade of difference, so we should
communicate in the unity of our material progress. The
fact is we do not, for the conception of width has, unfortunately, writes Douglas Jerrold,[16] been fatal to the idea of
depth.

An inhabitant of Mars who had last visited our planet at
the end of the eighteenth century, would today estimate
very differently the effects of the advance of science on the
spread of intelligence in the last hundred years. He would
assume, on hearing of the extension of communications,
that the separatist tendencies so prevalent in earlier centuries would have disappeared. On hearing of the adoption,
in all civilized countries, of compulsory education, he would
assume a wide diffusion of culture, the exaction by an educated electorate of new standards of logic from publicists
and of new standards of enlightenment from statesmen.
On hearing of the cheapness of printing, of editions of the
classics circulating at a price within the reach of all, and of
newspapers bringing the latest news from five continents
every hour to the notice of all classes, he would expect to

find the modern world accustomed to and exacting the highest standards in art and literature, the most sober and informed judgments on public affairs. Finally, when he heard of the growth of wireless telegraphy and broadcasting, he would feel assured that, whatever we may lack of leisure or interest, means at least exist for bringing home to all classes, by the most direct and effective methods, the facts of every problem, for breaking up class or sectional or national prejudice, and for combating and conquering ignorance.

In every one of these anticipations the inhabitant of Mars would be wholly wrong. The problems of ignorance, of irreligion, or class prejudice, of national, racial and class hatred which were visible on the surface of things a hundred years ago, have today struck roots so deep, so powerful and so diffused that they threaten the very foundations of our civilization. National war, first waged by Napoleon has reappeared in our own time to shake the framework of society and to destroy from without the last link between modern Europe and the great classical civilization which left as its legacy to history the conception of a super-national sovereignty. Meanwhile envy, born of ignorance and fed by material greed, threatens to destroy society from within.[17]

The reason for the breakup of neighborliness is because we have lost the common denominator of truth and the purpose of man. Refusing to recognize any other truth than subjective impression, and any other purpose than a purely transitory one, we have bent the resources of our work to further separation and alienation instead of into the bonds of unity and peace.

3. *Unemployment.* Why is the Church opposed to unemployment? Because man has bonds with God, with fellow man, and with nature, the latter of which is the basis of civilization. A man without work feels in some way that he is refused citizenship in the advance army of civilization and denied unity with fellow workers who by their work have earned a right to leisure. Leisure is earned; unemployment is unearned. Until his self-respect becomes completely destroyed, the unemployed man feels that he is not a part of the civilization in which he lives, because he has made no contribution to it. Unemployment, in the eyes of the Catholic, takes its biggest toll not from the

economic man, but from the *moral* man; its greatest
wound is not the empty pocket, but the empty heart; its
tragedy is not the loss of the pay envelope, but his right to
it; its danger is not that his body will starve, for he need
not starve in this country, but rather that his spirit will
die for want of something to mold and touch with his
hands. A man without relations to God, to fellow man,
and to nature is a marred man. If it be allowed to continue, he will develop into a perverted man, who will think
that society owes him a living, and that every possession
his neighbor has, has been filched from him; then he
needs only to hear a Communist lecture and he will be
ready to believe the greatest lie on earth — that the
Communist Worker is free.

Endnotes

[1] Cf. the discussion on "leisure work" in Kelso and Adler, *The Capitalist Manifesto, op. cit.*, 13-29. [Ed.]

[2] Étienne Vincent Borne (1907-1993). French professor of philosophy at Hypokhâgne at Lycée Henri-IV in Paris. Borne founded
the Mouvement Republicain Populaire (MRP), and the French
Christian Democratic Party, and was a columnist in the newspaper *La Croix* ("The Cross"). [Ed.]

[3] Étienne Borne and François Henry, *Le Travail et L'Homme*.
Paris: Desclée de Brouwer, 1937; translated as *A Philosophy of Work*. New York: Sheed and Ward, 1938. [Ed.]

[4] More accurately, According to Aristotle, slaves lack the capacity to acquire and develop virtue, and therefore cannot be trusted
with liberty. [Ed.]

[5] Cf. *Quadragesimo Anno*, § 135. [Ed.]

[6] Again, living *income* would be more accurate, given that the
right to own private property in capital as well as labor is inherent in the human person. [Ed.]

[7] 1 Cor. 3:18-23.

[8] "For the sake of the Lord." [Ed.]

[9] Cf. the motto of the Benedictines, *Laborare orare est*; "To work
is to pray." [Ed.]

[10] *Quadragesimo Anno*, § 53.

[11] "God help [me]." [Ed.]

[12] Given that the right to own capital is inherent in each person,
and, *e.g.*, even Monsignor John A. Ryan admitted that the "living wage" is a "secondary" or "derived" right (Ryan, *A Living*

Wage, loc. cit.), it would have been more correct for Sheen to have said that what each person has a right to is not a living *wage*, but a living *income*. [Ed.]

¹³ *Rerum Novarum*, § 40.

¹⁴ *Summa Theologica*, IIa IIae q. 66, a. 2.

¹⁵ *Ibid.*, § 38.

¹⁶ Douglas Francis Jerrold (1893-1964), British journalist well known for his support of fascism, believing that it was the best hope for the preservation of Catholicism as a political force, despite warnings and condemnations of fascism by, *e.g.*, Pius XI in *Non Abiamo Bisogno* ("On Catholic Action in Italy"), 1931. Jerrold's efforts were instrumental in convincing many people, even down to the present day, that forms of fascism, despite explicit statements to the contrary, are consistent with Catholic social teaching, *i.e.*, the natural law. Cf. Rev. E. Cahill, *The Framework of the Christian State*. Dublin, Éire: M. H. Gill and Son, 1932; Amintore Fanfani, *Catholicism, Protestantism, and Capitalism*. New York: Sheed and Ward, 1939; *Catechism of Catholic Social Teaching*. Westminster, Maryland: The Newman Press, 1960. [Ed.]

¹⁷ Douglas Jerrold, *The Future of Freedom*. London: Sheed and Ward, 1938, 84, 85.

7. Liberty and Labor

NOW THAT the basic principles are clear, it is possible to make some concrete applications to the labor problem itself. In the face of its sad history and the unemployment and poverty of the present, it is always a very difficult task to talk about the duties of labor. On the contrary, it is very easy for anyone who has any sympathy at all for the oppressed, to take sides with the apostles of revolution who are always taking labor's side, though labor itself does not realize that they are interested in it, not to liberate it, but to enslave it to their own wicked ends. We must be brave enough, even at the risk of being called anti-labor, or a Fascist, or a reactionary, or unsympathetic to the masses, to tell labor that the solution offered by revolutionists is impracticable. It simply does not work. Labor tried it in Russia and failed. We can profit by its sad experience in Russia and avoid being duped here.[1]

In a preceding chapter, recommendations were offered Capital to restore liberty; it now remains to offer recommendations to labor.

Labor must avoid learning that which Capitalism and Communism teach it; namely, labor is a commodity. If labor regards itself as Commodity then labor becomes something to be bargained for by the law of supply and demand as it is under Capitalism, or else it is something to be dictated to as it is under Communism. Once labor goes on the market as a thing, or as a tool in production, its worth is determined in exactly the same way as a ton of steel. The employer will not think of the employee as the person, or as the head of a family, but as a thing to be bought on the open market. This does not mean that the wage contract itself is unjust,[2] but only that the way the wage is determined was unjust. Once labor is bartered for solely on the basis of supply and demand, the laboring man is degraded and human society is endangered by its division into two groups, one of which attempts to buy cheaply, the other of which attempts to sell dearly. Because the world has been doing this very thing for decades, we almost took it for granted that a labor market was much the same as a fish market, except that in one case men were sold, and in the other case, fish. It was against just such a concept of labor that Leo XIII protested in 1891 in strong language:

> Religion teaches the rich man and the employer that their work-people are not their slaves; that they must respect in every man his dignity as a man and as a Christian; that labor is nothing to be ashamed of, if we listen to right reason and to Christian philosophy, but is an honorable employment, enabling a man to sustain his life in an upright and creditable way; and that it is shameful and inhuman to treat men like chattels to make money by, or to look upon them as merely so much muscle or physical power. Thus, again, Religion teaches that, as among the workmen's concerns are Religion herself, and things spiritual and mental, the employer is bound to see that he has time for the duties of piety; that he be not exposed to corrupting influences and dangerous occasions; and that he be not led away to neglect his home and family or to squander his wages. Then, again, the employer must never tax his work people beyond their strength, nor employ them in work unsuited to their sex or age."[3] ". . . the first concern of all is to save the poor workers from the cruelty of grasping speculators, who use human beings as mere instruments for making money. It is neither justice nor humanity so to grind men down with excessive labor as to stupefy their minds and wear out their bodies.[4]

This brings us to the exact nature of the danger facing labor. Labor is now in the deserved ascendancy; Capitalism is on the defensive; Labor both by right and by mood is gaining the upper hand. But instead of emphasizing human dignity and liberty, it is emphasizing its right to strike a good bargain. In other words, it is tacitly assuming that Capitalism was right in calling it a commodity or a chattel. It then proceeds in virtue of the superior power of corporate strength over the lesser power of the employer, to get what it wants. Though its unions (which are so necessary), it has the power to withhold the supply and therefore create a demand, as years ago the capitalists could withhold the wage because the supply was great. Labor is thus using exactly the same economic law which got it into its present mess. It bargains, not on the basis of the person, but on the basis of how much it can get out of an employer. Capital today is paying dearly, as labor yesterday sold itself cheaply. But at what cost? At the cost of social peace. As Pius XI has so well expressed it:

> Labor, indeed, as has been well said by Our Predecessor in his Encyclical, is not a mere chattel, since the human dignity of the workingman must be recognized in it, and consequently it cannot be bought and sold like any piece of merchandise. None the less the demand and supply of labor divides men on the labor market into two classes, as into two camps, and the bargaining between these parties transforms this labor market into an arena where the two armies are engaged in combat. To this grave disorder, which is leading society to ruin, a remedy must evidently be applied as speedily as possible.[5]

A perfect picture indeed of our present situation: "an arena where the two armies are engaged in combat." Capitalism and labor today agree on the basic principle: labor is a commodity; they differ on its price. They fight sometimes with the same weapons: force, violence, espionage; and at other times with different weapons: injunctions, picketing, advertising, and propaganda. On the capitalist side, General Motors Corporation, according to Senate Committee Report of December 21, 1937; between January, 1934, and July 1936, employed 200 spies against labor at an expense slightly less than a million dollars. On the labor side, radical influences have led the workingmen to sign their souls away, as they do in the ridiculous oath which is taken by the members of the International Typographical Union: "My fidelity to the union and my duty to the members thereof shall in no sense be interfered with by any allegiance that I may now or hereafter owe to any organization, social, political or religious, secret or otherwise."[6] On the side of the public — and the public always pays — in the United States during 1936, there were more working days lost than in any country of the world. According to the International Labor Office of Geneva the United States lost 13,901,956 days in 2,172 disputes, involving 788,648 workers.

There is no question here of saying who is right or wrong in these disputes, we are only saying that capital *was* wrong in telling labor it was *merchandise*, and labor *is* wrong in believing it. The result is, our country is divided into warring camps, in which two giants are coming to grips. So long as we continue on the assumption that labor is not personal but a commodity, we will all lose.

This class conflict can be avoided to some extent by labor avoiding unscrupulous organizers whose aim is not emancipation of labor, but the intensification of class struggle as a prelude to the revolutionary overthrow of society.

> . . .too few have been able to grasp the nature of Communism. The majority instead succumb to its deception, skillfully concealed by the most extravagant promises. By pretending to desire only the betterment of the condition of the working classes, by urging the removal of the very real abuses chargeable to the liberalistic economic order, and by demanding a more equitable distribution of this world's goods (objectives entirely and undoubtedly legitimate), the Communist takes advantage of the present world-wide economic crisis to draw into the sphere of his influence even those sections of the populace which on principle reject all forms of materialism and terrorism. And as every error contains its element of truth, the partial truths to which We have referred are astutely presented according to the needs of time and place, to conceal, when convenient, the repulsive crudity and inhumanity of Communistic principles and tactics. Thus the Communist ideal wins over many of the better-minded members of the community. These in turn become the apostles of the movement among the younger intelligentsia who are still too immature to recognize the intrinsic errors of the system. The preachers of Communism are also proficient in exploiting racial antagonisms and political divisions and oppositions. They take advantage of the lack of orientation characteristic of modern agnostic science in order to burrow into the universities, where they bolster up the principles of their doctrine with pseudo-scientific arguments.[7]

It is indeed interesting that John Lewis[8] himself warned of irresponsible labor agitators and the way they were attempting to convert ". . .trade unions into single units of workers within an industry known as 'industrial unions'." "Through this organization (Trade Union Education League headed by Communists) the revolutionary leaders in America are making a nationwide attempt to obtain control of the American Federation of Labor, reorganize the craft unions on the basis of " 'one big union' in an industry," *etc.*[9]

Class struggle is not the essence of the industrial order because bargaining with labor as merchandise, is a refusal to recognize human worth. The great mistake that is made in the matter now under consideration, is to possess oneself of the idea that class is naturally hostile to class; that rich and poor are intended by nature to live at war with one another. The exact contrary is the truth.

> Just as the symmetry of the human body is the result of the disposition of the members of the body, so in a state it is ordained by nature that these two classes should exist in harmony and agreement, and should, as it were, fit into one another, so as to maintain the equilibrium of the body politic. Each requires the other; capital cannot do without labor, nor labor without capital. Mutual agreement results in pleasantness and good order; perpetual conflict necessarily produces confusion and outrage.[10]

From this the Church deduces its first conclusion: "It is therefore entirely false to ascribe the results of the combined efforts of capital and labor to either party alone; and it is flagrantly unjust that either should deny the efficacy of the other and seize all the profits."[11]

The Church thus avoids two extreme errors: the error of Capitalism which claimed that Capital was entitled to all the profits; and the Marxist error that Labor is entitled to all the profits.[12] In between both is the golden mean that both Capital and Labor should share:

> . . . one class is forbidden to exclude the other from a share in the profits. This sacred law is violate by an irresponsible wealthy class who, in the excess of their good fortune, deem it a just state of things that they should receive eve-

rything and the laborer nothing; it is violated also by a
propertyless wage-earning class who demand for themselves all the fruits of production, as being the work of
their hands. Such men, vehemently incensed against the
violation of justice by capitalists, go too far in vindicating
the one right of which they are conscious; they attack and
seek to abolish all forms of ownership and all profits not
obtained by labor, whatever be their nature or significance
in human society, for the sole reason that they are not acquired by toil." ". . .each class, then, must receive its due
share, and the distribution of created goods must be
brought into conformity with the demands of the common
good and social justice, for every sincere observer is conscious that the vast differences between the few who hold
excessive wealth and the many who live in destitution constitute a grave evil in modern society."[13] "Every effort,
therefore, must be made that at least in the future a just
share only of the fruits of production be permitted to accu-
mulate in the hands of the wealthy, and that an ample sufficiency be supplied to the workingmen. The purpose is not
that these become slack at their work, for man is born to
labor as the bird to fly — but that by thrift they may increase their possessions and by prudent management of
the same may be enabled to bear the family burden with
the greater ease and security, being freed from that hand-
to-mouth uncertainty which is the lot of the proletarian.
Thus they will not only be in a position to support life's
changing fortunes, but will also have the reassuring confidence that when their lives are ended, some little provision
will remain for those whom they leave behind them.

These ideas were not merely suggested, but stated in frank
and open terms by Our Predecessor. We emphasize them
with renewed instance in this present Encyclical; for unless serious attempts be made, with all energy and without
delay to put them into practice, let nobody persuade himself that the peace and tranquility of human society can be
effectively defended against the forces of revolution![14],[15]

It may immediately be asked if this means that the
Catholic Church is in favor of a modification of the wage
system. The answer is definitely in the affirmative. "In
the present state of human society, however, We deem it
advisable that the wage contract should, when possible,
be modified somewhat by a contract of partnership, as is

already being tried in various ways to the no small gain both of the wage-earners and of the employers. In this way wage-earners are made sharers in some sort in the ownership, or the management, or the profits."[16]

But does not the payment of wage dispense Capital from any further interest? Leo XIII considered this objection:

> We now approach a subject of very great importance and one on which, if extremes are to be avoided, right ideas are absolutely necessary. Wages, we are told, are fixed by free consent; and, therefore, the employer when he pays what was agreed upon, has done his part, and is not called upon for anything further. The only way, it is said, in which injustice could happen, would be if the master refused to pay the whole of the wages, or the workman would not complete the work undertaken; when this happens the State should intervene, to see that each obtains his own, but not under any other circumstances.
>
> This mode of reasoning is by no means convincing to a fair-minded man, for there are important considerations which it leaves out of view altogether.[17]

This brings us to the heart of the Catholic solution. Why does it plead for elimination of class conflict by co-partnership? Why does it ask for a modification of the wage system? By what right does it claim the laborer is entitled to more than his wages? The answer is, because "a man's labor has two notes or characters personal and social."[18] "In this respect," writes the Holy Father, "it is like property."[19] Property is personal inasmuch as man has a real right to it; it is social inasmuch as property is destined for the good of all and hence the common good may condition the personal right.

Labor too has an individual and a social character. The individual aspect of labor is manifested by the obvious fact that the individual works and at the end of the day is tired. From the individual point of view, the worker is a total stranger to the industry, and is no more related to it than a manufacturer who sells tools to the industry.

But labor also has a social aspect. The worker is not only an individual but a member of a family and perhaps the head of one. Furthermore, he does not labor alone but in conjunction with capital and management to produce wealth. He works with other laborers and with his bosses and with raw material. There are three elements necessary for production: capital in the sense of finances, labor and brains in the sense of management (*Intellectus, Res et Opera*[20]). In contemporary parlance there are two: labor and capital. To ask which of the two is the more important is like asking which is the more important leg, the right or the left.

For his individual contribution the laborer receives a wage; for his social contribution he receives nothing. But he should. He should receive some return if there are any profits, for his social contribution to the creation of new wealth. This argument becomes all the more important with the divorce of ownership and control in capitalism. Since the owner or the stockholder has surrendered *responsibility, he has given up one of the essential notes of property and hence one of the essential titles to profits.* His claim to all the profits is less valid than under the traditional concept of property. To whom then should be given consideration? Certainly, to the *active* creators of the new wealth; namely, labor. The stockholder is only the *passive* creator; but since a man who contributes *his labor* is making a more *active* contribution should he not be given some share in the wealth he helps to produce? Hence the Church asks that "there be some modification of the wage system in favor of partnership so that wage earners are made sharers, in some sort, in the ownership, in the management or the profits" of industry.[21]

No industry has ever produced a thing without the functional cooperation of labor, capital, and brains. Labor's part in production is not merely individual, like a bird building its nest; it is also social or functional, somewhat like the role the lung plays in the human organism. The individual workers may be dispensed with, but no industry can dispense with workers cooperating with money and other human beings in the begetting of social wealth. Man is essentially a collaborating creature.[22] From the very beginning God called man to collaborate

with Him in the peopling of the earth, as the Divine command rang out to the first man and woman: "increase and
multiply." The collaboration was raised to the supernatural order, when, on the eve of His Passion, our Divine Savior bade man renew His sacrifice, from the rising to the
setting of the sun and unto the consummation of the
world, as there fell over the upper room the whispered
words: "Do this in commemoration of Me." Simply because
the world has become tremendously complex, does not
alter the fact that collaboration is still essential, and the
employer who thinks that his employee is less functional
than either himself or his capital, has failed to see that if
he dispensed with the functions of one he is cutting off
one of the legs of a three-legged stool. If a capitalist thinks
that labor is not a functional and integral part of his corporation, let him try to produce automobiles with only
money and machines.

1. *Profits.*[23] By profit sharing is here meant obviously a
share in the profits among the workers: (*a*) After the
worker has received a living wage, (*b*) after capital has
received legitimate profits, and set aside necessary surplus to entice new capital and to keep its plant in condition. To this suggestion of workers sharing in profits, Capitalism asks: "Why should the laborer share in the profits?
He has received his wages, assumes no risks and is entitled to nothing more." This objection forgets that the wages compensate the worker only for his individual useful-
ness, but not for his indispensable, social collaboration
with the employer and finances in the creation of wealth.
The two are quite distinct, just as each man is a person
with his own individual rights and duties, but at the same
time is a member of society, subject to its laws and capable of enjoying its privileges. It is not to the point to say
that the laborer assumes no risks. He does. He assumes
the risk of unemployment, insecurity, and even bad speculation on the part of the employer.

But immediately, the Capitalist objects: "Suppose there
are no profits. Will the worker share the loss as well as
the gain?" The answer is that the profit sharing does not
begin until capital has received a normal return to keep

the business solvent and pay a sufficient return to inves-
tors and other necessary expenses. Hence the objection
that the worker should share losses is not to the point.
There may be no surplus after all the necessary deduc-
tions have been made, but this does not mean the employer has received nothing: he receives possibly a normal
rate of interest on his investment, and certainly he receives his salary which is many times in excess of the
wage of his employee. If there are no surplus profits,[24] the
employer and the employee both get their salary; but if
there are profits why should not the worker share, to
some small extent at least, in the profits, for in the language of Pius XI: "By the principles of social justice one
class is forbidden to exclude the other from a share in the
profits."[25]

Why is it that some labor leaders are opposed to profit
sharing? John L. Lewis testifying before the Senate
Committee, November 30, 1938, rejected profit sharing on
the ground that the workers resented "paternalistic generosity," "the dollar in the hat," "the theory of largesse."
"Frankly, I think the profit-sharing idea is rather a delu-
sion and a snare in modern industry." Lewis was asked by
Chairman Herring of the Senate Committee if he believed
"the government is the only one in a position to provide
security for the workers." His answer was: "I do not see
how anyone else can do it."[26]

Why the "largesse" of the industry should be "paternalism" and not the "largesse" of the government is indeed
difficult to understand. One seriously suspects that the
psychology back of his opposition to profit sharing is not
that the workers would lose by it, but rather that by in-
tensifying their bond with industry their financial ties to
a labor leader might become less. The history of European
nations such as Russia and Germany prove that if the
worker had to have a *pater*[27] they would be better off if
they did not choose the government.[28]

Profit sharing is not and cannot be a compensation for
low wages; its purpose is not to make the workers slaves
to industry; neither is it to make them functional with
industry through sharing responsibility and its fruits. In-

creased wages through collective bargaining do not admit of infinite elasticity. There is a limit beyond which wages cannot go. Profit sharing admits the base of a living wage and at the same time provides that elasticity of increased returns when business is prosperous. The wage contract while just does not unite the worker to his work except for the security which the salary entails. A handout by a paternalistic government could give him exactly the same security. But a share in the wealth he has helped to create makes him a partner in the business. It gives him responsibility which is the attribute of liberty. It would seem obvious that labor will benefit itself not as it surrenders responsibilities, but as it assumes them. Security is the only negative side of liberty; it removes those economic obstacles which make freedom of choice either difficult or impossible. Liberty is choice with responsibility.

If I own an automobile and surrender the responsibility of buying gas to the Mayor of the city, and the responsibility of buying oil to the Comptroller of the city, and the responsibility of buying tires to the Senate of the city, and the responsibility of repairs to the House, I soon discover that I have lost my freedom to drive the car because I have surrendered responsibilities. Let the worker, in like manner, surrender his responsibilities either to a paternalistic government or a paternalistic labor leader, or a paternalistic employer and he by that very fact loses his liberty.

There is a further surrender of liberty by the failure of labor to demand its rights. Since it makes a social contribution to wealth, it has some right to share in that wealth produced. Labor would not and should not surrender its right to collective bargaining; nor does it believe, and rightfully so, that it is subject to the "paternalism" of a labor organization. Then why should it surrender its right to profits? And why should the acceptance of those rights be tainted with the charge of "paternalism"?[29]

2. *Management.* The Church also suggests that labor to some extent share management of industry. The choice is not whether the laborer shall take orders or give them; but rather he will merely take them or *participate* with

his fellow worker in some of the details of management.[30] Naturally, this does not mean that he shall help manage the finances, the purchasing operations, the marketing of the product, nor that his share in management will never extend beyond suggestions concerning sanitation, safety-first devices, the use of steel shovels rather than wooden hammers, *etc.* Rather, it means that labor shall share in the management of those things which affect both employer and employee alike, *e.g.*, wages, hours, working conditions. The Church suggests that in each industry there be a board composed of representatives of the employer and representatives of the employees. The basis for such a board is that "employers and employees who are of the same group join forces to produce goods and give a common service."[31] The Church rejects the economic theory that capital and labor are two independent groups bound together "by the position they occupy on the labor market," *i.e.*, one selling work, the other buying it. Rather, since both are collaborating for a common service, they should share to some extent in the processes which affect them both. The Church here tacitly denies that the employers have all the brains, as the depression[32] proved, nor that the employees have all the brains as the recession[33] proved. The laborer has some brains as regards the technique of his work, and as a person endowed with the same inalienable rights as an employer, he should be privileged to have some voice in the determination of that which is common to both. If such a board were set up in industries, including both representatives of employers and representatives of the organization of employees, the differences between the two would not be settled by violence and by espionage, but by reason, which is the mark of man. The result would be that workers would acquire greater self-respect and responsibility in the progress of business, the employer would find his peace of mind enhanced, and most likely his profits, and the public good would be better by increased production and decreased necessity of calling in police to halt a bloody battle. A meeting of employers and employees does not mean the extinction of labor unions, or that the only labor organizations must be company unions. In the three Scandinavian countries the employers' associations favor one big union because they find it easier to deal with it than with petty groups. There is no reason why representatives of industry and representatives of a trade unit cannot settle their difficulties without violence to the buyers and sellers of cheese.

3. *Ownership.* A third suggestion of the Church for collaboration is a share in ownership of industry. The Church immediately rejects the Marxian idea that labor creates value and is therefore entitled to all the returns. "The only form of labor which gives the working man a title to its fruits is that which a man exercises as his own master."[34] There is some labor which never results in a product, *e.g.*, chauffeuring, education, *etc.*[35] Furthermore, the material means of production are from one point of view just as essential as labor, for the employee cannot produce by twirling his thumbs. "What else is work but the application of one's forces of soul and body to the gifts of nature."[36] Since the employer does not "labor with his own property, he must form an alliance between his toil and his neighbor's property, for each is helpless without the other. . . . It is therefore entirely false to ascribe the results of the combined efforts of Capital and Labor to either party alone, and it is flagrantly unjust that either should deny the efficacy of the other and seize all the profits."[37]

But at the same time, neither can it be said that the employer and the raw materials and his plant are so exclusively the source of value that labor plays no role whatsoever. It is clear that the laborer should be enabled to increase his possessions so as to be "freed from the hand-to-mouth uncertainty which is the lot of the proletarian"; this would mean a *"wider diffusion of ownership."* That the laborer has a strict right to ownership in the industry where he works is very dubious.[38] But that he "share in some way in the ownership" as a result of "modification of the wage contract" by a "contract of partnership" is a consummation devoutly to be wished. There is little doubt then that with a quantitative increase in common wealth, there should be an increasing share in the ownership of that wealth by labor, for "it is only by the labor of workingmen that the State grows rich."[39] The worker does not become a co-proprietor of the industry because he works there, but he does become entitled to some kind of share of the value which he helped to produce there; in this sense there is some vague title to ownership.[40] Furthermore, since modern capitalism has distinguished *active* participation in industry such as labor and management and *passive* participation such as financial contribution through the purchase of stock, it has divided the two titles to profits; namely, control and ownership, and hence has weakened its claim. On the other hand since labor is extremely functional in the creation of *new wealth* and has taken over the *active* participation in industry which the stockholder has vacated, he has in some way "incorporated" himself to the industry and is therefore entitled to some greater recognition than a wage. A distribution of ownership could be effected in many ways, *e.g.*, by the issuance of labor shares. It would seem however, that this stock should not be the purely negotiable stock which the laborer could barter away at the exchange, as did the workers in a steel industry, but should be nonnegotiable, in order to intensify the laborer's bond with his work and to assure him annually a return over and above his wages.

Labor has three choices before it: (1) to work for a boss which is Capitalism; (2) to work for the State, which is Communism, or (3) to work for himself in the sense that he shares in some way in the "profits, management, and ownership" of industry. The Church begs labor to take a long view and to work for co-partnership in industry. The solution of the Church is the golden mean between a Capitalism which emphasizes only the individual aspect of labor, pays a wage, and ignores its social contribution; and Communism which emphasizes only the social side of labor and ignores man's personal rights. The Church insists that both suffer from the same fallacy; they look upon man only as a consumer. In both instances he receives only the power to purchase, which power is given to him either by the Capitalist or by the Bureaucrats. This,

claims the Church, is not liberty. Man is not just a consumer; if he were he would be little different than the
livestock kept for the market. Man's liberty consists more
in production than consumption; namely, the right to impress his personality upon things, to determine how they
shall be used, to use his free will in their disposition and
to be responsible in their making.

If labor is going to be concerned only with more and
more of created wealth — and there is no limit to what
one wants when the wealth is not*one's own — then labor
is on the way to its own enslavement. If labor is only a
consumer, what it consumes is regimented and planned
and dictated until the very meaning of independence is
forgotten. Then our social order will shift from a capitalistic error in which individual profits were confused with
the *common good* to the Communistic error, in which
greater production is confused with personal liberty. It
does not require much insight to see that Capitalism has
produced great evils because it dissociated *ownership* and
management; neither does it require much vision to see
that labor can fall into a similar error, by divorcing *organization* and *leadership.* Then, just as we had men manag-
ing a business who did not own it, so will we have labor
organizations owned by leaders who do not labor. Those
who work do not lead and those who lead do not work.

Both divorces are always bad for society, and peace can
be restored only by the restoration of *responsibility* to
both capital and labor, by making them both co-partners
in a common function for a common good. How willing is
labor to assist in carrying out this program? The answer
depends entirely upon whether labor cares to assume *responsibility* which is the mark of liberty.

The answer to the question is that labor is probably just
as much opposed to the above solution as capital, for just
as capital once said to labor: "You give me your work and
I will keep the profits," so now labor is saying to capital: "I
will take your profits but you can keep its headaches."
The restoration of liberty is impossible if neither capital
nor labor is willing to share responsibility. You can free
men politically as Lincoln did with a stroke of the pen, but

you cannot free them economically by giving them diffused ownership, unless they are willing to take the responsibility of that ownership. Capitalism has cost us
much. It has accustomed men to being so dependent on
others, that some want to be Communists and lose liberty
altogether, and others want to be just wage earners and
keep liberty only for Fourth of July orations. It is one of
the saddest commentaries on modern life that men do not
seriously want to be economically free citizens. If we must
find a reason for it, it is probably because since we
scrapped religion, we scrapped the word *duty* and retained only the word *right*.[41]

The Church is only asking that men begin to think of
property as they might of love, in the sense that to possess means also to be possessed. One is not possible without the other. The beatific vision consists in being oneself,
and at the same time being God's. The economic vision of
happiness likewise consists in possessing a garden, but
also being possessed by it, in the sense that you work for
it. Rights arise from possession; duties arise from being
possessed, and each is inseparable from the other. The joy
of a man being half possessed by the pipe he smokes, the
woman he loves, the field he digs, finds its counterpart in
the economic structure in possessing and being possessed
by the industry. Thus is he elevated to the dignity of a
producer-owner, a co-partner and a sharer, for if a man
surrenders all power of self-determination in regard to the
profits, management, or ownership of the place where he
works, he not only loses that special prerogative which
marks him off from a cow in a pasture, but what is worse,
he loses all capacity for determining any work, and this is
the beginning of a slavery which sometimes goes by the
name of security.

Liberty will not come immediately; there are present objectives which condition it, *e.g.*, right of organization, decent wages, and proper living conditions. We are not denying the necessity of these; we are only asking that labor
does not confuse *means* with *ends*, for then the last state
of the man shall be worse than the first. Labor should remember that the social conscience is awake, and that its

just rights will be vindicated. Reforms cannot be accomplished overnight. They are on the way, but in the meantime, let labor not be fooled by revolutionary apostles.

Finally, a plea for clarity concerning the term *worker*. Communist propaganda is misleading America into believing that the worker is the man who carries a dinner pail and that anyone who does not do so is an enemy of the worker. They are creating the impression that there is something uncommon in work, that it is a monopoly of the class, and in particular, the class that wears overalls, has big muscles, and carries a hammer, and it uses the term *democracy* to cover up the dictatorship of Russia. The term *worker* does not belong to a unique class. The Capitalist is a worker; the university professor is a worker, and the nurse is a worker. The worker from a Christian point of view means anyone who is active enough to procure for himself the necessities of life in order to secure the leisure for saving his soul, and who creates utility for his neighbor and spiritualizes matter so that civilization might advance.

When capital and labor both realize that they are both workers because both are persons, and that capital cannot exist without labor, and labor cannot exist without capital, a vision will come to both of them, a vision of a God who as the Lord of the universe, descends to this trivial earth of ours, in order to labor for over two decades as a carpenter in the little village of Nazareth.

Let not a class claim Him uniquely as their own as Christ the Worker. True it was that for the greater part of His Life He labored with His hands and practiced a trade. But He was not a member of a class as opposed to another class in society, for is the Redeemer the member of a class?

He stands in a unique relation to mankind as the only volunteer worker in the world. Labor was imposed on man as a result of primeval sin. Since He was without sin He was dispensed from its penalties. Furthermore, the Lord of the universe had no need of toiling with His universe. And yet He freely chose as the Son of God incarnate to join the ranks of labor. Because it was voluntary it was unique. He was not just a laborer in the sense that He was opposed to a capitalist who is living virtuously. This is the mistake many are apt to make. He was not just a poor man; He was a rich Person who became a poor man, for being rich He became poor for our sakes that through His poverty we might be rich. The very profession He chose, that of a carpenter, was a proof that He owned that upon which He worked and He worked that upon which he owned. He was not an employee working for a corporation; He was not an employer using capital to hire others to make it useful. He worked upon the universe He owned like an artist works upon the canvas he owns. Hence neither the employer nor the employee can alone invoke Him as their patron; neither can say He belonged to our class. He was outside all classes because He was the worker, and the worker is not the employee hating the capitalist; nor is the worker the capitalist enslaving the employee. The worker is he who by his work establishes bonds with God by submission to its penance; with neighbors by the creation of common *needs*; and with nature by giving it the imprint of a mind made to the image and likeness of God. It was the forgetfulness of these ends that made carpenters nail the Carpenter to the Cross; when that happens capital and labor both lose.

Endnotes

---

[1] The Labor Party of England for that reason refused to enter a popular front with the Communists, stating in their refusal: "We ourselves should regard Communist participation as an electoral liability rather than an asset. The Communist Party is subject to political directions from abroad: to this extent it is not allowed to determine its own policy."

Matthew Woll, the Vice-President of the American Federation of Labor also rejected the Bolshevik influence on Labor: "Speaking for nearly 4,000,000 American workers affiliated with the American Federation of Labor, I am authorized to say that American workers will not permit themselves to become embroiled in war to help save Stalin's dictatorship. The Soviet regime deserves no more support from organized labor in democratic countries, than do the governments of Hitler and Mussolini." — Joseph Shaplen in *New York Times*, February 16, 1938.

---

[2] "Those who hold the wage contract is essentially unjust are certainly in error." — *Quadragesimo Anno*, § 64.

[3] *Rerum Novarum*, § 20.

[4] *Ibid.*, § 42.

[5] *Quadragesimo Anno*, § 83.

[6] Books of laws of International Typographical Union (Jan. 1, 1938).

[7] *Divini Redemptoris*, § 15.

[8] John Llewellyn Lewis (1880-1969), American labor leader who served as president of the United Mine Workers of America from 1920 to 1960. He was noted for "steamrolling" opponents (including the government) to gain higher wages and benefits at all cost, and was considered ruthless in his strike tactics.

[9] Cf. Senate Document No. 14 of the 58th Congress.

[10] *Rerum Novarum*, § 19.

[11] *Quadragesimo Anno*, § 53.

[12] "Capital, however, was long able to appropriate to itself excessive advantages; it claimed all the products and profits and left to the laborer the barest minimum necessary to repair his strength and to ensure the continuation of his class. For by an inexorable economic law, it was held, all accumulation of riches must fall to the share of the wealthy, while the workingman must remain perpetually in indigence or reduced to the minimum needed for existence. It is true that the actual state of things was not always and everywhere as deplorable as the liberalistic tenets of the so-called Manchester School might lead us to conclude; but it cannot be denied that a steady drift of economic and social tendencies was in this direction. These false opinions and specious axioms were vehemently attacked, as was to be expected, and by others than merely those whom such principles deprived of their innate right to better their condition." — *Quadragesimo Anno*, § 54.

[13] *Quadragesimo Anno*, § 54.

[14] *Ibid.*, § 65.

[15] *Ibid.*, §§ 61-62.

[16] *Ibid.*, § 65.

[17] *Rerum Novarum*, §§ 43-44.

[18] *Ibid.*, § 44.

[19] *Ibid.*

[20] Literally, "The mind, the thing, and the work." [Ed.]

[21] By "partnership" in § 65 of *Quadragesimo Anno*, Pius XI clearly meant a private property stake, entitling the worker-owner to a commensurate share of the profits due to owners. Presumably because he did not see any way in which workers could become

owners without unjustly depriving current owners of their
rights, Sheen appears to interpret "partnership" as a moral, rather than a legal/contractual relationship. Kelso and Adler's
argument in Chapter 5 of *The Capitalist Manifesto* is more to
the point and consistent with the traditional understanding of
property: workers have a natural right to share in the ownership
of capital as it is added to the business, and this capital can be
purchased by the workers on credit repaid out of the future
earnings of the capital itself without depriving current owners of
anything except the virtual monopoly they now enjoy over ownership of future capital formation. [Ed.]

[22] Cf. "Man is by nature a political animal." Aristotle, *The Politics*, I.ii. [Ed.]

[23] Sheen's analysis here is clearly based on the assumption that
past savings constitute the only source of financing for new capital formation. It has, therefore, in large measure been supersed-
ed by Kelso and Adler's analysis in *The Capitalist Manifesto, op.
cit.* [Ed.]

[24] The concept of "surplus profits" is related to the Marxist "surplus value" and "the labor theory of value," and presumes as a
given that there is no free market. Sheen's use of the concept in
this context is thus somewhat equivocal, particularly in light of
the fact that he acknowledges that "capital" has a right to a just
return on investment. The free market, as the Medieval Scholas-
tics acknowledged, is (everything else being equal) the best
mechanism for determining just wages, just prices, and just
profits. See the discussion on the just price (including wages) in
George O'Brien, *An Essay on Medieval Economic Teaching*. London: Longmans, Green and Co., 1920, 102-158. [Ed.]

[25] *Quadragesimo Anno*, § 57. [Again, in light of the paragraphs
in *Quadragesimo Anno* preceding this statement, Pius XI's language implies not merely profit-sharing, but the right to receive
profits as a co-owner. — Ed.]

[26] Contrast "There is no need to bring in the State. Man precedes
the State, and possesses, prior to the formation of any State, the
right of providing for the substance of his body." *Rerum Novarum*, § 7. [Ed.]

[27] A play on words. Sheen contrasts the impersonal "largesse" of
the State or private employer, with the personal care of the "father of the family" — the *pater familias* — born out of genuine
concern and love instead of political or economic expedience.
[Ed.]

[28] Contrast Sheen's position with that of many of today's commentators on Catholic social teaching influenced by Tawney,

Ryan, Jerrold, Fanfani, *et al.*, that gives not only primacy to the
State, but total power, *e.g.*, "The State is the sole intercessor
available to the poor." Dr. Rupert J. Ederer, "Solidaristic Economics," *Fidelity* magazine, July 1994, 9-15. [Ed.]

[29] The popes and Kelso and Adler argue that this "social contribution" should be recognized by giving the propertyless workers
access to the means of acquiring and possessing private property
in capital. Sheen makes a weaker moral argument here than the
natural law legal argument the popes and Kelso and Adler use.
[Ed.]

[30] "Management sharing," an aspect of "Justice-Based Management" and "Justice-Based Leadership," can best be realized by
worker-owners voting their shares to elect members to the board
of directors, and ensuring that worker owners have guaranteed
board representation. [Ed.]

[31] *Quadragesimo Anno*, § 84.

[32] The Great Depression of 1930-1940. [Ed.]

[33] The "Depression within the Depression" of 1937-1938. [Ed.]

[34] *Quadragesimo Anno*, § 52.

[35] Sheen evidently means that there is no physical marketable
good that results; a service such as "chauffeuring" and "education" is just as much a marketable thing as a physical good. [Ed.]

[36] *Quadragesimo Anno*, § 53.

[37] *Ibid.*

[38] This statement is correct given Sheen's past savings assumption, *i.e.*, that the only source of financing for new capital formation is existing accumulations of savings. Workers have no
claim in justice to what is already owned by their employers or
anyone else. They do, however, have an equal right with everyone else to own future, as-yet uncreated capital, and to have full
access to the means of acquiring and possessing that capital.
[Ed.]

[39] *Rerum Novarum*, § 34.

[40] Again, this is a moral claim in charity, not a legal claim in
justice. Cf. *Rerum Novarum*, § 22. [Ed.]

[41] "The cause of the harassed workingman was espoused by the
'intellectuals' as they are called, who set up in opposition to this
fictitious law another equally false moral principle: that all
products and profits, excepting those required to repair and replace invested capital, belong by every right to the workingman.
This error, more subtle than that of the socialists who hold that
all means of production should be transferred to the state (or, as
the term it, socialized) is for that reason more dangerous and
apt to deceive the unwary. It is an alluring poison consumed

with avidity by many not deceived by open Socialism." — *Quadragesimo Anno*, § 55.

8. Liberty and the State

WITHIN FORTY YEARS the world has swung from a concept wherein man was isolated from society, to another extreme wherein man is absorbed by society. According to the present ideology of Fascism, Communism, and Nazism, the individual man has no value except as a fraction of the whole. Each man is merely a quantitative addition to the totality like another brick in a house. The collectivity continues to exist when he is gone. It alone has "immortality"; he is the stick tossed into the collective bonfire to keep it blazing for another generation. The society of the future is one for which he must make all manner of sacrifice, but it will never be a society of which any individual man can say "we," as he does of his family; it will be only an "it" and he will not be at its picnic.

Christianity teaches personal immortality. Totalitarianism teaches collective immortality. The latter could not scrap persons for wholes unless it invented a myth — the myth of the nation, the race or the class. Thus is man duped into believing that by the surrender of himself does he contribute to the collectivity. I say "duped" because it is man who is really conscious, not the race or the class; it is man who feels the pain, not the collectivity. Before conscious, feeling, rational, self-determining creatures could be induced to dispossess themselves of all that makes them men and not things, they had to be drugged with a myth that as they ceased to be they began to be precious. The Moloch of the collectivity must be satisfied, otherwise the Paradise of Communism and Nazism will not come upon the earth. Independent thinking and willing must be annihilated as an obstacle in the path of progress.

The myth of collectivism as the philosophy of Liberalism are both wrong, for neither considers man in his totality. Ignoring either the personal aspect of his nature or his social aspect they both distort liberty. *Liberty is born of the recognition of personal rights and flourishes in the recognition of social responsibilities.* Rights and duties are correlative, and one can no more have rights without duties, than one can have the concave side of a saucer without its convex side, or a square without four sides.

This brings us to the nature of man. Man is both personal and social; he is a *person* and a *citizen*. The reason for the double relationship is to be found in the constituents of human nature. Man is composed of body and soul. Though we deny this in theory, we acknowledge it in practice. Remorse of conscience testifies to this dualism through the conflict of the law of the flesh and the law of the spirit. Even dieting for the sake of health witnesses to it by the will imposing its discipline upon the body. Because man has a body he can eat; because he has a soul he can think and he can love. This is what the Church means when it says man is a rational animal — an animal with a mind.

Because man is in part material, he is a part of something therefore dependent. It is sheer nonsense for Rousseau[1] to say in the sense that he meant it, that "man is born free" in the sense of being independent of society. Rather he is born dependent. The very structure of his body makes him dependent on the family as a child, and later on, his incapacity for satisfying all the needs of his nature makes him dependent on society. It is the nature of all material things to be a part of something and related to other material things in a universe; so interrelated are they that modern physicists call it "organic." An apple is a part of a tree; a tree is a part of an orchard; an orchard is a part of a farm; a farm is part of a state, and so the dependence grows in ever increasing complexity. In like manner, man as he is presently constituted, is dependent on society. He unites with other men in society in order to supply those things necessary for human development which neither he alone, nor the family can satisfy. "The proximate end and proper function of the State," writes Leo XIII, "is to attend to what is useful to man in the things *that are passing.*"[2] Our dependence on society becomes more acute as civilization becomes complex. We need only to be deprived of electrical power for five minutes to realize our dependence on society, for by failure on that score alone thousands are deprived of communication by illumination, radiation, and to some extent nutrition. The material element in man is the basis of his relation to and his dependence on others. By it, man is a part of society, one in a social organism, a member of the human race, a man among men, a citizen in a state, a soldier in an army, an individual in a group bound to the social whole for the sake of the common good. In more technical language man is an individual, and to be an individual means to be one man among men.

But because man is a social being, it does not follow that man has no personal rights. Man is composed not only of a body but of a soul. Being spiritual, the soul cannot be a part of anything. Faith, for example, being a spiritual concept is not a section or a part of anything in the same way that the heart is a part of the human organism. In like manner, since man has a soul which is immaterial, he is not a part of anything, but a whole, total and integral. He can choose his own end, he can determine means in relationship to those ends; he is endowed with rights which flow from his spiritual nature, and possessed of liberty which is the heritage of his spirit, or in the more technical language of the Church to indicate the independence of man, man is a person. It is because he is a person that he has rights.[3] Rights are claims of moral beings on one another; even when we speak of rights to things they are claims on persons. Peanuts have no rights. A person is his own; a thing is another's.[4]

In virtue of man's dual nature, he is therefore a part of a whole, a citizen in the State, and yet possessed of rights independent of the State; a soldier in an army and yet a captain of himself; bound to the State and yet the State is bound to him; immanent in the social order, and yet transcendent to it. He is in the State — but not of it — an entity belonging to two worlds; a political animal, and a theological creature. As an individual, he is a member of society and is bound to work for his good; as a person, he is a creature of God endowed with rights by God which no earthly power can take from him. It was the cognizance of this double role of man, personal and social, which explains the answer of our Lord to those who asked Him if it was lawful to pay tribute to Caesar. "Render unto Caesar the things that are Caesar's, and to God the things that are God's."[5] "Render to Caesar the things that belong to Caesar," because you are dependent on society and are bound to work for the general welfare of Caesar. But "render unto God the things that are God's" because you have a soul, which makes you independent of society and responsible to a destiny which lies beyond the stars.

Two conclusions follow from the nature of man, *viz.*, he is independent of society and yet dependent on it. Possessing a soul or better, as a *person*, he has intrinsic sacredness and possesses rights which the State did not create nor confer, and therefore rights which the State cannot take away. These "inalienable rights" the Declaration of Independence rightly recognizes as the endowments of the Creator, and since they are Creator given, they cannot be creature taken away. Such is also the official position of the Church as explained by Leo XIII "For the laws of nature and of the Gospel which by right are superior to all human contingencies are necessarily independent of all modifications of civil government, while at the same time they are in concord with everything that is not repugnant to morality and justice. They are, therefore, and they must remain absolutely free from political parties, and have nothing to do with the various changes of administration which may occur in a nation."[6]

Though man is independent of the State because a person possessed of rights, he is at the same time dependent on the State because an individual and therefore bound by duties to the State. "Let there be no question of fostering under this name of Christian Democracy any intention of diminishing the spirit of obedience, or of withdrawing people from their lawful rulers. Both the natural and the Christian law command us to revere those who, in their various grades are above us in the State, and to submit ourselves to their just commands. It is quite in keeping with our dignity as men and Christians to obey, not only exteriorly but from the heart, as the Apostle expresses it, for conscience sake, when he commands us to keep our soul subject to the higher powers."[7]

If we are to find an imperfect analogy for man in his relation to society, it might be the human body. Certain organs in the body have what improperly might be called their own "personality," *e.g.*, the heart, because no other organ can pre-empt its rights nor fulfill its duties. There is a uniqueness and independence about its nature and operation. But though it glories in its independence, it is still dependent, for it cannot function apart from the human organism. In some such feeble way man is in the State, but not wholly of it. Being spiritual man has a destiny beyond the State; namely, the salvation of his soul; being social, man has a destiny in the State. He has certain rights independent of the State, but he is also dependent on the State and cannot isolate himself normally from it. Against the myth of the collectivity it must be asserted that man is not a part of the State, because as a *person* he stands alone, *sui juris*, captain and master of his own fate and destiny, with his own *personal* perfection to attain even though the whole world opposed it. "Fear not those who kill the body."[8]

On the other hand, against Liberalism, though the State may not interfere with his *personal* end, it must on the contrary foster it by providing the material setting necessary for its attainment. This does not mean the State is built to lead men to heaven; that is the function of the Church. But it does mean the State is built to arrange the temporal affairs for the common good of men who are on their way back to God. The State then is not an outcome of a common agreement, but the result of human nature.[9] The State did not create human nature, and therefore may not nullify its rights. Like the family, the State owes its existence to the law of nature which moves individuals to dwell in society. As St. Thomas puts it: "Man is not related to the political community in the entirety of his being."[10]

What then is the purpose of the State? To "enable men to live a virtuous life" or to promote the common good. But what is the "common good"? "Civil society," writes Leo XIII, "exists for the common good, and hence is concerned with the interest of all in general, albeit with individual interests in their due place and degree."[11]

When we say the State exists for the "common good," two conclusions follow: (*a*) The State does not exist for itself as a race, or a class, or an abstraction, but for the welfare of the people, whether they be Aryans or non-Aryans; proletarians or non-proletarians, members of a political organization or not. (*b*) The common good is not to be considered in such a general way as to ignore the welfare of individuals, *e.g.*, the poor or the unemployed.

The common good is superior to any private good, and hence in case of need it may set aside the interests of individual citizens. The common good is therefore the good of the whole and of its parts, a good which subordinates man to society inasmuch as he is *social*, but also a good which respects man as a person ordered directly to God and his eternal end. Man is independent as regards *his value* — immortal, spiritual, and God-destined. He is dependent as regards his *function* — social, bound to the common good, functioning somewhat like an organ in an organism. Therefore man has both right and duties. Society in like manner has rights and duties; rights as regards its end — the fostering of the common good; duties as regards its respect for inalienable rights which the State did not give and therefore cannot take away.

> For one and all are we destined by our birth and adoption to enjoy, when this frail and fleeting life is ended, a supreme and final good in heaven, and to the attainment of this every endeavor should be directed. Since, then, upon this depends the full and perfect happiness of mankind, the securing of this end should be of all imaginable interests the most urgent. Hence civil society, established for the common welfare, should not only safeguard the wellbeing of the community, but have also at heart the interests of its individual members, in such mode as not in any way to hinder, but in every manner to render as easy as may be, the possession of that highest and unchangeable good

for which all should seek. Wherefore, for this purpose, care must especially be taken to preserve unharmed and unimpeded the religion whereof the practice is the link connecting man with God.[12]

Two errors are possible concerning man's relation to society: isolation and absorption. Individualism or Liberalism ignored man's social responsibility. Collectivism and the Totalitarian State ignore the personal, incommunicable, and inherent dignity of man. As a citizen he is for the State, but as a person the State is for him, for man alone has eternal destiny, man alone is the source of all earthly values. Man alone is the fountainhead of Liberty, Truth, and Justice and before that supreme value the State must bow. As an end for whom the State exists, the State serves him; as a means without which the State could not exist, he serves the State.

Two conclusions follow: Liberalism, out of which the world is passing and of which Capitalism was the economic expression, conceived the State as negative in function with no other duty than to prevent interference with individual rights. In the end this meant only the right of the strong to survive. The State in this outmoded view had no other duty than to protect rights and repress injustice. Hence the common appeal to the State to protect "property rights" and the violent protest against the violation of constitutional rights and the charge of "undue interference," if the State attempted to limit individual rights for the common good.

Such a false view of liberty is derived from Spencer and Kant, who declared that "every man has freedom to do all that he wills, provided he infringes not the equal freedom of any other man."[13] If this view were true, adultery would be right if the adulterer gave the same privilege to the husband of the violated woman. This makes the individual the supreme arbiter of what is right, and excuses theft, vice, and economic injustice provided one does not deny the same right to others. This concept of liberty so completely ignored the objective standard of *the common good* and the general welfare, that in practice it resulted economically in the right of the strong to oppress the

weak. When one challenges it, one is met with shouts of
protest against the invasion of individual rights and liberties, but that is because such men understand liberty only
as *my* liberty. Private interpretation of liberty is not liberty but license. It is grounded on the worst of all illusions
that liberty is absolute, and that each man is a king, or
maybe God. To such a mind the master is the enemy of
freedom; authority is the denial of liberty. The amassing
of wealth into the hands of the few, and the impoverishment of the masses is the eloquent proof that too many
individuals in modern society have insulated themselves
from their social responsibility. Those who amass great
fortunes and use them for their own selfish ends, justify
their selfishness by saying that the worthy always come
to the top and the indigent always stay at the bottom
where they belong. This was the modern expression of the
Calvinistic heresy that worldly prosperity is a sign of
God's favor; it was a modernization of the philosophy of
the Orientals who came to Job and told Job that he suffered because he deserved it; he was on a dung heap because he sinned; he was an underdog because he had no
brains.

Liberalism, Capitalism, as its economic aspect, and Individualism are dying; they may be already dead, though
they do not know it, because the tombstones have not yet
been erected. Unfortunately, in too many instances Liberalism was wounded and killed, *not by a reaffirmation of
the person and the rebirth of liberty*, but by the opposite
error of the Totalitarian State or Collectivism which denies that man has any inalienable rights and refuses him
all opportunity to develop his personality. Man is so absorbed into the group or the class or the race that he may
not do or think anything contrary to the will of the dictator. The dictator, in his turn, justifies himself by saying
that the good of the whole is whatever he demands. The
only morality in such a view is State morality; the only
conscience, State conscience; the only end is the glorification of the nation, race, or class. Freedom in this theory
resides not in man but in the State; rights are born not in

the soul, but in the group. Man is not a social person, but a part of a whole and as such is a means to an end.

One of the most remarkable expressions of the Totalitarian fallacy is that prophecy of Communism by the Russian novelist and philosopher Dostoievsky, who in his work *The Possessed* written in 1871 gave such an accurate description of the extinction of liberty under Communism that we would believe it was written in Moscow this very year. "Starting from unlimited freedom, I arrived at unlimited despotism. Mankind is to be divided into two parts. One-tenth enjoys absolute liberty and unbounded power over the other nine-tenths. The others have to give up all individuality and become a herd, through boundless submission, willed by a series of regenerations, to attain primeval innocence, something like the Garden of Eden. They will have to work, however. The measures for depriving nine-tenths of mankind of their freedom and transforming them into a herd through the education of whole generations are based on the facts of nature and highly logical." "Shigalov is a man of genius," says Verhovensky later.

> "He has discovered 'equality'! He suggests a system of spying. Every member of the society spies on the other, and it is his duty to inform against them. Everyone belongs to all, and all to everyone. All are slaves and equal in their slavery. In extreme cases Shigalov advocates slander and murder, but the great thing about it is equality. To begin with, the level of education, science and talents is lowered. A high level of education and science is only possible for great intellects, and they are not wanted. . . . They will be banished or put to death. Cicero will have his tongue cut out, Copernicus will have his eyes put out, Shakespeare will be stoned — that's Shigalovism. Slaves are bound to be equal. . . . In the herd there is bound to be equality, and that's Shigalovism.

> ". . . To level the mountains is a fine idea. . . . Down with culture. We have had enough science! Without science we have material enough to go on for a thousand years, but one must have discipline. The thirst for culture is an aristocratic thirst. The moment you have family ties or love you get the desire for property. We will destroy that desire; we'll make use of slander, spying; we'll make use of incred-

ible corruption; we'll stifle every genius in its infancy. . . .
Complete Equality! Only the necessary is necessary, that's
the motto of the whole world henceforward.

"Slaves must have directors. Absolute submission. . . . But
once in 30 years Shigalov would let them have a shock and
they would all suddenly begin eating one another up, simply as a precaution against boredom. . . . Listen . . . we'll
make an upheaval. Do you know that we are tremendously
powerful already? I have reckoned them all up (those who
will be with us). A teacher who laughs with children at
their God is on our side. The lawyer who defends an educated murderer is one of us. The schoolboys who murder a
peasant for the sake of sensation are ours. The prosecutor
who trembles at a trial for fear he will not seem liberal
enough is ours. Among officials and literary men we have
lots, lots . . . and they don't know it themselves. . . . When I
left Russia the dictum that crime is insanity was all the
rage. I come back to find that new crime is simply common
sense, almost a duty; anyway, a gallant protest. . . . We'll
mend things — if need be we'll drive them 40 years into
the wilderness. But one or two generations of vices are essential now; monstrous, abject vice, by which a man is
transformed into a loathsome, cruel reptile. That's what we
need. . . . We will proclaim destruction. Why is it that idea
has such a fascination? We'll set fires going. . . . We'll set
legends going. Every 'Scurvy' group will be of use. Out of
them I'll pick you fellows so keen they'll not shrink from
shooting, and be grateful for the honor of a job, too. Well,
there will be an upheaval! There's going to be such an up-
set as the world has never seen before! Russia will be
overwhelmed with darkness, the earth will weep for its old
gods."

What Dostoievsky did for the Russians in *The Possessed*
Heine[14] did in a monograph on Germany over a hundred
years ago.

It is the greatest merit of Christianity," he writes, "to have
assuaged the joy of the German in brutal bellicosity, but . .
. when, one day, the Cross of Christ is broken the savagery
of the old warriors, the wild Berserker wrath, will break
forth anew in all the barbaric fury of which our Nordic po-
ets tell in song and saga. Even today the talisman of Christianity has begun to rot, and the day will come when its
power will piteously collapse. Then will the old stone gods

arise from the accumulated rubbish of the past. . . . When
that day comes . . . take good care, Frenchmen, and do not
interfere with those affairs which we are settling among
ourselves. Take care neither to fan the fire not quench it . .
. Do not laugh at my advice. . . . German thunder is admit-
tedly German; it is not very agile . . . but it will come one
day and . . . you will hear an explosion such as has never
yet occurred in the history of the world.

The hour will come, when, like spectators in an amphithe-
ater, the nations will crowd around Germany to watch the
great tourney. I warn you, Frenchmen, keep quiet and
above all do not applaud. . . . Take care! I wish you well,
and for that reason I tell you bitter truths. . . . You have
more to fear from a liberated Germany than from the entire Holy Alliance, with all its Croats and Cossacks. . . .
Never disarm . . .

It is the characteristic of a halfwit, when he learns of an
abuse to condemn the use: to say none shall drive an automobile because some automobiles kill pedestrians or no
one shall have wine because some get drunk, or that none
shall have property because some freemen ignored the
poor. The more balanced mind rejects both Liberalism and
Totalitarianism, because he refuses on the one hand to
isolate man from social responsibilities which is to endanger liberty by making man a bull in a china shop. On the
other hand he refuses to absorb man into the collectivity
which destroys liberty by making man an apple in the
collective applesauce.

Somewhere there is a golden mean in which Truth is
not determined either by an individual, or by the State,
but by consonance of the mind with the objective world,
natural and human law and Divine Authority; in which
liberty is neither doing what I please, nor doing what a
Dictator extorts, but a liberty in which I am free to choose
between good things in the social order in order to attain
the perfection of my personality and the salvation of my
soul; a society in which each man as a citizen has a function like an organ in an organism, and therefore has definite duties to perform, certain social responsibilities to
shoulder for the sake of the common good; but a society
also in which every citizen is a *person*, to each of which

the State is a servant in order that the virtuous life of
each be not impeded but assisted to the end that through
the virtuous living of each person, the State itself will be
virtuous and the Kingdom of God will be filled with the
children of liberty. This will mean another kind of liberty
than indifference, and another kind of liberty than necessity; a golden mean in which the citizen is for the State,
and the State is for the person, for liberty as we said before is born of the recognition of personal rights and flourishes on the recognition of social responsibilities. Then we
shall have the rebirth of liberty, which will not be doing
what one pleases, nor what the dictator dictates, but doing what I *ought to do.*

Endnotes

---

[1] Jean-Jacques Rousseau (1712-1778), Swiss philosopher and
political scientist whose ideas helped inspire the French Revolution. He is noted for his theory of the "social contract."
[2] *Libertas Praestantissimum,* § 21.
[3] Technically, Sheen has it backwards. A man is a person *because* he has rights; a "person" is "[a] man considered according
to the rank he holds in society, with all the right to which the
place he holds entitles him, and the duties which it imposes."
"Person," *Black's Law Dictionary*. St. Paul, Minnesota: West
Publishing Company, 1951. [Ed.]
[4] This is, essentially, the same as saying that "property" is not
the thing owned, but the right to be an owner, and the bundle of
rights that define what an owner may do with what is owned.
[Ed.]
[5] Matthew 22:21.
[6] Leo XIII, *Graves de Communi Re* ("On Christian Democracy"),
1901, § 7.
[7] *Ibid.,* § 9.
[8] Matt. 10:28.
[9] A particular State may result from agreement among men, but
the need for the State is built into human nature. [Ed.]
[10] *Summa Theologica,* Ia IIae q. 21, a 4, ad. 3.
[11] *Rerum Novarum,* § 51. [As explained by Father William J.
Ferree, S.M., Ph.D., the common good is that vast network of
institutions within which human beings acquire and develop
virtue, that is, become more fully human. See *Introduction to
Social Justice*. New York: Paulist Press, 1948, 26-30. Thus, the

common good is the manifestation of humanity's capacity to acquire and develop virtue. — Ed.]

[12] Leo XIII, *Immortale Dei* ("On the Christian Constitution of States"), 1885, § 6.

[13] Herbert Spencer, *Social Statics*, c. 4, § 3.

[14] Johann Heinrich Heine, born Harry Heine (1797-1856), German poet, essayist, journalist and literary critic. A convert from Judaism (at which time he changed his name), Heine was influential in the "Young Germany" movement. As an expatriate he spent the latter part of his life in Paris. [Ed.]

9. Liberty and the Republic

ONE OF THE METHODS of Communist propaganda in the United States is to speak of Communism as "democracy," in order to hide its dictatorship. Stalin's agents in the United States plead for a union of the two great democracies: Russia and America.

Naturally when the Communists call Russia a democracy and not a dictatorship which it really is, they are distorting the meaning of democracy. The Stalin agent in the United States recently said when advocating a union of Russia and America: "The Communist party is the most energetic, systematic and vociferous defender of democracy."[1] There is no doubt about Communists being the most vociferous, but the question is, do they believe in democracy? We know they talk about it as they were told to do by Moscow at the 7th Congress, but talk is cheap. The point is: Do they believe in it? The one way to settle this question is to go to official Communist documents themselves.

1. When the Communists use the term *democracy*, what do they mean, *American democracy* or *Soviet democracy*? Notice that in the above quotation the Stalin agent says: "Defender of democracy," not "defender of American democracy." Note furthermore that the Communist oath does not swear to defend America and its Constitution but to work for the establishment of "Soviet America." Furthermore, the official document of the Communist Party states that "We Communists are unswerving upholders of *Soviet Democracy*, the great prototype of which is the proletarian dictatorship in the Soviet Union."[2] In other words, when a Communist uses the word *democracy*, he uses it to mean Soviet Democracy, the prototype of which is not America but Russia. He uses the term *democracy* in the same way a gold-brick salesman uses the term *gold*.

2. Their brand of democracy is impossible without a revolution. This means in the concrete that our present form of government must be overthrown before Soviet Democracy can be established. "Soviet Democracy presupposes the victory of the proletarian revolution."[3] If they are upholders of American democracy why do they want to overthrow it by a revolution? If you believed in the beauty of flowers would you put a bomb under them? If they love the American flag (they are always careful to attack our institutions alongside of one) why did the American agent of Stalin testify before the 71st Congress[4] that the Communist workers in America "have only one flag and that is the red flag"? If they love American democracy why do they uphold Soviet democracy which presupposes, as their official program puts it on page 36, "the violent overthrow of armies, police bureaucratic hierarchy, the judiciary, parliaments" and the "complete suppression of opposition"[5] and the "task of systematically and unswervingly combating religion"[6]?

3. If Communism believes in American democracy why did the Stalin agent in the United States bring to Moscow on July 27, 1935, a ninety-minute report on Communist activities in the United States? Since when do loyal Americans make reports to foreign powers? The Stalin agent in the United States who made this report to Moscow was a candidate for President in 1936.

4. If the Communists in the United States believe in American Democracy, why did the Stalin agent testify before a legislative committee of New York State on June 30, 1938, that the Communist Party of the United States "is a part and parcel of the Communist International of Moscow, looking to the teachings of Marx, Engels, Lenin and Stalin, and that the Communist Party in the United States *never vetoed a single order from Moscow*. Everything we had to pass on we agreed with."

5. If Communists believed in democracy, why did our American government on November 16, 1933, make the Russian Commissar Max Litvinoff (Finkelstein) promise that the Soviets would not permit "any organization or group, which has as an aim the overthrow or the prepara-

tion for the overthrow of, or bring about by force of a change in the political or social order of the whole or any part of the United States." Certainly the only reason America made the Soviets sign that pledge was because it knew the insidiousness of Communism. The Communists have not kept the pledge, but that is not their fault, but ours. When a man knows the termites are eating the roof over his head, it is his own fault that the roof falls on him.

Stalin forgets his own tactics and asks the citizens of the United States and other democratic countries to aid Russia in the case of attack. In his letter to Phillipovitch, Stalin expressed this plea to the citizens of democracies; namely, "to organize political aid by the working class of bourgeois countries for the working class of *our country* in case of a military attack upon our country."[7]

Without laboring the point suffice it to recall one final reason why we must not be fooled by the Communist plea for "democracy." Democracy means, in the plainest language, the right to dissent; it recognizes freedom of speech and press even to those who do not believe in democracy; it even permits Communism to talk revolution.

But Communism does not grant this right to dissent. Article 125 allows freedom of speech only on condition it be used to support Communism. We would hardly say we had freedom of speech in the United States if politicians could talk, and newspapers could print, and commentators could broadcast only in support of, let us say, the Republican Party. Suppose the Democratic Party sent all Republicans to labor camps; suppose they purged Maine and Vermont? Would that be Democracy? And yet that is precisely the condition which prevails under Communism.

The official Communist newspaper admits that Communism permits no different point of view: "The Constitution does not admit nor can it admit any other political party. The question has been settled once and for all and can never be discussed again. The partisans of the liquidated class enemies no longer exist among us; neither do the parties which represent them."[8] The Party and the government under Communism are one; under a democracy they are distinct. When one realizes that less than

1½ percent of the total population of Russia's 170,000,000 belongs to the Communist Party, one immediately realizes that its 98½ percent are subject to its whims, its fancies or its terror. They have elections it is true, and with a secret ballot, but the secret ballot is a farce if one cannot choose between parties. In theory they may choose between men of the same party, but in practice out of 1,143 districts in the last elections there were only 1,143 candidates. Even a certain number of candidates nominated by the people were liquidated before they could take their seats in Congress, because they were not suitable to Stalin. Among them such generals and commissars as Alksnis, Bokis, Ozoline, Daveltianov, Goulbrot, Nazarova, Bhrakanov.

H. I. Phillips commenting on the election in which the people had only one candidate from which to choose wrote:

> The laugh of the year was the recent national election over in Soviet Russia. It gave the world its first national election with one ticket in the field. Ninety million voters voted as one man. And the one man was Stalin. Final returns which are still trickling in show that the people, given a chance to vote yes or yes, decided unanimously to vote in the affirmative. 'The voting was carried out with the utmost decorum and in an atmosphere that was wholly festive and peaceful' said a Russian dispatch. Why not? It was merely an experiment in putting a cheer in writing. Guards were stationed around all the voting booths to see that no voter was influenced by anybody except official influencers. And the voters were given plenty of time to vote as Stalin's conscience dictated. Latest stories by eye-witnesses to the greatest demonstration of outdoor mass shadow boxing ever held in any country say it was an unforgettable spectacle to see millions of voters filing to the polls and deciding whether to vote 'Okay, boss' or 'Okay boss' without a moment's hesitation. But the Russians seem to have enjoyed it and there are reports that thousands stayed up in the Russian Times Square to cheer the election returns, proving that the farce was a landslide. If there is a Russian Literary Digest it must have had the softest job in literary history. Think what it would mean if America held an election on the Stalin plan. Mr. Roosevelt would announce that he was im-

mensely satisfied with himself and his associates and that the re-election would be held on Tuesday, a week from tomorrow. Jim Farley would have one ticket printed and distributed to all voters, explaining that the custom of having an opposition ticket was old-fashioned and only complicated elections anyhow. The slogan would be 'Vote early and blindly!' And can't you imagine those voting machine instructions? (1) Pull the only lever you will find in the only direction it will go. (2.) Wait for the click. When you hear it you will know you have voted as ordered. (3.) Leave promptly. If anybody molests or tries to change your vote it will be more than illegal; it will be a miracle.

Once Americans realize that Communists who talk "democracy" are really the enemies of democracy, they will prove not only their own intelligence but also their right to be citizens of a democracy. Now for the second question: Is America a Democracy? In the strict sense of the term, No! We are a republic, a representative republic as Article 4, Section 4 of the Constitution implies. Democracy means a direct rule by the people; a republic means an indirect rule by the people, *i.e.*, through their duly elected representatives. Each state of the union is a republic in the sense that in it sovereign power resides in the people, which power is exercised by representatives responsible to them. The union of all the states makes the United States a republic of republics.

There is no reference in the Constitution to "Democracy" in the strict sense of the term. James Madison writing on our Constitutional form of government says:

> Democracies have been spectacles of turbulence and contention; . . . a republic, by which I mean a government in which the scheme of representation takes place, offers a different prospect and promises the cure for what we are seeking. . . . In a democracy people exercise the government in person; in a republic they administer it by their representatives. Under the confusion of names, it has been an easy task to transfer to a republic observations applicable to a democracy alone.[9]

President Roosevelt apropos of the Ludlow amendment wrote: "Our government is conducted by the people through representatives of their own choosing. It was with singular unanimity that the founders of the republic agreed upon such a free and representative form of government as the only practical means of government by the people."

In the light of this distinction, how describe the present tendency among the "democracies" of the world? They are failing because they are ceasing to be republics and are beginning to be democracies, *i.e.*, they are allowing the impulses and passions of citizens directly to influence government rather than indirectly through the more calm, deliberate influence exercised through elected representatives. In other words, republics fail because they become democracies in the narrow sense of the term. The people's front in France, the popular front in Spain; the general strikes in France and formerly in England and yet in the future for the United States; the multiplication of pressure groups, high-powered propaganda with stereotyped messages to Congress sent out by one propaganda agency and signed with fake signatures and "marches on the Capital" — all these are symptoms of a tendency to substitute mob rule and pressure government for government through normal channels. Our position is not that those who do these things are not exercising their rights, but rather that in exercising them they are confusing democracy as a goal with democracy as a method. Their goal is right; namely, the preservation of sovereignty by the people; their method may become dangerous by making the sovereignty express itself through pressure rather than through representatives. A salesman has a right to knock at a door to sell his wares to the housewife, but he abuses that right if he threatens to sleep on her front porch until she buys.

Certain forces in national life attempt to create the impression that those who make the most noise are the most representative of the people; and that if ten thousand of organized minority stage a mass demonstration for a certain piece of legislation, then it must be the will of ten million. Just as in education there is a tendency to equate knowledge with measuring, so too there is a tendency in government to equate democracy with majority. Where does sovereignty lie? In the people? Yes. But who are the people? Are the "people" the "majority" in an election? If so, then sovereignty would not lie in the people but in the majority. Government, such as our own, means basically one thing: recognition of minority rights through majority rule. The majority party is a trustee not only of its program but, what is infinitely more important, of minority rights. The majority has no mandate for absolute power, for it is not the source of the rights of the minority and therefore cannot take them away. The majority in a republic does not equal what is right; it only equals what is popular. The majority can follow iniquity and untruth as well as truth, despite the optimism of Rousseau regarding the intrinsic goodness of human nature. Once we equate majority with sovereignty then there is no guarantee that the majority will serve freedom rather than destroy it. Once the passion for justice is lost, then the unity of men by submission to Righteousness and Justice gives way to a mechanical unity based on the votes of the majority. From that point on, the creation of majorities, real by election, or simulated by organized minority propaganda becomes the supreme, dynamic, and moving inspiration of classes, groups, and special interests, and always at the expense of the general wellbeing and peace of the nation. Then mob rule becomes sovereign and human rights its slave.

Dictatorships have profited by our confusion between the sovereignty and majority and carried universal suffrage to its absurdity in the plebiscite. Why do Hitler, Mussolini, and Stalin hold an election, when there is only one Party, one policy, and one candidate in the field? Because democracies taught them that might in suffrage is right in government. If they can by propaganda, terror, or purges effect a 100 percent plebiscite, they feel vindicated, even in the eyes of democracies.

A dictatorship is a rule by one man, but it is well to remember that is not the only kind of tyranny. If we had a Communist democratic front government here in America, we would probably suffer just as much from it as the citizens of Spain and we would lose as many rights. What makes a dictatorship bad is not the fact that there is one man at the head, but rather because in practice, that one man generally identifies his dictatorship with the source of all rights and liberties, and the common good. A majority elected by the people could do exactly the same, confusing votes with the ceding of rights.[10] The one great truth which must not be surrendered is that basic minority rights, in the sense of human rights, endure regardless of the arithmetic of an election.

It was in order to forestall arithmetic-democracy, mob rule, pressure-group government that our Founding Fathers developed a system of checks and balances to preserve rights and liberties amidst the shifting of political power. In addition to the imperfect way of preserving them by allowing minority opposition, they set up a government of checks and balances to preserve and respect minority rights. Hence, bicameral legislatures, elected on the basis of population, required more than an ordinary majority to effect important changes, *e.g.*, an amendment to the constitution.

America, if we may speak in technical language, is a republic in which the people rule through representatives and a government where rights and liberties of the minority endure even under majority rule. Its continuation depends on its not becoming a democracy in which capital becomes a political weapon for selfish profits, and labor becomes a political weapon for selfish power, but a form of government in which both recognize that they find their greatest liberty in submerging class interests for common good. A republic can survive only on the condition that it refuse to capitulate before any show of force, whether it be Capitalism and its display of credit, or labor and its display of organization, or Communism and its display of pressure groups of clergymen, lawyers, and educators, at the same time fearlessly telling them all that not one of them is the nation. Then liberty will mean something more than indifference to good and evil; then right will mean something more than rule by majority; then rule by the people will mean something else than rule by mobs.

In theory, we are a republic; in practice we must be just that. As Ross Hoffman[11] has so well expressed it:

. . . one doctrine of the State that involves neither an atheistic denial of spiritual reality nor submission to the mysticism of superpersonal national organisms, is the doctrine of the Republic. Unfortunately, in a world that has so largely lost its historical memory and faith in the Christian God and therefore is searching to find some substitute absolute, not much thought is given to that sane republicanism which is the common political tradition of Christendom. Most men, indeed, appear to have no notion of what a Republic actually is, fancying vaguely that it is merely a State without a king. The Christian political thinker, however, knows what it is; knows that it is the public thing maintained by a multitude of private 'things,' that is not an absolute but contingent reality; that it belongs to the community, not the community to it. Only where it is upheld, and by a community which in its turn recognizes a dependence on yet higher powers, can men discharge freely and in reasonable peace their dual duties to Caesar and to God."[12] . . . "How great has been our fall from the old republican idealism![13]

Source of Rights

If the majority is not the source of rights and liberties, what is the source? This is a question which every nation must ask at its birth and which every Constitution must answer. The correct answer is: Our rights come from God. Pilate, the Roman Emperor, was reminded of this by a Prisoner who stood before him and who really was his judge: that he had no power except from above.

That is why Christianity enjoins obedience to the State. "Let every soul be subject to higher powers: for there is no power but from God: and those that are, are ordained of God. Therefore he that resisteth the power resisteth the ordinance of God."[14] St. Peter likewise bids his Christians "fear God, honor the emperor."[15] And the emperor was Nero!

If God is the ultimate source of rights and liberties, what is their proximate source? The person. Only a person has rights, because only a person has a reason and a will. A stone has no rights; a donkey has not rights; but an infant has rights; a drunkard has rights; an imbecile has rights.

But why, it may be asked, is a person the proximate
source of rights? Because a person can do two things
which no chemical, plant, nor animal can do; namely, determine his own goals and purposes and secondly, choose
the means to attain them or reject them altogether. Man
does no know his end by instinct as a dog, nor unconsciously as an acorn; he decides it by reason. Since he
alone can determine his own ends, he alone has right to
attain them. Since man's self-perfection cannot be attained fully without the submission of his intellect to
truth and of his will to goodness, then he has a right to
live, as life is the condition and the means of the attainment of that end.[16] The rights of the person are derived
from the *good*, in the sense that every being is directed to
that which is good. The proximate source of human rights
then is not the State (Hegel), not the social contract of
individual wills (Rousseau), not the emergence of new bio-
logical factors (Spencer), not the will of the majority, not
the socially useful, not a Constitution, not a Dictator, nor
a Parliament, but a person made to the image and likeness of God, endowed with the power of self-determination and therefore the right to self-realization, both in
this world and the next.

The supreme value of the world is the person; not all
visible creation and all the wealth of nations is as a grain
of sand in the balance compared with the worth of a single
man. To save man, the supreme value of earth, the Cross,
was erected at the crossroads of the civilizations of Jerusalem, Athens, and Rome. Such is the measure of his
greatness.

Unlike the beasts of the field, man does not exist for the
sake of the species, for these individuals die that the species may survive. Rather each person is a possessor of a
unitary value, which not even the State absorbs, for the
State exists for man, not man for the State. Man has
rights anterior to any State, which the State may recognize but not create. The human person and his family,
being prior to the State, have inalienable rights, such as
the maximum of personal liberty and economic wellbeing
consonant with the laws of God.

Such is the traditional concept of the source of rights which is today the essence of Catholic social teaching and the basis of Americanism. Americanism, as understood by our Founding Fathers is the political expression of the Catholic doctrine concerning man. Firstly, his rights come from God, and therefore cannot be taken away; secondly, the State exists to preserve them. "We hold these truths to be self-evident . . . that they are endowed by their Creator with certain inalienable rights, that among these are life, liberty and the pursuit of happiness. That to secure these rights, governments are instituted among men, deriving their just power from the consent of the governed."

The recognition of the inalienable rights of the human person is Americanism, or to put it another way, an affirmation of the inherent dignity and worth of man. This does not mean humanity but each human; not mankind but this man; not man in the abstract but in the concrete. As a political document it affirms what the Gospel affirms as religion: the worth of man. Christ died on a cross for him, and governments are founded on account of him. He is the object of love theologically and politically — the source of rights, inalienable and sacred because when duly protected and safeguarded, he helps in the creation of a kingdom of Caesar which is the steppingstone to the Kingdom of God.

The exact statement of our problem today is not the forgotten man, in the sense of the hungry man, but the forgotten man in the sense of forgotten human worth, and forgotten human dignity. It is rather important to hearken back to this elementary doctrine of the source of rights to avoid two dangers threatening Americanism — one from the outside, and the other from the inside. Outside, the danger is in those Totalitarian States which hold that the State is the source of all human rights. Mussolini, for example, stated that the State "is the creator of right."[17] If he carried this out in practice, it would follow that the Fascist citizens could enjoy only those rights which the State granted.

Hitler has forgotten human rights even more, for to him the source of rights is not the "State as an economic organization, but a race organism."[18] This in practice means that only Aryan men have rights; hence the persecution of Jews.

Finally, there is Soviet Fascism or Communism, where not the nation as in Italy, nor the race as in Germany, but the Party is the source of all rights. Hence in the Soviet Constitution one reads through ten chapters and one hundred and seventeen articles before one comes to a mention of a right, only to discover that the first right mentioned is the right to work. Given the Party as the source of rights as in Russia, it follows that the Party has the right to purge its dissidents, as Hitler claims the right to exile the non-Aryans. Man under Nazism, Fascism, and Communism is not a historical entity, but only a social atom awaiting absorption into the mass. The only geniuses such collectivities can produce are saints; namely, those who challenge Caesar's claim to be God. If Shakespeare lived in Russia he would be purged; if Jeremias lived in Germany, he would be persecuted; and if Washington or Lincoln lived in any one of these Totalitarian states they would be reduced to impotent silence, for in such regimes only the servile survive. The Totalitarian regimes fit man to the group which is just as bad as fitting a man's head to his hat. Freedom lies politically in the liberation of man from the mass, not in his submission.

So careful is our Constitution of the rights of man that the first ten amendments to the Constitution, called the Bill of Rights, protect the sovereignty of the people against the encroachment of Federal powers, and Article Nine reminds us that when rights are conferred by the Constitution it must not be assumed that these are the only rights which man enjoys. The danger to America from the outside lies in the infiltration of Fascist, Nazi, and Communist ideologies which deny these sacred, inalienable rights of human personality.

On the inside, the danger lies in those who would regard the Constitution as expressing only a mentality of the eighteenth century or no longer being adequate for our times. Among such influences are those of the editori-

al writer of the *New York Times* who says that Freedom
and Democracy are "a heritage from the British and
French revolutions";[19] or that the Constitution was an
expression of the individualism of the Enlightenment;[20] or
that "every tribe needs its totem and its fetish and the
Constitution is ours";[21] or that "in an age where Reason is
God, constitutions or fundamental creeds are always *supposed* to be the result of rational thought on the part of
our forebears" and "the language of the Constitution is
immaterial since it represents current myths and folklore";[22] or that we must get rid of "an unremitting search
for universal truth."[23]

Such men confuse the temporal background of a truth
with the truth itself. It is just like saying that because the
Egyptians counted two and two in terms of pyramids,
therefore two and two no longer equals four because we no
longer count pyramids but skyscrapers. The doctrine of
the inalienable rights of man, founded on the worth of
person may be stated during the days and in terms of the
language of Deism, or the Enlightenment or Rationalism,
but that does not make the truth expressed any less true.
The American Constitution and the Declaration of Independence are the temporal expressions of the only solid
basis upon which any government can be built; namely,
sovereignty of the people through the affirmation of the
intrinsic rights of man.[24] If we wanted to find immediate
sources for the American doctrine of human dignity, one
could trace it better in Burlamoqui[25] and Victoria[26] than
Locke.[27] Dr. James Brown Scott[28] of the Carnegie Foundation gives this interesting bit of history concerning the
proximate and probable origin of Jefferson's statement of
sovereignty. Robert Filmer[29] left among his manuscripts,
when he died in 1653, a work called *Patriarcha* which was
published in 1680. It was a defense of the divine right of
kings and a rejection of the doctrine of the popular sovereignty. In defending his thesis, Filmer attacked the contrary position, the best expression of which he found in *De
Laicis* of Cardinal Bellarmine which ran as follows:

> Secular or civil power is instituted by man; it is in the peo-
> ple unless they bestow it on a prince. This power is imme-

diately in the whole multitudes as in the subject for it; for this power is in the divine law, but the divine law has given this power to no particular man. . . . Power is given by the multitude to one man, or to more by the same law of nature; for the commonwealth cannot exercise this power, therefore it is bound to bestow it upon some one man or some few. It depends upon the consent of the multitude to ordain over themselves a king, or consul, or other magistrates; and if there be a lawful cause, the multitude may change the kingdom into an aristocracy or democracy.[30]

Thomas Jefferson wrote that "to secure these rights, Governments are instituted among men, deserving their just powers from the consent of the governed." Jefferson knew and said the ideas to which he was giving form were not his own. Jefferson had Filmer in his library. It was his custom to score the passages in books which he liked. It is interesting that the only passage marked in Filmer was the above quotation from Cardinal Bellarmine. Dr. Scott concludes,

If we of the United States were to have a patron — and in our case a political saint — (Protestant though we be) we might indeed do well to choose the Cardinal and sainted Bellarmine, who, strange as it may seem, has perhaps the greatest claim to the gratitude of the people of the United States, because he stated and defended in advance those principles of government which the United States have made their own and upon which their government firmly rests.

The Constitution of the United States and the Declaration of Independence are not the sources of the doctrine of the intrinsic value of man, but only its confirmation. They are merely the sanction of a traditional doctrine, and the affirmation that these natural rights are also civil rights. If we scrap the basic principle that man is of inherent worth, and set up the class, for example, as supreme, then only the class has a right to survive and purging is justified; then the moral conscience is abolished for class conscience; then we have a government of men which is subject to psychological aberrations instead of a government of men subject to law which is the guarantee of liberty.

Against such dangers from the inside, Washington warned us, and it might be well to recall the warning once again.

> Toward the preservation of your government, and the permanency of your present happy state, it is requisite not only that you steadily discountenance irregular opposition to its acknowledged authority, but also that you resist with care the spirit of innovation on its principles, *however specious the pretexts*. One method of assault may be to effect, in the form of the Constitution, alterations which will impair the energy of the system, and thus to undermine what cannot be directly overthrown. But let there be no change by usurpation; for though this, in one instance, may be the instrument of good, it is the customary weapon by which free governments are destroyed. The precedent must always greatly overbalance, in permanent evil, any partial or transient benefit, which the use can at any time yield.[31]

Since the tendency of the modern world is to the absorption of man into the collectivity; since men today are quite generally treated as robots or as means to an end, the most needed emphasis is the emphasis on the personality of man. Underlying all of our political and economic chaos, and all our plans for social reconstruction, is the basic question of man. What kind of an order are we going to build for the future? Are we going to build a society which will hold only soldiers, or a society which will hold only workers, or a society which will house only a race, or are we going to build a society which house men, that is to say, human beings composed of body and soul, members of two kingdoms but using one as the steppingstone to the other, by completing their destiny in the God from whom they came. No slave can ever lose the hope of freedom. No force can ever have power over the testimony of a clear conscience so long as we uphold the sacredness of human personality. This proposition should be evident to anyone: that since our rights and our liberties come from God therefore no State can take them away; since the soul is the source of these inalienable rights and liberties no earthly power can touch them. Now turn the proposition around. Suppose we were told that there was one country in the world which not only denied the existence of God but blots out religion from its land; suppose we were told that in the same country it was denied that man had any soul and therefore no rights which he could call his own; what kind of a society would we expect to find? Slavery! We find that society in Russia, and something very close to it in Germany. There is no escaping this vital truth, that the denial of the soul is the beginning of *all tyranny and all dictatorship*.[32]

Now if the source of man's rights and liberties is to be found in God and in the soul, who is doing most in America to preserve the essence of Americanism or the sacredness of human worth? Is our present system of nonreligious education which forgets God and dissolves man into a chemical entity doing anything to preserve the rights of man? Is a system of education which forgets that moral training is far more important than intellectual training, and that brain power without will power is rationalized evil, doing anything to preserve the rights and liberties of man? It is religious education, whether it be Catholic or Protestant or Jewish, which is contributing most to the preservation of Americanism, for religion and the rights of man go hand in hand. The decline of human liberty in the world is in direct ratio with the decline of religion. Religion and tyranny grow in indirect ratio. That is why those States which are most antireligious, are most antihuman. Nazism and Communism know they cannot control man and make him subservient either to the race or the class until they strangle the Church which says that man has rights independent of any race or any class. Hence, any attempt on the part of the Church to minister spiritually to citizens who want something else to feed upon, than the husks of the economic, is regarded as "counterrevolutionary" as it was in Spain, or as "anti-Nordic" as in Germany, or as "reactionary" as in Russia. Naturally, if the State is the supreme object of worship, any citizen who claims the right to worship God, is to be regarded as guilty of treason. The punishment of such "treason" becomes persecution, by the simple fact that the State possesses those instruments of force which can compel shameful obedience on the part of weaklings, or impose glorious death on the part of the strong. It is because of just such brute force that Mexico, Germany, Russia, and Spain have exiled from their lands, the noblest of their citizens — those who loved their country most because they loved God more. Man will always have an object of worship, and if he forgets the true God, someone will make him a new deity. That new deity forged on the anvil of politics is the modern State. Nabuchodonosor[33] of old not only demanded that his statue be adorned but that at a given signal the adoration of other gods should cease. Our modern Nabuchodonosors have trumpeted the same command: Render unto Caesar even the things that are God's. Refusal means either exile or persecution.

Though the State exists for man and not man for the State, love of country is in the Christian concept a form of the virtue of *pietas*.[34]

Patriotism, however, is rapidly becoming a lost virtue; too many of our citizens think of freedom only as the right to make a speech; of tolerance as indifference to right and wrong; of liberalism as the surrender of tradition, constitutions, and the value of a person; and of democracy as the catchword to involve America in international brigandry.

Love of country needs once more to be revived, otherwise we shall perish for no other crime than because we refused to love. Patriotism has a negative aspect and a positive aspect and one cannot be divorced from the other. Negatively, patriotism implied strong opposition to all anti-American activities.

From the first point of view, if we are to maintain Americanism, we must remember that there are not two, but *three* anti-American ideologies: Communism, Nazism, and Fascism. The difference between the three to an American is like the difference between theft, burglary, and larceny. Every true American knows that he cannot be pro-Communist, or pro-Nazi, or pro-Fascist without being anti-American. But the problem is: How know whether an organization is Communist, Fascist, or Nazi? The answer is very simple: A truly American organization is opposed to all three. Hence any organization which condemns one without condemning the others is, to say the least, suspect.

For example, if any organization says it is immoral for Mussolini to set up a Fascist state in Abyssinia, or for Hitler to set up a Nazi state in Austria, then let it also admit that it is immoral for Stalin to use agents to set up a Soviet state in America.

Which of the three offers the greatest danger to America? No clear answer can be given because they operate differently. Nazism and Fascism attack from without, but Communism attacks from within; Nazism and Fascism rob you by breaking down your front door. Communism robs you after it has been your house guest for a week end. As far as internal dangers are concerned there is no doubt Communism is the most dangerous. Their tactics are more clever. They use non-revolutionary language to attain revolutionary ends.

The Communist tactics in the United States can be made clear by a parable: One day a dozen rats got into a house and ate cheese, meat, ham, and crackers. The housewife set traps and caught six of the rats. The other six remaining rats, fearful of being exterminated, organized a popular front with a rattrap salesman who told the lady of the house that her greatest danger was not rats but bedbugs; another popular front the rats organized with professors, who told the housewife that statistics proved that 60 percent of children in the village of Squedrenck lost their fingers in rattraps in one year; finally the rats organized a popular front with some sentimentally inclined social leaders who told the housewife that by using rattraps she was guilty of the reactionary crime of "rat baiting." The poor housewife, so overcome by such influential nitwits, gave up use of rattraps entirely — and now the rats run the pantry.

The moral is obvious. Communism creates the bogey of Fascism in order that it may work unmolested, as Fascism creates the bogey of Communism. Which comes first? Historically, Communism comes first, as it did in Italy, and in Germany. There would be no Mussolini or Hitler in the world today if there had been no Communism, just as there would be no rattraps if there were no rats. If Americans want to keep Fascism out of America, and we all do, then the best thing for us to do is keep out Communism which generates it by force of reaction. Did you know that 19 governments in Europe have outlawed the Communist party, because of their revolutionary intentions? Both Fascism and Communism are founded on the bogey of fear — one on the fear of the "Red terror," the other on the fear of Fascism. Whether or not we fall prey to either depends upon our gullibility; and, curiously enough, those who have been most taken in by the Communist propaganda in the United States are not the workers, or the poor, but the "intelligentsia," that is, those who think they know but do not know that they don't. It is easier to get a university professor to join a Communist front organization than it is to get an unemployed father. Communism has ceased to have an appeal to the workers — they are too close to life's realities to be fooled. That is why it has turned to the intelligentsia who are not nearly so clever. We are supposed to be an alert and intelligent people, but the Communist front organizations prove that many Americans can be taken in hook, line, and sinker and maneuvered not only into defending Communist interests throughout the world but also into assisting them to create the situation they desire for the successful culmination of their revolutionary strategy.

But Patriotism is not just a negation of anti-American activities; it is above all the affirmation of a love of country as a reflection of our love of God. It is about time we stopped talking about our aches and pains and began to think of the happiness of being Americans. There are three blessings for which we should be grateful.

1. *Economically* we are better off than any nation in the world. The laboring man in the United States has a right to strike in protest against unjust wages, hours, and working conditions. He has no such right under dictatorships. Russia forbids the strike under Article 131, classifying it as sabotage for which death is often the penalty. The Italian Law of April 3, 1926, the German Labor Act of January, 1934, agree with Russia in the refusal to grant

the worker this basic right. In Italy the per-capita bank deposit is $47; in Germany $89; in Russia $9.5; in America $423. In Italy there are 30 gallons of milk available per person, per year; in Russia 35; and in the United States 95. In Italy there are available in units of electricity 275 kilowatt hours per person; in Germany 550; in Russia 190; in the United States 900. If the people in those countries packed up and moved by auto tomorrow, how many would have to walk? In Italy, for one that would ride, twenty would walk; in Germany for one that would ride, ten would walk; in Russia for one that would ride, 150 would walk; and in the United States there are enough cars for *all* to ride.

2. *Politically* we have much to be thankful for. Note the difference between the American and Totalitarian regimes: Here in America, man is the source of rights; there, the collectivity is the source of right. Here the State exists for man; there man exists for the State. Here the State recognizes inalienable human rights; there the State grants them — and since it gives man rights it can also take them away. Here the Government is distinct from the Party; there the Government *is* the Party, which means there is no right of dissent. Here freedom resides in man; there freedom resides in the collectivity — in the race as in Germany, in the nation as in Italy, and in the class as in Russia. Here a man can render to God the things that are God's, and to Caesar the things that are Caesar's. There, they say, even God derives His existence and authority from Caesar. Here a Communist or Nazi or Fascist may attack the government openly or undermine it from within; there they would be shot for the same offense. Here the moral conscience exists independently of the State conscience; there the moral conscience is abolished for the sake of the collective conscience. Here a man has personal value apart from the mass; there he is a drop of blood in a race or a cog in a machine or a soldier in an army. For this blessing above all others we should get down on our knees every day and thank God we are Americans.

3. We should be thankful also for our *religious* blessings and the right to adore God according to the dictates of our conscience. The conflict of the future is not between democracy and dictatorship, but between a State-religion and a God-religion. Two of the dictatorships have already made this clear: Russia and Germany. They know they cannot possess man body and soul until they dispossess religion which says the soul belongs not to the State, but to man and to God. It might be well to mention here that the gravest danger facing civilization is the present union of Germany and Russia. Their political ideologies are somewhat different, though not very different, for Germany is like a half-cooked beefsteak, brown on the outside but red on the inside. They have this in common: they both hate religion. That hate is so basic that it dwarfs other differences of a political or economic character. Pilate and Herod were mortal enemies but they became friends the day they condemned our Lord. So too Hitler and Stalin who were enemies now embrace and become friends over the body of the same torn and bleeding Christ as they unite for the same unholy cause to drive God from the earth He has made. The elements of a battle between brotherhood in God and comradeship in anti-God already exist in germ in the present world situation. When it comes then shall the loyalties of men be tested; then shall men feel in their hearts the deep and hidden thrill of what is only now a catchword: "For God and Country." There is no escaping this truth and let us deeply engrave it in our minds: The denial of the soul is the beginning of all tyranny and dictatorship.

If democracy is to survive, it must take more cognizance of religion. Why? Because a democracy assumes that citizens will always act in the interest of justice, righteousness, and virtue. But justice, righteousness, and virtue are inseparable from a conscience and a conscience is inseparable from a moral law, and a moral law is inseparable from religion with a Lawmaker whose nature is Goodness. Let religion die out of the hearts of citizens and the virtues essential for democracy die with it. What then? Then democracy will mean the right to choose what is wicked and immoral; then right will mean not what is truly right but only what is popular. With all our talk about democracy let us not forget that it is possible for a democracy to vote itself out of democracy. The result of such surrender of religion and abandonment to popular fronts of foreign ideologies will be chaos and enthroned injustice. To restore some kind of order the State will then have to impose its own idea of religion on the people, and that is the beginning of tyranny for the nonreligious State becomes the antireligious State; and the antireligious State becomes the persecuting State.

Let us not forget that there are two kinds of tyrannies: not only the tyranny of the minority, as in Russia where less than 2 percent of the population belong to the Communist Party and control the other 98 percent, but also the tyranny of the majority. One can be just as bad as the other. A democracy that loses religion can be just as intolerant to its minorities as a dictatorship which loses religion.

The decline of patriotism in America is due to a decline of religion. As men cease to love God, they also cease to love their neighbor. No one proves this better than Matthew, the author of the first Gospel. He was at one time as unpatriotic a citizen as ever lived: his land was overrun by a foreign power, his fellow citizens lost many of their civil and political rights — and yet he welcomed the foreign power to his bosom for the basest of all motives, financial booty. He became a publican, that is, a collector for the Romans, thus not only selling out his countrymen, but even filching them to enrich himself by becoming subject to the invaders. One day while collecting his taxes and counting his profits, our Divine Savior passed by. "Come, follow Me,"[35] He said to Matthew, and Matthew, with no other promise than a peace which shown in the Divine Countenance, became an Apostle, an evangelist, and a martyr. He became more than that — the greatest patriot in the Gospels. His Gospel might be called the Gospel of Patriotism. Tirelessly he unfolds the glories of his people, the traditions of his land, and the prophecies of its spiritual triumphs. Time and time again he goes back to the past, turns over the pages of Isaias, Jeremias, Micheas, David, and the Kings; ninety-nine times to be exact, he quotes from the glorious pages of his people, and crowns it all with the thrilling message: You are a great people! From Israel comes the Savior; from our clouds comes the Messias; from our earth the Redeemer. Hail! Christ is your king.

He became a patriot because he found his God.

Endnotes

---

[1] *Washington Post*, November 28, 1938.

[2] Georgi Dimitrov, *The Working Class Against Fascism.* London: Modern Books, Ltd., 1935, 126.

[3] *Ibid.*, 36.

[4] House Repost No. 2290.

[5] *Ibid.*, 49.

[6] *Ibid.*, 53,

[7] *Daily Worker*, Thursday, February 17, 1938.

[8] *Izvestia*, June 15, 1935.

[9] James Madison, *The Federalist*, No. 14 ("Objections to the Proposed Constitution from the Extent of Territory Answered"), November 30, 1787.

[10] "Of all the ways and practices of liberal democracies, that which has been the most effective in bringing them to their present position of discredit is the failure of leaders actually to lead. Despite appearances, liberal democracies are dependent on leadership even more so perhaps than other more authoritarian forms of government; for, in authoritarian systems, the springs of authority are more firmly established at all the levels of the political organization, while, in liberal democracies, their natural tendency to weaken the springs of political authority must be counterbalanced by a higher level of personal and moral authority on the part of their leaders. Now, liberal-democratic leaders can hardly be said to have shown the courage and self-control which are necessary for the acquisition of moral authority."

"At the outset it may be said that, through the operation of the set of the current axioms and postulates on liberty, equality, democracy, capitalism and labor which we have endeavored to analyze above, liberal-democratic leaders have seldom had a sufficiently clear perception of the organic nature of the State and, even when they have had it, they have often lacked the courage to say so and to act accordingly. Steeped in the prejudic-

es of the day, they have accepted in all its disastrous implica-
tions the statistical conception of democracy, *i.e.*, the view that
numbers of votes, no matter by whom, how, or on what occasion
given, decide the issues before the community." — Salvador de
Madariaga, *Anarchy or Hierarchy*, New York: Macmillan, 1937,
49, 50.

[11] Ross John Swartz Hoffman (1902-1979), conservative historian, Catholic convert (1931). Hoffman was instrumental in the
revival of the thought of Edmund Burke after World War II.
[Ed.]

[12] Hoffman, *Tradition and Progress, op. cit.*, 128, 129.

[13] *Ibid.*,106.

[14] Rom. 13:1,2.

[15] 1 Pet. 2:17.

[16] The sun *must* rise in the east; man *ought* to realize the full
potentialities of his personality. *Ought* is the mark of freedom.
Cf. Fulton J. Sheen, *The Cross and the Crisis*. Milwaukee, Wisconsin: Bruce Publishing Company, 1938.

[17] Mussolini in *Enciclopedia Italiana*, Article *Fascismo*.

[18] Hitler, *Mein Kampf*, p. 165.

[19] October 17, 1937.

[20] Carl Becher, "After Thoughts on Constitutions" in *Yale Review*, Spring, 1938. For an excellent refutation. Cf. *Thought*,
June, 1938.

[21] Max Lerner, "Constitution and Court as Symbols," in *Yale
Law Journal*, Vol. 46 (1937).

[22] W. Arnold Thurman, *The Folklore of Capitalism*. New Haven,
Conn.: Yale University Press, 1937, 27, 29.

[23] *Ibid.*, 59-71.

[24] See Cardinal Satolli's characterization of the U.S. Constitution and the Gospels of Jesus Christ as "the Magna Charta of
humanity." Rev. John Ireland, *The Church and Modern Society*,
I, 127, quoted in Rommen, *The State in Catholic Thought, op.
cit.*, 370. [Ed.]

[25] Jean-Jacques Burlamaqui (1694-1748), Swiss legal and political theorist who is credited with a strong influence on America's
Founding Fathers. [Ed.]

[26] More commonly "Vitoria." Francisco de Vitoria, O.P. (*cir.*
1483-1546). Spanish philosopher, theologian and jurist, founder
of the Salamanca School of philosophy, noted for his contributions to the theory of just war and international law. Because of
his idea of a "republic of the whole world" (*res publica totius or-
bis*) he has been called the "founder of global political philosophy." [Ed.]

27 John Locke FRS (1632-1704). English political scientist, philosopher, and physician known as the "Father of Classical Liberalism." He is regarded as one of the most influential of the Enlightenment thinkers and one of the first of the British empiricists. His social contract theory greatly influenced the development of epistemology and political philosophy. His writings influenced Voltaire and Rousseau, many Scottish Enlightenment thinkers, as well as the American revolutionaries, although some authorities believe that the influence of Algernon Sidney, who adhered more closely to the thought of Bellarmine, was greater. George Mason, who may have read Bellarmine directly, seems to have had more influence on the United States Declaration of Independence than Locke on the question of essential human nature and dignity. See John Clement Rager, S.T.D., *The Political Philosophy of Blessed Robert Bellarmine*. Washington, DC: Catholic University of America Press, 1926. [Ed.]

28 James Brown Scott, J.U.D. (1866-1943), American authority on international law. [Ed.]

29 Sir Robert Filmer (1588-1653), chief theologian of James VI/I Stuart of Scotland/England, and proponent of the divine right of kings. [Ed.]

30 Robert Bellarmine, *De Laicis, or, The Treatise on Civil Government*. New York: Fordham University Press, 1928, 25-27. N.B.: This is a different translation. See Rager, *op. cit.* [Ed.]

31 George Washington's *Farewell Address to the People of the United States*, 1796.

32 Walter Lippmann, *The Good Society*. Boston: Little, Brown and Co., 1937, 383 ff.

33 Nabuchodonosor II (*cir.* 605-562 B.C.), Chaldean restorer of the Second Babylonian Empire, under whom it reached its zenith. He was noted for the many temples and monuments he built and restored. Cf. Diodorus Siculus, II, 95; Herodotus, I, 183. Nabuchodonosor is mentioned in the Old Testament, particularly in the Books of Jeremiah and Daniel. [Ed.]

34 Responsibility, sense of duty, piety, *etc.* [Ed.]

35 Matt. 4:18-22.

10. Limits of Freedom

FREEDOM IS THE POWER to do what we *ought*. A man can do many things, *e.g.*, shoot his wife, steal his neighbor's cabbage, or punch his competitor's nose. But he *ought* not to do these things, because all his rights involve corresponding duties. The power to act a certain way is not the right to act any way. Liberty as a *physical* power to do whatever one pleases is quite distinct from the *moral* power to do what one ought. The power to do evil is not the same as the right to do evil. The power to violate traffic laws is not the beginning of the freedom to drive, but its end. The individual who appeals to the Declaration of Independence and its "inalienable right to liberty" to justify his right to feed firecrackers to wild animals in the zoo will soon discover that the word *liberty* is not subject to private interpretation. When liberty becomes arbitrary it becomes anarchy. Even the anarchists who hate all rule abide by their own rules. Order is the balance between liberty and authority. Freedom consists in the wise sacrifice of liberty. The pendulum of a clock is free to swing in rhythm only on condition that it be attached to a fixed point. If it sacrifices that much liberty it is free to swing, but not otherwise. In like manner, liberty has a fixed point; namely, law, either divine or human; so long as liberty serves the purpose of rationality, purpose, and law it is most free in its exercise. Leo XIII has well expressed the relation of liberty to law as follows:

> Such then being the condition of human liberty, it necessarily stands in need of light and strength to direct its actions to good and to restrain them from evil. Without this the freedom of our will would be our ruin. First of all there must be *law;* that is, a fixed rule of teaching concerning what is to be done and what is to be left undone. This rule cannot affect the lower animals in any true sense, since they act of necessity, following their natural instinct, and

cannot of themselves act in any other way. . . . In other
words, reason prescribes to the will what it should seek after or shun, in order to pursue the eventual attainment of
man's last end, for the sake of which all his actions ought
to be performed. This ordination of *reason* is called law. In
man's free will, therefore, or in the moral necessity of our
voluntary acts being in accordance with reason, lies the
very root of the necessity of law. Nothing more foolish can
be uttered or conceived than the notion that because man
is free by nature, he is therefore exempt from law. Were
this the case, it would follow that to become free we must
be deprived of reason; whereas the truth is that we are
bound to submit to law precisely because we are free by our
very nature.[1]

Applying this to the social order, no society can exist
without setting limits or "fixed points" to liberty. Society
has obviously such a right, for man as a citizen exists for
the common good, as the hand functions for the good of
the body. The State may therefore curb certain rights of
individuals for the common good. The "common good" is
not "class good," nor "race good." The common good of the
State in the language of Leo XIII is "public wellbeing and
private prosperity. . . . The immediate end is social peace,
that is, the organic blending of individual and social activities as to produce social harmony. The proximate end
which is temporal prosperity, *i.e.*, intellectual, economic,
artistic and moral."[2] Negatively this means the State
must put no obstacles in the way of the spiritual development of individuals. When the State limits or conditions certain rights of citizens it does so not out of a denial
of inalienable rights, but because too selfish an adherence
to them would destroy that common good, as too selfish an
adherence to property rights would prevent my neighbor
having city water in his home. The employer who would
pay only the "wages he pleased" even though they were
starvation wages, could not accuse the State of unjust aggression, if it insisted on a living wage. The "liberty" of
that individual employer would be lessened but the general level of liberty would be increased. The State may in
certain extreme cases take over private property, *e.g.*, for
the purpose of defense in war. This it would not do if the
personal right to property were absolute and unlimited.[3]

As there are limitations to the right of property so there are the limitations to the "right to life."[4] Every man has a right to life, but that right, like all rights, is limited to some extent in the citizen by the common good. If the right to life is interpreted as the right to take another man's life, society has a right to curtail the right. The right to life must include the right of another man to defend his life, and this may involve as a matter of necessity the right to take the life of the aggressor or more normally for the State to do it.

Every man has the right of association, *i.e.*, to enter freely into groups or societies to defend particular interests, *e.g.*, study clubs, labor organizations, religious communities.[5] But this right of association is not so absolute that it is independent of the common good. The right to association does not include the right to organize against public safety nor national security. Neither the capitalist's right to form employer's associations and monopolies, nor the laborer's right to organize are absolute; both are socially conditioned, and both can be revoked if they endanger the general weal. Liberty must be respected in its exercise and in pursuit of what is good and compatible with the social order. But it can be restricted in an individual who uses it to injure himself, *e.g.*, a drunken driver. Furthermore, the State has a right to add its support to the weak to protect their liberty against the strong, *e.g.*, legislation favorable to the poor. The order of society is an equilibrium between liberty and restraint. If there is only restraint or authority there is despotism; if there is unlimited *liberty*, there is anarchy.

What is the absolute limit of liberty in society? What is the last point beyond which a man may not go in the exercise of freedom? There is in all things a point where not only the worm turns, but also rights. There is a point beyond which a man may not eat without losing the benefit of eating; there is a point in tickling beyond which it ceases to be funny and begins to pain; there is a height beyond which birds may not fly, without ceasing to be free to fly; so too there are limits beyond which right may not go without surrendering the right itself. And what is that

limit? When a right is invoked to destroy a right. If I invoke my right to property to steal your property, or if I
invoke my right to liberty to take away everyone else's
liberty, or if I invoke my right of free speech to destroy
your right of free speech, then I have passed that limit of
freedom, and I must surrender my rights, because I have
ignored the *purpose* and nature of the rights.

The State has a right to check the liberty of any of its
citizens who amass financial and economical power dangerous to the common good. It would not justify the State
in depriving every citizen of productive property as Communism would do, but it would justify it in legislating
against unrestricted control of money and credit, or property. The principle of self-preservation applies to the
State as well as to man, though in different degrees.[6] An
unwarranted challenge to the common good justifies the
State in curtailing individual rights and liberties. Since
the State exists for man, man would suffer deeply in body
and soul, economically and socially, if the State collapsed,
just as the fingers suffer if the hand is injured.

Since one of the most talked about liberties today is the
right of free speech, it is important to inquire (a) whether
free speech is a natural right, (b) whether it has any limits. Undoubtedly, it is a right in the sense that it implies a
moral and legal freedom from all undue interference in
the exterior manifestation of one's opinions. It is a *natural*
right because speech is an inseparable attribute of human
nature. Man is the only animal who really talks, and he
talks because he has a rational soul. But freedom of
speech is not only a *natural* right, but also a civil right for
without it, it would be impossible to conduct a representative government. There are many subjects which are matters of opinion, none of which are inimical to the common
good, or the Divine law, or the sacredness of human personality. "In regard to all matters of opinion which God
leaves to man's free discussion, full liberty of thought and
speech is naturally within the right of everyone; *for such
liberty never leads men to suppress the truth*, but often to
discover it and make it known."[7] Freedom of speech and
press are fundamental rights safeguarded by the due pro-

cess clauses of the fourteenth amendment of the Constitution. As the Supreme Court put it, "The very idea of a government, republican in form, implies a right on the part of citizens to meet peaceably for consultation in respect to public affairs and to petition for a redress of grievances."[8] The right itself must not be curtailed, but only the abuse.[9] By such liberty minorities are protected; by it they register their protest and influence opinion; by it knowledge grows through challenge and opposition; and by it the State grows, for its collective wisdom is conditioned by the individual contributions of its citizens. A State without free speech is without criticism, such as Germany, Russia, and Italy; under such regimes life is conditioned upon keeping the collective mouth shut. The "purges" of Russia mean that there the right of speech is the right to echo, and then one must fear that the echo is not in keeping with the Party line.

Immediately after religious liberty, free speech is one of the first rights mentioned in the Constitution of the United States. "Congress shall make no law . . . abridging freedom of speech, or of the press; or the right of people peaceably to assemble and to petition the government for a redress of grievances."

Granted that it is a right, does free speech have any limitations? Like all social rights it is socially conditioned, and like all natural rights its exercise is subject to the common good.

In order to understand its limitation, it must be kept clearly in mind that speech is not an end, but a *means*. Speech is like an automobile; it is a vehicle of communication; instead of transporting men it transports ideas, but transportation or communication is not the same as the purpose of the journey. The morality of a journey is not to be judged by the means of transportation used, but by the purpose or end of the journey. A robber is not guilty because he uses an automobile to rob a bank; he is guilty because he used the automobile for the purpose of robbing a bank. As my right to an automobile does not give me the unlimited right to drive over public gardens, so neither does my right to free speech give me the right to drive

over the gardens of public decency. The right to free
speech must be judged by the purpose or the end for
which the speech is used.

What is the end of free speech? In the State it is the furtherance of the common good. This does not, in non-
Totalitarian States, mean a slavish adherence to the Party line; it means the right to rational dissent. I say rational dissent because speech being a rational power,
must be used rationally. Since then the common good is
promoted through justice, truth, and it is destroyed by
vice and injustice, it follows that freedom of speech is conditioned by the way it serves the ends for which governments are instituted. Freedom of speech is therefore not
an unlimited, unbounded absolute right to say anything
one pleases, any more than the right to the "pursuit of
happiness" mentioned in the Declaration of Independence
gives one the right of breaking in a department store to
sleep on one of its comfortable beds. Neither is freedom of
speech license of speech. Civil law, for that reason, does
not permit the circulation of immoral literature through
the mails, nor false statements injuring the character of
others, nor even misleading advertising. Postal laws and
local legislation of various kinds prove that the First
Amendment to the Federal Constitution and Free Speech
guaranteed in a State Constitution are not unlimited
when public decency is at stake, for the right to speech is
not the right to injure the just rights or claims of others.
Just let a believer in absolute freedom of speech mount a
soapbox and give a speech advocating the assassination of
the President of the United States, and he will find that
that right, like all rights, functions in society and to some
extent is subordinated to the common good of society.
There are too many in America today who believe that the
larynx is sacred, and that any attempt to throttle its vo-
calizations is an infringement on liberty. The larynx is no
more sacred than the hand, and like the hand does not
always do the right thing. The hand may not be used to
abuse another man's nose, so the larynx may not be used
to abuse another man's reputation, nor the general welfare of all men. As the Supreme Court of the United

States in the Gitlow case declared: every Constitutional right implies responsibility and if one is allowed freedom of speech, it is because he is responsible for his utterances, but at no time may he "abuse this freedom by utterances inimical to the public welfare, tending to corrupt public morals, incite to crime or disturb the public peace."

This decision of the Supreme Court is but an echo of the official teaching of the Church.

> Men have a right freely and prudently to propagate throughout the State what things soever are true and honorable, so that as many as possible may possess them; but lying opinions, than which no mental plague is greater, and vices which corrupt the heart and moral life, should be diligently repressed by public authority, lest they insidiously work the ruin of the State. The excess of an unbridled intellect, which unfailingly end in the oppression of the untutored multitude, are no less rightly controlled by the authority of the law than are the injuries inflicted by violence upon the weak. And this all the more surely, because by far the greater part of the community is either absolutely unable or able only with great difficulty, to escape from illusions and deceitful subtleties, especially such as flatter the passions. If unbridled license of speech and of writing be granted to all, nothing will remain sacred and inviolate; even the highest and truest mandates of nature, justly held to be the common and noblest heritage of the human race, will not be spared. Thus, truth being gradually obscure by darkness, pernicious and manifold error, as too often happens, will easily prevail. Thus, too, license will gain what liberty loses; for liberty will ever be more free and secure, in proportion as license is kept in fuller restraint.[10]

It is no escape to say that both truth and falsity should be allowed equal rights, because in the conflict truth will conquer in the end. The catch here is in the word *end*. How far off is the end? Is there not a danger that the truth will have an "end" before the end? Must we allow countless thousands to die of cancer and take no precaution to prevent it because health has always won in the end? Must human persons be sacrificed for a distant good which they cannot personally enjoy?

Furthermore, since the wicked more readily use unscrupulous methods there is more chance of their end being more quickly attained than the good ends of the good.
Such a theory of equality of right and wrong, truth and
error, we should not allow for health and disease, and certainly we should not allow it for the mind or soul. It is
ethically wrong because it excludes a solution of life's
tragic torments for the generations who offered themselves up as guinea pigs in the experimental period. It is
but little consolation for human beings, conscious of the
affinity of their minds for truth and their will for goodness, to know that long after they have gone down to their
graves, generations yet unborn will enjoy the fruits of
their unnecessary contradictions and trials. Such a theory
of freedom is but another phase of the modern tendency to
use persons as instruments and means instead of regarding them as sources of unitary value. No future state of
humanity on this earth can possibly expiate the suffering
of Peter and Paul on this earth, and to allow evil and disease to spread unchecked in the hope of a victory for truth
and health is to be without compassion for men. Furthermore, may not, during this period of trial, the apostles of
evil have more methods of propaganda at their disposal
than the apostles of truth? The modern press proves this
to be the case. By disregard for truth minds may become
so weakened that they are no longer impressed by what is
said, but by the emphasis with which a thing is said. Such
is largely the mentality of our day when truth equals rep-
etition; if a thing is repeated often enough modern minds
believe it must be true. Such is the psychology of both
propaganda and advertising. When then a state adopts a
policy of permitting socially injurious error, it neglects its
duties to the present generations and to generations yet
unborn who expect to reap something else than the harvest of our errors.

There is no such thing morally or legally as the unlimited right of free speech. Our civilization has so insisted
on the word *right,* that it has forgotten there is such a
thing as the word *duty* or *responsibility.* All rights imply
duties. I have no right without someone else having a cor-

responding duty. Right implies duty in another, either the duty of non-interfering or else the duty of helping. There is a way then of judging the morality of freedom of speech and that is by the way it serves the end of the State; namely, the furtherance of the social good and the temporal prosperity of its citizens. As men think only of their rights and nothing of their duties to the State, they will more and more regard any restriction of unlicensed speech as a violation of their "inalienable rights." It is indeed interesting that subversive orators who preach revolution against the government and who speak of that right as inalienable could never give a reason why it is inalienable. They seek to set up a regime where the State is supreme, but if the State is supreme and the source of all rights, then no right is inalienable.

This of course does not mean unlimited right to preach their revolutionary doctrines, for the Court continues: "These rights may be abused by using speech or press or assembly in order to incite to violence and crime." The point is that the rights of freedom or speech may not be curtailed, but only the abuses of that right. In the Gitlow case[11] the defendant was found responsible for a "manifesto" advocating the overthrow of government by violence. In the Whitney case[12] the defendant was found guilty of willfully and deliberately assisting in the forming of an organization for the purpose of carrying on revolutionary class struggle by criminal methods. The same ruling was handed down in the Burns case.[13]

Descending to the concrete; are the Communists and Nazis, from a political point of view and from the American point of view, to be denied the right of freedom of speech? This question is apropos because very few in America are today fooled particularly by the new tactics of Communism. Moscow ordered the Communist Party of the United States in 1935 to soft pedal its revolutionary talk without soft pedaling its revolutionary aims. As Manuilsky[14] told them: "tactics change, but the end, revolution, remains unchanged." The cooing of the Reds about democracy is just so much camouflage and Trojan horse tactics destined to fool the gullible. The question here at hand is not then the right of the Communists to talk "peace, democracy, jobs" and the jargon of the "front," but the right to use these tactics to gain the end of "the overthrow of the existing government" and to "purge the old dross of society" as their Official Program states, and to carry out their pledge made with clenched fists to "sovietize America" and make it one with the "fatherland of liberty," Russia. A democratic society, such as we call our own, must tolerate subversive orators as St. Peter Claver[15] tolerated fleas.

The Communists, as citizens, have a right to express ideas. They have the same right to freedom of speech as anyone, but they have no right to abuse it. It is not their expression but their permanence and diffusion and acceptance which endangers the common good. Until that final point is reached, not the force of the United States, but common sense will deal with them. Collegians during Prohibition loved to drink, not because they enjoyed drinking, but because they loved to flaunt convention. Revolutionary ideas of Communism affect collegians today like liquor during Prohibition — it gives them a sense of elated transcendence and condescending superiority to the masses. But there is no reason to be hysterical about it. There is never an army without some soldiers in the "jug"; nor a club without its unpaid members, nor a picnic without its ants, nor a bridge game without its kibitzer. So long as they are all in a minority a democracy must grant them the privilege of "letting off steam." Of course, if instead of ten ants on the picnic tablecloth, there were a thousand, then something would have to be done to preserve the picnic.

The United States Supreme Court in *De Jonge v. Oregon*[16] nullified the decision of Oregon courts. De Jonge was an admitted Communist who spoke to strikers at a Communist meeting but said nothing about the Communist revolution. The Supreme Court held unconstitutional and as repugnant to the Fourteenth Amendment Oregon's statute which made it a crime to advocate or teach orally or by writing crime, violence, sabotage, *etc.*, as the means of effecting an industrial or political change or revolution. Chief Justice Hughes said, in his decision: "While the States are entitled to protect themselves from the abuse of the privileges of our constitutions through an attempted substitution of force and violence in the place of peaceful political action in order to effect revolutionary changes in government, none of our decisions go to the length of sustaining such a curtailment of the right of free speech and assembly as the Oregon statue demands in its present application."

The attitude of America toward Communists politically must be very much like that of the man who allowed bees to swarm all over his head and shoulders and neck. They did not annoy him particularly, they just tickled him. But one day one of the bees stung him on the nose, and then rising in indignation he said: "Just for that, now you all get off." Immediately the Communists will retort through their Civil Liberties League that the government denied them the inalienable right of "freedom of speech." By that time, however, they will be too blind to see that they wanted the right of freedom of speech for themselves only to deny it to others. As Douglas Jerrold has put it "Of all arrogance and folly the most crass is that of those politicians who go on identifying freedom with their right to talk, even when the subject of their talk is the further restriction of the liberties of other people."[17]

It is not likely that the government of the United States will be called upon to restrict their freedom of speech, because the natural good sense of the American people will not accept a system which has so failed in Russia and there destroys freedom of speech altogether. Communists will probably continue for a time to be to the United States what flies are to a cake, but there is no need of burning down the house to kill the flies. From an American point of view their freedom to continue preaching subversive doctrine is proof of their own impotency.

But the evil should not be permitted to grow unduly, lest it be difficult to conquer, and also because Communism generally begets Fascism. Historically Fascism has arisen as a reaction against Communism. A wise government will dispense itself from the necessity of either.

For to nourish hate in the name of love, to use violence in behalf of freedom, to talk beneath an American flag as a protection for supplanting it by the red flag; to sing the *Star Spangled Banner* as a snare for forcing the singing of the *Internationale*[18]; to use freedom to destroy it — is a proof of madness, the earmark of a traitor, and the cancer on the body politic.

Walter Lippmann[19] has stated the position well from an American point of view:

> No man may invoke a right in order to destroy it. The right of free speech belongs to those who are willing to preserve it. The right to elect belongs to those who mean to transmit that right to their successors. The rule of the majority is morally justified only if another majority is free to reverse that rule. To hold any other view is to believe that democracy alone, of all forms of government, is prohibited by its own principles from insuring its own preservation. There is nothing in the principles of democracy that requires a people to surrender democracy or relieves them of the obligation to defend it. In many countries of the world today there are armed bands of men, using the democratic liberties of free assemblage and of free speech for the overthrow of democratic liberties. Is there any doubt that democratic governments have the right to suppress them? That there is no democratic right to destroy democracy and that revolutionists against democracy may be tolerated only if they are so weak as to be negligible? A free nation can tolerate much and ordinarily its toleration is its best defense. It can tolerate feeble Communist parties and feeble Fascist parties as long as it is certain they have no hope of success. But once they cease to be debating societies and become formidable organizations for action, they present a challenge which is suicidal to ignore. They use liberty to assemble force to destroy liberty. When that challenge is actually offered, when it really exists in the judgment of the sober and the well informed, it is betrayal of liberty not to defend it with all the power that free men possess.[20]

The argument that the Communist party is only a political party in the United States is to betray a colossal ignorance of facts. One needs to be familiar with their literature to know that the Communist party of the United

States is a section of the Communist International of Moscow.

1. Earl Browder[21] who is the "front" man of the Communist Party in the United States (the real heads of the Communist Party in the United States as far as ruling spirits are concerned are Jack Stachel and Alex Bittleman and the Moscow representative of the Communist International who in the May Congress of 1938 was introduced as Comrade Brown) testifies before the McNaboe Investigation Committee of New York in 1938 that the Communist Party of the United States was affiliated to Moscow and that the Communist Party of the United States had "never" refused to accept the orders from Moscow.

2. The Official Program of Communism to which the Communist Party of the United States subscribes states: "The conquest of power by the proletariat does not mean peacefully capturing the ready-made bourgeois machinery by means of a parliamentary majority. . . . The conquest of power by the proletariat is the violent overthrow of the bourgeois power and the destruction of capitalist state apparatus, bourgeois, armies, police, bureaucratic hierarchy, the judiciary, parliaments."[22]

3. The American expression of this revolutionary doctrine is to be found in *Ultimate Aim*, published by the International Publishers of New York, 1935. "The replacement of one social system by another, *i.e.,* the replacement of the rule of one class by the rule of another, is only achieved by means of the *violent overthrow* of the ruling class, by means of *revolution*. It is impossible for the working class to come to power in any other way than by the method of revolutionary overthrow of the rule of the bourgeois, by the method of *proletariat revolution*."[23]

4. Immediately after the conclusion of the Tenth Convention of the Communist Party in New York, May 31, 1938, the Communist Party of the United States sent a telegram of greetings and pledges to Stalin as head of the Communist International of Moscow.

5. Communists in their pledge to the Communist Party of the United States do not say they will defend the

"American Republic" but "international democracy." In the same breath they declare Russia is the "only real democracy."

6. The New Constitution of the Communist Party of the United States provides that its emblem shall be "the hammer and the sickle" which is the same as the hemophilic government of Moscow.

7. The recruits under the Constitution of the Communist Party do not say: "I do solemnly swear that I will support the Constitution of the United States . . . " but "I pledge firm loyalty . . . and full devotion . . . to the true principles of the Communist Party . . . and for the establishment of socialism."

8. No truly American party is interested in a revolution against the United States government which would be made through alienating the loyalties of the sailors and soldiers from their country. But Earl Browder in his book *What Is Communism* tells us that the "Communist Party acts as the organizer and guide of the workers." "The Revolution does not simply *happen;* it must be *made. . . .* But soldiers and sailors come from the ranks of the workers. They can be and must be won for the revolution. *All revolutions have been made with weapons which the overthrown rulers had relied on for their protection.*"[24]

9. An American party is interested in the preservation of American democracy and yet the *Official Program* of Communism circulated and sold by the American Communist party speaks of the "violent overthrow" of the government and "The conquest of power by the proletariat is the violent overthrow of bourgeois power, the destruction of the Capitalist state apparatus, bourgeois armies, police, bureaucratic hierarchy, the judiciary, parliaments, *etc.*"[25]

Cognizant of these facts the *New York Herald Tribune* wrote soundly in an editorial:

> It is entirely right that a democracy should err on the side of tolerance. Its survival as a democracy depends on its jealous defense of the principle that all citizens should be free to hold and express their opinions, however unorthodox, and to organize, if they please, for the advancement of

their views. This principle is embedded in the Constitution of the United States. On the other hand, its recognition has always been subject, in law and popular custom, to the rule of reason: Libel and obscenity are ruled out and there are other necessary curbs, notably against disturbance of the peace or incitement to violent revolution. The government of a democracy has not only the right but the duty of self-preservation.[26]

With this preamble we would approach the puzzling problem of dealing with Communists. In Russia, Communists have shown themselves opposed to every tenet of democracy traditionally associated with the word, including freedom of speech, of assembly and even of conscience. American Communists are avowedly bent on altering the American system to conform with their ideology, and they have been allowed to organize in a formal political party and, like any other such party, to appeal to the electorate upon the assumption that their appeal was to the ballot, not to force. They have their press, their meetings, their candidates for office. In this particular jurisdiction, at least, the only lines drawn in their case are those which limit agitation of whatever sort. Subject to police discretion, they may not indulge in parades and meetings calculated to disturb the peace and they may not openly advocate the overthrow of the government by force or conspire secretly toward that end.

This treatment is on all fours with American ideals and we are glad to applaud it. The law is clear and the principles are sound. But the application is beset with difficulties. There is excellent ground for believing that these American principles have been very badly abused by many Communist leaders as well as by a certain portion of the rank and file. And the very practical question arises, Where should the line be drawn?

So far as the leadership goes, the Communist party in this country is by no means a purely American institution. It is an offshoot of the Comintern,[27] dominated by Russians; includes in its membership a large fraction of foreigners, and the evidence that its leaders take their orders from Moscow is strong enough to put upon them the burden of proof. In other words, the question is to what extent, under the shelter of our fundamental principles, we have been nursing an organization whose object is not only to induce revolution (and by no means peacefully, if its activities in the labor field are any criterion) but to induce it in the interest if an alien power.

The tests are clear. The difficulty is, as we say, in applying them. In so far as Communism fails to meet these tests it is not entitled to the protection of our institutions and it should be suppressed. The need is, first of all, for the facts. The sooner our authorities establish the truth and act accordingly, the better.

The strategy of these twin phenomena is the same. The aims of both movements are best realized in democratic countries, not by the organization of powerful and open political parties — such parties would not have a chance on earth in any country with a tradition of freedom — but by having their adherents in every party, and by "boring from within" every kind of social organization.

The enrolled membership of the Communist Party gives no inkling of its real size or the amount of influence that it wields, in the trades unions, for instance, and over the Government in Washington, particularly over certain independent agencies of that Government.

Strict followers of the Moscow party line may call themselves "Liberals," or "Progressives," or "Democrats," or "New Dealers," or even "Republicans."

The form of organization with which they work is the "cell" or the "fraction."

It is a tiny, secret and closely knit unit inside a trades union, or a Government agency, or a WPA[28] project, or a newspaper, or an editorial office, or any other instrument that affects social organization or instruments of opinion.

This fraction takes orders, according to the party line, and *by policy* never reveals itself for what it is.

Secrecy is essential to it. If the members of a trade union, for instance, should know that John Smith, who is advocating this or that course of action, is merely acting as an instrument of the Communist Party line, and that the busy little groups who are advocating his ideas are a "fraction," then the workers would revolt, for the American worker is a very independent soul. But he often does not know it, and it is Communist tactic to see that he does not know it.

THE BRAKE which the Communists exercise over liberals who know what is going on is the fear that exposure will give aid and comfort to the Fascists.

This is also a Communist tactic. The Communist Party is the greatest aid to Fascism in the world today.

It inspired Fascism and Nazism in the first place, as in the course of time, I shall try to show. It gave to both, but particularly to Nazism, its entire technique of organization. It has on numerous occasions made a direct alliance with Nazism.

The Nazi church has canonized two saints — Horst Wessel[29] and Shlageter,[30] and the latter was first canonized by the Communists.

INSIDE GERMANY, the first advocate of "national bolshevism" was the Communist Party, under instructions dictated from Moscow. And when Nazism triumphed in Germany, because it is a far more efficient revolutionary program and, for the masses, particularly the unemployed and the small impoverished white collar class, a far more attractive creed, the Communists went over to it, almost in a body.

In fact, it may develop that Nazism and Communism, instead of being two churches, really represent a schism in the same church, and a schism that may yet be healed.

If it is healed, they will fight side by side against democracy. In the present situation, they are fighting from both sides, from the "left" and from the "right" against democracy, and outside and openly, but inside, and secretly, and both of them as the friends of democracy.

IT IS TIME that democracy took the offensive. That involves primarily a more vigorous intellectual and spiritual conception of what democracy is and is not.

And the offensive demands exposure. The American people have one inalienable right, as free men. That is the right to know what is going on.

Endnotes

[1] *Libertas Praestantissimum*, § 7.

[2] *Ibid.*, § 21,

[3] What Sheen describes is a limitation on the exercise of property, not on the right to be an owner. When a State commandeers things for war or exercises eminent domain, the owner must be offered just compensation. [Ed.]

[4] This statement and the discussion that follows make it clear Sheen refers to the exercise of rights, not an abrogation of the naturals rights of life, liberty, and property. These and other rights remain inherent — inalienable — in every human being, but no right, regardless how absolutely held, may be exercised in any way that harms the right holder, other people, groups, or the common good as a whole, or in any way that prevents others from exercising their rights. [Ed.]

[5] *Quadragesimo Anno*, § 87. [Ed.]

[6] *Ibid.*, §§ 105-106.

[7] *Libertas Praestantissimum*, § 23.

[8] *U.S. v. Crickshank*, 92 U.S. 542, 552.

[9] See the Foreword, viii-ix.

[10] *Libertas Praestantissimum*, § 23.

[11] *Gitlow v. New York*, 268 U.S. 652.

[12] *Whitney v. California*, 274 U.S. 357.

[13] *Burns v. U.S.*, 274 U.S. 328.

[14] Dmitry Manuilsky (1883-1959), noted Bolshevik and supporter of Lenin. [Ed.]

[15] St. Peter Claver, S.J. (1581-1654), Catholic missionary noted for his work with African slaves in the New World. [Ed.]

[16] *De Jonge v. Oregon*, 299 U.S. 353.

[17] Jerrold, *The Future of Freedom*, op. cit., 121.

[18] The Communist Anthem. [Ed.]

[19] Walter Lippmann (1889-1974), American writer, journalist, political commentator, and founding editor of *New Republic* magazine. He is noted for introducing the concept of "Cold War" and for the neologism "stereotype." [Ed.]

[20] Walter Lippmann in *New York Herald Tribune*, February 5, 1935.

[21] Earl Russell Browder (1891-1973), American labor leader and politician, noted as General Secretary of the U.S. Communist Party during the 1930s and 1940s. [Ed.]

[22] See pp. 36, 37, Program of the Communist International, 1936 edition.

[23] *Ibid.*, 8.

[24] *Op. cit.,* pp. 163, 165. Italics his.

[25] *Ibid.*, 36.

[26] *New York Herald Tribune.*

[27] The "Communist International," also known as the Third International (1919–1943). An international communist organization founded in Moscow. The goal of the Comintern was to work "by all available means, including armed force, for the overthrow of the international bourgeoisie and for the creation of an international Soviet republic as a transition stage to the complete abolition of the State."

[28] Works Progress Administration (1935-1938), renamed the Works Projects Administration (1938-1943), a government-funded New Deal program to create jobs for unskilled labor on public works projects. [Ed.]

[29] Horst Ludwig Wessel (1907-1930), Nazi Party activist and SA-Sturmführer murdered in 1930. Reasons for the murder are vague, ranging from allegations of non-payment of rent to revenge for Wessel's presumed involvement in the death of a Communist Party youth. Wessel was the composer of *Die Fahne Hoch* ("The Flag on High"), more commonly known as [*Das*] *Horst-Wessel-Lied*, which became the official anthem of the Nazi Party, and the unofficial anthem of Germany. He was adopted as "patron saint" by the 26th Destroyer Wing of the Luftwaffe, and the 18th SS Volunteer Panzergrenadier Division. [Ed.]

[30] Albert Leo Schlageter (1894-1923), member of the German Freikorps, executed for acts of sabotage against the French occupation following the First World War. He was regarded by many as a martyr for German nationalism, especially by the Nazis after they rose to power. [Ed.]

11. Liberty and Equality

IT USED TO BE THE FASHION to praise the rich; now it is the fashion to curse them. Formerly the rich were identified with prosperity; now they are identified with exploitation. The mood has changed; the fashion has gone into reverse; the wealthy are now on the defensive and the forgotten man is exalted. The "have's" have been unseated and the "have-nots" are in the saddle.

It is very easy to believe that the former view is right and the present one wrong, or *vice versa*. The truth is both are wrong. A civilization is on the down grade when it measures itself by the number of its millionaires; and decay has already set in when the have-nots do not wish to become rich like the millionaire, but merely wish to have what he has, regardless of how they get it. From an extreme wherein there were great and even unjustified inequalities, the world has suddenly reacted to an extreme of equality which abolishes all classes and reduces citizens to the monotony of "workers" or "race." Such is the solution of Soviet Fascism or Communism, Nazism, and Fascism.

A correct understanding of equality requires a knowledge of its history, and its various interpretations. There are three possible views concerning equality:

1. Equality understood in the political sense.
2. Equality understood in the economic sense.
3. Equality understood in the spiritual sense.

1. Political Equality

As with liberty, equality was conceived by political philosophers of the eighteenth century as a reaction or a protest against *unjustified privileges*. Just as liberty was falsely defined as the absence of constraint, so equality was erroneously defined as the absence of privilege. The

185

French Revolution definitely marks the inauguration of this kind of equality, for it broke down and destroyed all the ranks, hierarchies, and aristocracies then existing. It happened that the inequalities existing at that time were not so much economic as political. Society at that time was not divided as ours on the basis of income or wealth, but on the basis of privilege. The aristocracy controlled legislation, wealth, education, government, and profession. The masses or the common people could not rise, because their social position was rigidly fixed; certain professions were not opened to them; the peasant for example, could not ordinarily become a lawyer. Even the control of education was denied the common people on the ground that if they had it, they would be insolent to their superiors.

It was only natural for an attack to be made against this snobbery; it was also and even more natural for the attack to be dictated by the nature of inequalities then existing. But since the inequalities were of a political character, the revolution took on a political character which sought to destroy all privileges standing in the way of equality.

The victory was won; the aristocracy was abolished; hierarchies wiped out, and political impediments against the common people abrogated, as there rang through the French and American constitutions the stirring message: "All men are created equal." From now on, everyone would have the privilege of paying taxes, since the government is the government of all; education became generalized as the son of a peasant sat next to the son of a prince; professions, legal, medical, and military, were opened to all; arbitrary inequalities based on rank and privilege were eliminated while competition and worth, not birth nor blood nor title, decided who would be on top.

Because the world of those days understood equality only in the political sense, as freedom from legal restrictions, it did not foresee its possible effects. It was falsely assumed that once everyone was made equal before the law and given the right to vote, that economic inequalities would soon disappear. The masses revolted against the aristocracy not because the aristocracy had more wealth, but because they had more privileges. The masses reasoned that if they could have the same political rights and privileges as the lords, they would soon have as much money. Since all the existing inequalities were attributed to favoritism, it seemed to them logical to conclude, that once favoritism was broken down everyone would soon be rich. Such an argument falsely assumed that a man was a millionaire only because he had a "pull," hence if everyone had a "pull" everyone would be a millionaire.

Such was not the case. The "push" is as important as the "pull." Furthermore, no one seemed to have vision enough to foresee that the inequalities of the lord and the peasant would one day become the inequalities of capital and labor. It was wrong to confuse opportunity with equality. Political equality of all men before the law is no guarantee of economic equality; in practice it may unfortunately mean the opportunity of becoming economically unequal. Tawney[1] who describes this situation better than anyone else, sums up the above in these words: "Thus it was that by condemning the inequalities of a monarchial past, the revolution blessed the inequalities of the industrial future."[2] A new aristocracy arose, this time not of blood but of money. With the invention of machinery the peasants were replaced by the proletarians. A few of the lowly did succeed in rising to the positions of preeminence and wealth, but they were but a poor compensation for the millions who did not so rise.

The legally privileged and the legally underprivileged gave way to two new economic classes: the few controlling wealth on the one hand, and the masses working for wages on the other. Political equality of all men before the law was attained, but economic inequality took its place. The new millionaires took the places of the lords, and the under-privileged of the aristocracy became the wage earners of capitalism. Wealth crept into the hands of the few as privileges had done in the generation before, while impoverishment and dependence became the usual lot of the masses.

Here was a new situation which had to be remedied. How handle the new inequality of wealth? How establish economic equality? Communism gave this answer: all economic inequalities are due to the ownership of productive property which makes it possible for the man who owns to exploit the man who does not own. If then by a revolution which "purges the old dross of society" (Official Program of the Communist International) one does away with private ownership of productive property, one also does away with inequalities. Fascism and Nazism do not go so far, though they both control economic processes to a great extent. Since Communism pushes the Fascist solution to the extreme we shall here be concerned with it as Soviet Fascism. As the French Revolution stressed political equality, Soviet Fascism stresses economic equality.

2. Economic Equality

From protest against *unjustified privileges* which characterized the French Revolution, Communism goes to the extreme of suppressing even *justified privileges*. Communism interprets equality not politically, but economically. Men are presumed to be equal, if they share the same things, *e.g.*, all eat apples grown by the State tree. This places equality not in man, but *outside* of him; not in what he is, but in what he has; not in his dignity, but in his possession. In order to secure economic equality, Communism puts all productive property into the hands of the State. There are to be no classes, for there is no property with which to make classes; there are to be no differences of parties, for the State allows only one Party — the Communist. This is equally true of Fascism and Nazism. In other words, a leveling process sets in by which everyone is beaten and hammered on the dictator's anvil until all look alike, think alike, live alike, and will alike. Men become as interchangeable units like spare parts of an automobile, it being presumed that any individual can fulfill any function because all are "workers."

There are two defects in Communistic leveling and standardization: Firstly, Communism purchases equality by the suppression of freedom, for it refuses to admit that man has any other rights except those given to him by the

State.[3] Freedom thus becomes identical with obedience to the will of the dictator. Secondly, Communism does not restore equality.

Property, as we have seen, is the economic guarantee of human liberty, the external manifestation of inner responsibility. Deprive man of the right to fashion things according to his own will, and you deprive him, at one stroke, of the social basis of his freedom. By suppressing personal ownership of productive property the equality of Soviet Fascism becomes equality of dependence on the State, and dependence is the death of liberty. The French Revolution made all men equal before the law; the Communist revolution makes all equal before the dictator. But equality is not freedom.

The second defect of Communistic equality is that it does not secure the equality of which it boasts. It does away, of course, with big bankers, but in their place it gives Red Commissars; it eliminates the classes based on wealth, but creates new classes based on privilege. This is bound to be in any order where administration is distinct from *ownership*. Robbers share a loot in common, but the quarrels begin when it must be decided who will divide the spoils. And if a regime begins by injustice, the workers must not expect, if they have any brains at all, that it will not end in injustice. Thus it is that from a Capitalist evil by which wealth creates privilege, Communism goes to the opposite evil where privilege creates wealth.

Neither the French Revolution nor the Communistic Revolution gave the equality they promised; the French did not, because it defined equality in terms of *politics*; the Communistic did not for it defined equality in terms of *economics*.

3. Spiritual Equality

The Catholic view of equality considers it not politically, not economically, but spiritually. Equality has its roots neither in law, nor in things, but in man. It may be summed up in the form of two propositions: (1) All men are equal; (2) all men are unequal.

Naturally, these two statements refer to different things, and so they do; the first refers to the *essence* of human nature; the second to its accidents.

I. All men are equal *substantially* in the sense that all men (*a*) have the same nature, *i.e.*, are composed of body and soul; (*b*) have the same end which is union with perfect Life, Truth, and Love which is God; and (*c*) have all been redeemed by our Divine Savior Jesus Christ. As Leo XIII puts it:

> If we consider that all men are of the same human race and of the same nature and that they are all destined for the same ultimate end, and that they have all been redeemed by Jesus Christ — and if one considers the duties and rights which flow from this oneness of origin and destiny — then all men are equal.[4]

II. But as regards the accidents of human nature, not all men are equal; for example, they differ in intelligence, industry, talent, health, race, taste, character, virtue, physical energy, and the like. This distinction between the substantial equality of men and their accidental inequality is derived not only from right reason but is also sanctioned by the teaching of our Lord Himself.

1. All men are equal because they all possess a soul made to the image and likeness of God. All have the same fundamental rights and duties, hence He recommended: "Do unto others as you would have them do unto you."[5] The Gospel belongs to no one class but to mankind for "even the poor have the Gospel preached to them."[6] The race or class means nothing, for, if He willed it, He could raise up "children of Abraham from the very stones."[7] The externals do not matter for God is no respecter of persons.[8] Under the surface all men are the same, hence the command "Preach the Gospel to every creature."[9]

Not only have they the same nature, but they have the same end — an eternal life conditioned by the novitiate of this life. Each soul must appear before God at judgment and before Him all are equal, for each "will be judged according to his works."[10] The wealth of a Dives will not influence the scales of justice in his favor, for the beggar Lazarus will have a higher place. "Even the harlots and the publicans will enter the Kingdom of Heaven before the Scribes and Pharisees."[11] Different talents may be given to different men, but they will all be judged equally not by *what* they received, but by how well they used it; for each one will appear as he *is;* not as he seems to be. This is the essence of equality.

2. But though men are equal because they have the same nature and because they have the same end, it does not follow that there are no accidental differences between them. Our Lord often speaks of the different talents given to different men. Some receive ten, others five, and others one talent. "He who received much, of him much will be expected."[12] In forming His Kingdom, our Lord chose 72 disciples; out of them 12 Apostles[13]; out of them 3 favorites, and out of them all His visible representative on earth and the head of His Church — Peter. But at the same time that our Lord acknowledged inequalities He reminded them all they were gifts of God, and He corrected undue estimation of gifts by humility. The left hand was not to know what the right hand did, for "he that exalteth himself shall be humbled, and he that humbleth himself shall be exalted. He who was Master of all was to be the servant of all"[14] for by this would men know His disciples — that they loved one another.

Three practical applications follow from the Catholic doctrine that equality is not in law, nor in wealth, but in man.

a) Since all men are equal by nature and by destiny, and since men are unequal by their talents, gifts, characters, and dispositions it follows that the society in which men live must not be a dead level in which all are "workers" or "Aryans," but rather a society which recognizes both equalities and inequalities; namely, a hierarchical society. Society has been called a *body politic* and this designation is correct in the sense that society is like an organism. Just as the human body is made up of many members unequal in function, so too is society made up of different levels and classes. Society is not formed of a classless class of "workers"; it is made up of different groups forming a hierarchy. It is built not like a plane but like a pyramid. Inequality is as essential to society as the difference between the heart and the lung is essential to a human body. There is no energy without difference of level; electrical power cannot be generated when water is at a level; rivers cannot be harnessed unless there is a falls. Suppress differences of level and the hierarchy of powers and you deprive man of his mill, his dynamo, his steam engine.

> Differences of level in society are of no less importance. A society lives, thanks to the play of tensions formed within it, precisely by the differences of level which it contains. Without inequality therefore, collective life would lose all its value as a field of experience. The web of life is made up of these differences. Culture, art, love, history, would be poorer without the inequalities of life, and the effort upwards, which is one of the most deeply rooted instincts in social man, would disappear in a society leveled to an average which would have to be perforce very modest.[15]

In this hierarchy of society, there are equalities and inequalities. There are equalities as regards the nature of man; there are inequalities as regards his function. All men are equal in *value*, *i.e.*, as human beings endowed with immortal souls and possessing rights and privileges independent of any State, for the State exists only to preserve and protect these values. But as regards their *function*, men are unequal. They are unequal because their accidental differences fit them better for one role or vocation in society than another. Men and groups differ because of their function in society, just as the heart differs from the lung in the human body. But though the organs differ one from another, they must function not for their own selfish interest, but for the good of the whole body. In like manner, as regards functions man and his groups are not transcendent to the State, but subject to it so that the common good of all will result.

A hierarchical society avoids the extreme of Liberalism which recognizes political equalities but which does little to remedy economic inequalities, and the extreme of Fascist states, whether Italian, German, or Soviet wherein economic or racial equality swallows up natural inequalities and liberty.

For the past century or more, society has been organized on a contractual basis.[16] The bond between men was a contract. Rights were contract rights; duties were contract duties — not human rights and duties. In a contractual society men say "You do this for me, and I will do that for you." For example, in the *economic* field: the justice of a wage was not determined by human dignity, but by the contract into which a laborer entered. For a capitalist the wage was just if the laborer accepted it; for the laborer the wage was just if the capitalist accepted the union demands. Labor under such an arrangement is a mere chattel. In the consumer's field articles were sold not at a just price, but at a contract price, *viz.*, the highest price the consumer could and would pay after an artificial demand had been created by advertising.[17] In the field of property, the sole right to ownership was contract. The owner assumed he could use his property any way he pleased, even for his own selfish ends, if he had a deed or contract to it.[18] In the field of religion, the attack upon the Church became contractual: "What has the Church ever done for me?" Those who asked this question were invariably the ones who would have been tremendously embarrassed by the question: "What have you ever done for the Church?" The prevalence of divorce, the breakdown of family life and so many other symptoms of a society which ignored the *function* of a husband and wife, and thought only of relationships as contractual and breakable at will.

The growth of violence is another consequence of a contractual society, in the sense that violence is an attempt to make amends and reparation for inequalities in contract. Labor "takes it out" on Capitalism; and Capital "takes it out" on labor. Everyone has to pay for his wealth. In the international field, peace is sought not on the basis of justice and order, but on the contractual basis of "balance of power." "You fight with me and I will fight with you." Peace thus becomes anonymous and nations who shout it the loudest are always those who are most prepared for war. The spectacle of Soviet Ambassadors running about the world with doves of peace on their shoulders and possibly the greatest war machines of the earth behind their backs, proves that peace for them means a breathing spell until they are strong enough for war.

b) This brings us to the Christian solution, which, starting with justified equalities and justified inequalities, arrived at a hierarchical society in which there is status or function. Status means "standing" and implies that the bond between men is not *contract* but *function;* not a *bargain* but a *service*; not rights alone, but rights inseparable from correlative duties. Status depends on function and implies that society is not made up of isolated entities who enter into a bargain with one another, but living organisms which live a common life and serve a common purpose. The basis of the social relation then is not the fact that one man has a contract with another man, but because all are organic to the same body politic. As the heart has a function in the body, and the ear another function, and the eye another, so likewise have the legal group, the automobile group, the medical group, *etc.*, different functions; and yet they cannot function apart from one another for their own selfish interests any more than the eye can live apart from the ear. The basis of division of society under such an arrangement is not privilege which comes from blood, nor power which comes from wealth; nor is it an elimination of all groupings by the denial of human rights and the reduction of all "workers for the State," but rather a differentiation based on service to the common good.[19]

Inequalities are born of liberty. Because men are free to determine their own role in society, *vocationally* as the Encyclical puts it, a pyramid of classes results.[20] Even in nature, indeterminism is the law of inequalities, *e.g.*, papers in a windstorm. They take different positions because they lost the paperweight which determined them to one position. Man, being rational, is free to determine his own proximate goal, profession, or rank. To the extent you suppress freedom you suppress justified equalities.

Suppress the freedom to disagree politically and you establish the forced equality of an electorate voting 100 percent behind a dictator; suppress the freedom to live in a city of a million, or a city of a quarter of a million as the passports of the Soviet citizens do, and determine where they shall live, and you get the forced equality of habitation. Suppress freedom of conscience and you get forced equality of State worship. It is indeed an interesting confirmation of the thesis that Germany and Russia who have most suppressed the natural right of freedom have the greatest unjustified equality — either the equality of race or the equality of class. In proportion as the world moves in the direction of dictated equality, it by that fact moves away from liberty.

c) This brings us to the third and final point — not all inequalities are wrong. There are justifiable equalities; namely, all men are equal in basic human rights. There are also justifiable inequalities; namely, those based on different talents, temperaments, and functions. Soviet Fascism never makes a distinction and hence never sees that inequalities are not necessarily wrong. It assumes that because some are rich and others are poor, therefore there is an injustice. This does not necessarily follow. The foot is not equal to the brain in the hierarchy of the body, for one can live without a foot, but not without brains. But because they are of unequal importance in the organism it does not follow that I do my foot an injustice by always walking on it instead of walking on my head.[21]

The inequalities which Communism condemns are not based on their love of justice — for there can be no justice without God: rather they condemn inequalities on account of envy. Communism hates the man who has more, whether he earned it lawfully or not, because he wants to have his wealth, even unlawfully. Communism believes that inequality come from economic structure instead of from human nature. It falsely assumes that just as soon as society stops paying incomes to the bankers, industrialists, and landlords, shareholders, and all the owners of productive capital, class warfare will cease and everyone will be equal because the State owns all. They put the finger on the wrong cause: the mere transfer of title from private individuals to the State will not cure inequalities, because what makes inequalities is not property, but *who* owns the property, and *who* divides the property. Inequalities will result under common ownership, as long as there are dishonest men and so long as administration is distinct from ownership. "One kind of privilege in particular would, therefore, be ineradicable in a socialist state. That is the privilege of ruling it. In a planned economy some must make the plan and administer it, the rest obey and be administered to. It is impossible to imagine how from the exercise of such vast power there could be eliminated all the familiar characteristics of supreme privilege. Perhaps it might be done by stipulating that those who are to exercise this power shall be eunuchs chosen by lot, imprisoned like the queen bee, and then, when they have served a fixed term, put to death with Aztec ceremonial, and buried with honors! Some such arrangement might discourage the struggle for place and power. But if communist rulers are to be less drastically dealt with, if they are to be trained for their special tasks and provided with the conveniences, the freedom, and the authority which the exercise of responsibility requires, they will live better and be more important than other men."[22]

The fact is that evil which produces wrong inequalities, is not in things, but in men; and the good which produces healthy inequalities is not in property but in persons. It was on the division of the spoils of violence, that Stalin, Kamenev, and Zinoviev quarreled, and it is at that point Red leaders will always quarrel. Communism or Soviet Fascism forgets that envy applies not only to property but also to privilege. A classless class can no more purge men of acquisitiveness or aggression than it can purge noses out of human faces. Acquisitiveness is in the heart not in titles of property.

It is not inequalities as such that men hate; it is the unjust inequalities which repose upon no spiritual superiority that they hate. The wrong inequalities are therefore those which deny to all the right to enjoy the common heritages of civilization, according to their state of life and their role in the hierarchy of society. Soldiers do not envy their fellow soldier whose heroism saved his regiment, for which heroism he is promoted to a captaincy. But the poor do justly[23] hate the son of a wealthy father who never earned a cent in his life and divides his time between yachts, divorces, and drink. There is the basic reason for the growing hatred of rich — some of them have not justified their wealth. Wealth is a responsibility, and if he who owns it is irresponsible in his stewardship, he must submit to public disapproval. But to say that because some rich men are irresponsible, therefore rich men must be purged is to miss the point. The rich man who justifies his wealth by magnanimity, public service, and charity proves his right to wealth.[24]

The modern talk about equality and the classless class is born of our loss of heroes. We have lost the justifiable envy[25] of the *righteous* and we have left only the *selfish envy* of wealth. We look up to things instead of to persons. The restoration of society will come only through an elite, not of blood nor dollars nor party loyalty, but an elite to whom the rest of society can look for its inspiration. The ancient Greeks looked up to the heroes of Homer; Catholicism looks up to its saints; boys look up to the athletes, and in each instance they recognize a power which they have not, but which they wish to have. So too society needs an aristocracy which will be as independent of a bank account as was St. Francis of Assisi; which will be as detached from snobbery, as a King St. Louis IX; and which will be as full of faith in God, as the eleven thousand religious who were killed in Spain,[26] for no other crime than because they loved Christ. The revolution of the future will be spiritual. The masses cannot save themselves alone, for they need a leaven to lift them up. Unless this leaven come from the spiritual aristocrats who make the necessary rupture with selfishness, there will be only chaos.

A social order cannot be reconstructed by starting with equality, for inequality is necessary to society. But it can be reconstructed on the basis of a hierarchy in which the unequals, both politically and economically, are equalized by having that which is necessary for their function. But this hierarchy cannot be organized without religion which puts a premium on justice, honesty, and self-sacrifice. This is not easy to achieve. It is false to think that we can save society by assaulting either the Kremlins of Fascism or Communism. These are easy enough to overcome; their ramparts easy to take; their walls are easy to scale; their soldiers are easy to scatter. What is hard is to conquer our own duplicity, our sin, and our selfishness.

Endnotes

[1] Richard Henry Tawney (1880-1962), influential English economic historian, Christian socialist (Anglican). His best known work is *Religion and the Rise of Capitalism* (1926). [Ed.]

[2] Sheen misquoted. It should read, "The movement which equalized legal rights condemned the inequalities of the feudal past; it blessed the inequalities of the industrial future." R. H. Tawney, *Equality* (1929). New York: Rowman and Littlefield, 1964, 101-102. [Ed.]

[3] Communism has "led to the disregard of the most obvious differences between human beings, even those which Nature has rooted in the deepest recesses of life, that, for instance between man and woman, a natural distinction which, with the most persevering foolishness, the nineteenth and twentieth centuries have sought to obliterate with an equalitarian prejudice which has deprived the feminist movement of much of its beneficent effect on the legal and social emancipation of woman." A worse form "consists in denying, or ignoring, the irrational elements in collective life, all the imponderabilia the delicate shades of character, the differences which constitute the salt of society. The graces, the arts, the value of fruitful leisure, the creative power of the unexpected, the virtues of luck — all that which cannot be reduced to figures, to rule or to general laws — is neglected or forgotten by the politically minded liberal democratic masses. Yet these elements of inequality remain in collective life as strong as ever, and the average human being, unspoilt by politics, holds them instinctively, even at times against the grain of his conscious opinions, because they belong to deeper levels of life than the merely political." —Madariaga, *Anarchy or Hierarchy, op. cit.*, 35, 36.

[4] Leo XIII, *Humanum Genus* ("On Freemasonry"), 1884, § 26.

[5] Matt. 5:1-5.

[6] Matt. 11:5.

7 Matt. 3:9.

8 Matt. 22:16.

9 Mark 16:15.

10 Rom. 2:6.

11 Matt. 21:31.

12 Luke 13:48.

13 Luke 10:1-24.

14 Matt. 20:25-28.

15 Madariaga, *Anarchy or Hierarchy, op. cit.,* 101.

16 The problem Sheen focuses on here is not the problem with contract *per se.* Contract based on natural rights is the basis of civil society. Contract, however, assumes equality of status between the parties to the agreement, and this is clearly not the case in modern society. Where the parties to a contract are of different status yet treated as if they were equals, injustice results. Modern society assumes that humanity's equality of nature before God automatically gives equality of status before man, which Sheen points out is clearly not the case; human dignity is thereby offended by forcing non-equals to behave as equals. [Ed.]

17 Again, what Sheen rightly criticizes here is the insistence that people who are not equal in status being treated as if they were, in fact, equal in status when that is clearly not the case. The workers and consumers are obviously not equal in bargaining power to the capitalist, and are forced into a disadvantageous position by that lack of power. Had workers an alternative to wages for income, and consumers an alternative to production than what the capitalist offered, such as capital ownership offers, they would be equal in status to the capitalist, and the agreed-upon wage or price would be just. [Ed.]

18 Sheen notes here the distortion of the rights to and of property that necessarily accompanies reliance on past savings to finance new capital. The natural right to be an owner is eroded in capitalism, and abolished in socialism, while the socially limited and defined rights of property — the use or exercise — become construed as absolute in both systems, exercised by a private elite in the former, and a bureaucratic elite in the latter. [Ed.]

19 Put another way, no contract or law can force an equality of status that does not exist. Only widespread and direct ownership of capital can vest people with the equality of status essential to participating in civil life based on contract. Agreements (contracts) must otherwise take into account any differences of status, *e.g.,* contracts between adults and minors may be voidable at the will of the minor, while wage contracts between em-

ployers who own capital and workers who do not own capital should have certain protections built in for the workers. [Ed.]
[20] This appears to be a reference to *Quadragesimo Anno*, §§ 77-87, which describes the principle of subsidiarity. [Ed.]
[21] "The fact that classes exist is but the social manifestation of a natural phenomenon, *i.e.*, the existence of human beings endowed with a greater or lesser spirit of initiative on which, as on a more or less powerful stem are engrafted combinations of qualities and defects — of tendencies, to use a neutral word — in unlimited numbers. Just as with a forehead, two eyes, a nose, two lips, a chin, and two cheeks, framed up with hair or with the lack thereof, nature can produce fifteen hundred millions of different faces, so by combining relatively small numbers of tendencies nature can produce fifteen hundred millions of different characters." — Madariaga, *Anarchy or Hierarchy, op. cit.*, 112.

"That the pressure of economic conditions should have reduced this problem to one of classes, and the problem of classes to a mere matter of income, is natural but regrettable. Inequality is not to be measured along the vertical scale only and by the income unit only; it spreads sideways as much as up and down, in quality as much as in quantity, and the more dimensions it possesses the richer the life and the culture of the land and of the people which it graces with its presence." — *Ibid.*, 108, 109.
[22] Walter Lippmann, *The Good Society*. Boston, Massachusetts: Little, Brown and Co., 1937, 81, 82.
[23] Hatred of another person is never just. Sheen probably meant "understandably," not "justly." [Ed.]
[24] More accurately, the right to the equal opportunity to acquire and possess wealth. This does not, however, take away the rich man's God-given rights in what he owns. This cannot rightfully be taken away by human agency except for cause, by following due process, and offering just compensation. [Ed.]
[25] Again, Sheen probably meant "understandable" here rather than "justifiable," and, possibly, righteous "wrath" or "anger" instead of the deadly sin of envy. [Ed.]
[26] This is a reference to the numbers of professed religious (*i.e.*, priests, nuns, monks) who were killed by the "Republicans" (communists) during the Spanish Civil War. According to Archbishop Antonio Montero Moreno, the number was 6,832. See *Historia de la Persecucion Religiosa en España 1936-1939*. Madrid: Biblioteca de Autores Cristianos, 1961. [Ed.]

12. Liberty and Asceticism

TWENTY YEARS AGO the world had too little discipline;[1] today it has too much of the wrong kind. Under the old order of Liberalism, discipline was regarded as unjustified restraint, license was glorified as "self-expression," and mortification was frowned upon as a "survival of the Middle Ages." The freeman was he who was subject neither to prohibitions nor inhibitions. The young who left the lights and glamors of the world for the shades and shadows of the cross where saints are made, were presumed to have done so because they had been disappointed in love. The convent or the monastery were looked upon as religious Foreign Legions into which the young entered because they had lost their lovers. The truth was — they entered because they found their Lover. Morality to the Liberalist generation was not a relation of action to law and purpose, but a statistical average of the way men and women lived. Right was what the majority did; wrong was what the minority did not. Freedom of thought became so free that it became freedom from thought or thoughtlessness. If men in those days behaved with the same abandon and utter disregard of human purposes, as they thought, chaos would have been upon us long before this. They even rewrote the Gospels and all texts bidding men to "take up the cross daily"[2] and "lose your life to save it"[3] were rejected as antiquated and unsuitable to our times; the belief in the Divinity of Christ was presumed to have been eaten away by "the acids of modernity." At least Mr. Walter Lippmann told us so. Instead of adjusting their lives to dogma, men began to adjust dogmas to their lives. They suited religion and morality to the way they lived. God was made to dance to the tune of their new physics, and theology made to reel to the music of biology. Men were free, it was believed because they were no longer restrained.

Now, all this has changed. From a world of all freedom and no restraint, we have gone to a world of restraint and no freedom. From an order in which there was no self-denial, the world has reacted to a denial of self. The Totalitarian regimes are all founded on the ascetic principle: "Do Penance for the Kingdom of man is at hand."[4] Asceticism has become the fashion; men must now sacrifice both what they are and what they have. Individual liberty must be surrendered for the sake of the new myth: the race and the class. "Purges have become fashion." It is a fact that no political system in the course of the past 1,900 years has carried this asceticism as far as Soviet Fascism and Nazism. Indeed it is unlikely that it would have so successfully preached political asceticism had not Calvary's Cross of mortification cast its shadow upon the world. Under religion men had learned to be mortified for the sake of their eternal destiny. When they forgot religion, Marxism seized upon asceticism and bent men once more to its yoke, not for the sake of their souls but for the sake of greater production. Mortification once was the unmistakable mark of good men; Marx and Lenin made it the badge even of the evil.

The world was ready for such a recall to asceticism, for it had already been surfeited with the license of individualism. It was looking for something which would make demands upon the soul, and it found it in Marxism. Many things had to be given up in order to enter its kingdom. The angel with the flaming sword stood guard before its paradisical gates, bidding each one who would enter to surrender his personality for the sake of the collectivity. Absolute submission to the party line was ordered under penalty of a bullet in the back on Kremlin stairs; private productive property had to be surrendered as the condition of possessing all; even family had to be surrendered as a challenge to the State, in order that the worker might be the unit of the new order. Soviet Fascism came to use exactly the *same means* Christianity has always used, before for a totally different end. From now on it contended, men must be disciplined not for the sake of their souls, but for the sake of social wealth. Modern ears no longer hear the plea for "self-expression," or if they do, they hear it from liberal reactionaries. Today they are hearing the plea for violence, both from Christianity and its enemies of Soviet Fascism and Nazism. It is indeed a remarkable fact that Christianity no less than Communism preaches violence. Lenin said that he cared not if four-fifths of the world were bathed in blood so long as the other fifth was made Communist. Our Blessed Lord preached that the "Kingdom of Heaven is gained by violence and only the violent shall bear it away."[5] Eye must be plucked out, hands cut off, members maimed, a daily cross must be carried, and even life must be lost before entry can be made into His Kingdom.

But there the analogy ends, and up to this point it is quite superficial. The principal differences between the asceticism advocated by Soviet Fascism and the asceticism of Christianity are threefold. Firstly, Communist asceticism is *imposed;* Christian asceticism is *voluntary.* Consider private property. Neither the Communists nor the Carmelites, for example, own property. In both there is the asceticism of possession. At one time they both had it. The Communist had his taken away; the Carmelite gave hers up. In other words, the Communist *had* to take the "vow of poverty" in the sense that he may not own productive property, the Carmelite did not. The detachment in the first case was commanded; in the second case it was free. A Soviet Fascist of Moscow receiving a small salary at a nut and bolt factory today, does not look out upon the shop he owned in 1917 in the same way the Carmelite looks out upon her home. He looks back upon his shop with regret and wishes he could once more be responsible for productive property. With the Carmelite it is different. A few years ago when the cloister of a Carmelite convent was opened to visitors, one of them pointed to a beautiful home on the other side of the valley which belonged to a wealthy newspaper owner. "Sister," she said, "if, before you entered here, you could have lived in that home and had all that goes with it, would you have given it up for Carmel and its cross?" The Sister answered: "That was my home."

Communism does not believe in private property, therefore it says, no one shall own it. Everyone *must* take the vow of poverty. Such asceticism is the death of liberty. Our Blessed Lord recommended to the rich young man that he sell all he had and give to the poor, but He did not take away the young man's property by force. Communism does not believe in democracy in the sense that it permits only one Party to which everyone must submit. Quite different is the call of the Savior who bade the Apostles follow Him, but He did not purge the disciples of Capharnaum[6] as "Trotskyites" because they refused to walk with Him again or found His sayings "hard."[7]

Communism does not believe in God, therefore no one shall adore God. It imposes atheism as the last asceticism of the human spirit and denies in Article 124 of its Constitution the freedom of propagandizing religion. Our Lord on the Cross, in the face of the enemies of religion did not smite them dead, but prayed for them, for they knew not what they did. He left men free to be irreligious, but the irreligious Communists will not leave men free to be religious.

The asceticism of Communism leaves nothing to free choice; everything is imposed by force. They rend everyone else's garments, sprinkle ashes on everyone else's head, chastise everyone else's body and turn the nation into a vast madhouse where everyone has the vows without ever taking them. It is very much like Calvinism which held that a man was determined to heaven or hell independent of his merits. As God decreed, so his destiny was fixed regardless of whether he lived well or badly. Under such a fatalism, man was not free to be a saint or to be a devil. God made him what he is, not himself. Communism too is like Prohibition. The Prohibitionists did not want a glass of wine at dinner, so they decided no one else should have it. There is a common thread running through them all; Puritanism without dances, Prohibition without wine, and Communism without property. The masses all had to take the "vows" of the leaders whether they wanted to or not. Instead of asking man: "Will you take this woman as your lawful wife?" the new asceticism says: "*You will* take this woman as your lawful wife." Confronted with the problem of abuse they destroyed the use, and face to face with the fact of selfishness they took away everyone else's liberty. Like some vegetarians who would deny meat to anyone else, Communism forces its views down everyone else's throats, an expedient which proves profitable only to the unascetic Red leaders of the new asceticism.

The Church contends that if asceticism is forced it becomes tyranny. Our Lord never went about forcing men to take up a Cross because He took one, nor nailing them to it, because He willed to be fastened, nor snatching away wives and mothers from husbands and children because He had no family, nor abolishing wedding feasts because He had none, nor forcing everyone to sleep under starless skies because He had no roof. All these detachments He left to the free choice of His disciples saying, "Do you think you can drink of this chalice?"[8]

It is not so with modern ascetic. You either do what the Dictator dictates or you do not do at all; you either have a certain kind of blood flowing through your veins, or your blood may not flow at all within the borders of his empire; you either accept the State as the Church, or you suffer the consequences of making "politics" out of your religion; you either use your speech and your press to further their systems, or you go down to the supreme oblivion of death. Freedom ends when force begins. It is good and well to have discipline and mortification, but unless you leave each man free to do it, you destroy its value. A vow of obedience exacted by force is not a binding vow, any more than a promise to marry at the point of a gun is a valid contract. The restoration of asceticism is a consummation devoutly to be wished, but our last state will be worse than the first unless we leave it to the free assent of man. Taking away wives from husbands by force does not make them chaste, any more than confiscating productive property makes men devoid of the passion of greed. It is voluntary discipline the world needs and not an imposed discipline. The Church, for example, has recognized the sanctity of Simon Stylite[9] who spent most of his life perched on the top of a marble column away from the bustle of men, but the Church has never said that every man who wishes to be a saint must live on the pinnacle of a skyscraper. The Church canonized the Little Flower,[10] but refused to force any woman to enter a convent. The Church teaches that consecrated chastity is higher than the married state, but it will condemn the man who says marriage is wrong. The Church delights in her children who take the vow of poverty and surrender productive possessions of their own, but condemns Communism which says that personal ownership of productive property is wrong. The Church teaches temperance and praises the total abstainer, but rejects the reformer who says that liquor in itself is intrinsically bad. St. Thomas à Becket[11] as Archbishop wore a hair shirt under his gold and crimson in order that he might get the benefit of the hair shirt and the people might get the benefit of gold and crimson, but he never pulled hair shirts forcibly over the sheep of his flock. Briefly, Communistic asceticism, because it is forced, is *dispossession*; Christian asceticism, because it is voluntary is *liberation*.

This brings us to the second difference between Communistic or Nazi asceticism and Christian asceticism. The former asceticism is always on the same level, *i.e.*, it never lifts one into another kingdom; it only changes one's place in the same kingdom. Christian asceticism bids you die to time to live to eternity, and to die to the world to live to Christ. Communistic asceticism bids you die to time to live in time. It keeps you always on the same level and forever on the same plane. You mortify yourself to the economic only to find yourself again in the economic. You forcibly give up wealth, but only to be faced with its struggle under the name of privilege; you give up productive ownership only to end in consumptive ownership; you die the death of individual selfishness only to be incorporated to collective selfishness. This is extremely unsatisfying. We want to be more than we are when we mortify ourselves. The only reason for dying is to discover a new life. Easter must be more than a sunset on Good Friday. If we give up property we want something more than property for our surrender. All asceticism implies elevation to a new order, a brighter life, a nobler kingdom.

Such is the philosophy of Christian asceticism. Asceticism is not a sleep. You do not go to bed to wake up to a new job. You wake up beyond the need of laboring at all. Nature itself proclaims the lesson that the death of asceticism is a birth to a higher life. Plants die in order to live in the animal; animals die to live in the kingdom of man; and man dies to himself by mortification in order to live a Godlike life in Christ. "Unless you die to yourself you cannot live in My Kingdom."[12] In the Christian plan you die to this world to live in the next world, not to a bettered existence in this one. It is not worth passing through a revolution with its social upheaval and pillaging of tabernacles just for the sake of transferring the privilege of wealth from the envious Capitalists to the newly envious Commissars. But it is worth denying oneself all the pleasures of this world to be lifted into an order where there is no more blood to be shed, no more brothers to hate, for all are one in God who is Peace and Love. Purely economic adjustments and the transfer of titles of property from Capitalists to Communists is not worth the imposed asceticism. After all our enforced Golgothas and scourgings we wake up in the same bed in which we went to sleep, only the walls we gaze upon are now red instead of blue. Asceticism is hard even when voluntary, and anyone who practices it has a right to demand something more in return for it than a political upheaval and reshuffling of wealth. No man is going to deny himself very much if he is still going to be the same man. He wants to be different, to have new blood in his veins, new thoughts in his head, new brothers to love, new causes to serve, and no more battles to be fought. No earthly revolution is worth its cost. The revolutionists juggle and reshift the wealth but they do not cure the cause, for they merely substitute their avarices for someone else's. The Communist philosophy of violent asceticism is therefore nothing but snobbery — the cheap snobbery of wealth. Why should the masses undergo the travail and woes of a bloodshed just to find the money in someone else's pockets and the palaces in someone else's hands?

Someday the masses will see that such asceticism is not worth the price, for it gives only a religion of killing instead of a religion of rising from the dead. It purchases no new freedom, for the freedom of revolution ends too often in the negation of freedom. It did this in the French Revolution and it did it again in the Russian Revolution. America entered the World War to make the world safe for democracy and there is no one living today who can tell what the world gained by turning poppy fields into Haceldemas of blood.[13] We were not purged by the shedding of blood; rather were we almost drowned by the wailing of mothers' tears, as we woke up to new states wherein men were widowed of their rights and liberties. We dunged our battlefields with dead, but we reaped no harvest. We cut the body of civilization until it bled, but we did not heal. We crowned mankind with thorns but we gave him no halo of light; we left the world where we found it after all our sufferings and mortifications, because we went down to death not for the sake of a kingdom beyond earth, but merely for slogans, for commerce, and for power.

No asceticism is worthwhile which leaves us the same creatures, with the same passions, the same selfishness, and the same conceits. Surrender of inalienable rights, of property, of personal liberty, and of conscience, which the new asceticism demands is too high a price to pay for a mechanical or racial relation with our fellow men, and if we pay it, we are cheated. Man's happiness does not consist in having *more* of what he already has; he wants a state where he never has to ask for more. He does not want more food; he wants food which will dispense from hunger; a drink which will dispense from thirst; a mansion which will dispense with the rent collector. It is not a better world he wants, but a new world; not a more abundant life, but life abundantly; not life, but Living; not education, but Truth; not security, but Freedom. And not one of these lie here below, but only beyond in the Kingdom of God. Given that supernatural vocation of man, then asceticism even of the most violent character is worth the price, for it ushers us out of this mundane order into the efflorescence and perfection of our personality in the God for whom we were made. A revolution which turns a man inside out alone is worth effecting for "what doth it profit a man if he gain the whole world and lose his immortal soul?" Our Divine Savior who came to teach us this asceticism which lifts us out of this world, never preached it more fervently than when men asked Him to come down from the Cross.[14] "To come down" would have been to admit that man takes a cross only to walk the same earth again. To refuse to come down means that one takes a cross to leave this world. The revolution which ends by stepping down from a Cross and walking the earth again on Calvary is not a revolution, but a defeat. The real revolution demands so much detachment from the world that the very earth itself must consider us as dead and inter us into its womb. Through that momentary victory does the earth suffer its greatest defeat, as it gave up its dead on Easter when the King of kings walked in the newness of His Resurrection.

The final difference between the two asceticisms is that Communism believes in violence to neighbor, while Christianity believes in violence to oneself. Both believe in violence, but the violence of each issues in different objectives because inspired by different motives, love in the case of Christianity and hate in the case of Communism. Communism teaches the spirit of revolution, while Christianity teaches the revolution of the spirit. The violence of Communism is against others such as the "reactionaries," "Fascists," "Trotskyites," "Capitalists," "priests," "Christians." The violence of Christianity is against pride, egotism, selfishness, greed, avarices, concupiscence, and hate. The Communist purges his neighbor; the Christian mortifies himself. The Communist sees the mote in his neighbor's eye, but never the beam in his own. He mortifies his neighbor's liberty, but never his own license; he disciplines his neighbor's possessions, but never his own avarice; he scourges his neighbor's politics, but never his own intolerance. His swords are all directed outward, but never inward where the real trouble lies. This kind of asceticism which gives everyone else the aspirin when it has the headaches, and which cuts off everyone else's hand when the gangrene is in its own, is not the asceticism of salvation. The truest kind of reformation begins with self. The examination of one's own conscience is the hardest of all revolutions to begin and only saints have the courage to do it. Selfishness is not cured by Communism any more than putting all the toys of children in the same park cures the children of rickets. It is not property which causes our social disorders; it is the selfishness of those who own property; it is not money which is the root of evil, but the excessive desire of it. Hence all the revolutions in the world against institutions will never make a new world; they will only shift possessions from one exploiter to another. Neither will they do away with classes for whatever names you use, there will still be two classes left; the leaders and the led. Violence against neighbor and hate will reshuffle the classes but it will not do away with class conflict. It may get the foxes chasing the hounds instead of the hounds chasing the foxes, but it will not do away with the chase.

The only successful revolution, and it is one which can never be completely realized here below, is violence against the baser passions of self. The spirit of charity can make economic communism succeed, because it eliminates jealousy, vanity, strife, and avarice. Religious communities of nuns and religious orders of men are communistic in the broad sense that they share all things in common, own no productive property personally, but enjoy only its consumptive use. Communism of this kind works because love of God and love of neighbor are paramount. Lenin made the great mistake of trying to turn Russia into a monastery without charity. He wanted common ownership but without the spirit of love. Such an arrangement is just as impossible as honest bookkeeping without the virtue of justice. You cannot turn men loose in an orgy of hate against Capitalism and democracy and religion with the promise of booty and expect them to be peaceful and just and submissive once the booty is won, any more than you can initiate national health by spreading germs. If men are taught to lie during the regime of the Democratic Front, they will still want to lie under the dictatorship over the proletariat. Only when justice and charity are rooted in the souls of men can we expect any measure of social peace. This idea can be illustrated by the story of two monks, one of whom was attempting to explain to the others how quarrels arose in capitalist countries and how purges arose in the Soviet Fascist and other Fascist countries over property. One thumped down a stone and said: "This stone is mine." The other, full of a spirit of charity said: "All right, take it." The other said, "Oh, no. You must say, 'it is mine'; then we can quarrel about it and have our class conflict." So the second monk said: "It is mine," and the first answered, "All right, take it," and the whole fight ceased because there was charity. Both of them had been so used to using violence against themselves, that they were incapable of using it against their neighbor. Of such revolutions of the spirit peace and justice are born, but if we are only to revolutionize our neighbor and not ourselves, then we will revolutionize nothing. We will only lay waste the earth.

The question before the world today is not whether we will or will not be ascetic; rather it is which kind of asceticism will we practice? Will it be voluntary or will it be dictated? Will it use persons as means to the glorification of a race or a class, or will it exalt persons as the supreme value of the earth? Will it be for the Kingdom of God, or the kingdom of Caesar? Will it be to lift us to another and higher order, or will it be merely to change our positions in the same order? The selfishness of the world must be cured — both the individual selfishness of Liberalism and the totalitarian selfishness of Fascism and Communism. How cure it? There are only two choices open to us. Either we will cure our selfishness freely by mortification, or others will attempt to cure it for us by the destruction of our personality. Liberty is at stake in the choice. Mortification because it is personal, is free; Dictatorship because it is collective, is forced. Only by surrendering our selfishness voluntarily can we preserve our freedom. The asceticism of the cross is the condition of liberty, but no man can be forced to take the cross. That must be done voluntarily. That is why He came to teach us to take up a cross daily, preached that lesson by seemingly being its prisoner. Truth nailed to a cross compels nobody. Riven hands cannot be violent against neighbor; pierced feet cannot seek out the dissident; parched lips can but weakly preach to the agnostics. There was only the loving gesture of the eye to bid all men to come to that cross. If Crucified Truth were turned into coercive truth, all Christianity would have failed. Dictators believe that men can be forced into asceticism; they cannot. They can only be solicited into it. Selfishness must be surrendered; it cannot be conquered. And it will surrender to no Power except Love that is selfless enough to die that others might live. Only under the radiating asceticism of Calvary can selfishness be killed and liberty made to survive, and only on condition that modern man reverses the process by which he drove God out of the world and onto a gibbet will he find the freedom and peace he craves.

It is not the sinner we must liquidate; it is sin. It is not the Capitalist we must purge, but sinful Capitalism; it is not our neighbor we must hate, but ourselves for hating our neighbor, for the Kingdom of Heaven is gained by violence of this kind and only the violent shall bear it away.

Endnotes

[1] Sheen appears to be referring to the "Lost Generation" of the 1920s, noted for its rejection of traditional moral values in the wake of the First World War. [Ed.]

[2] Luke 9:23.

[3] Matt. 10:39.

[4] A twist on Matthew 3:2, "Repent, for the Kingdom of Heaven is at hand." Cf. Pope Paul VI, "If you want peace, work for justice," a twist on *Si vis pacem, para bellum*, "If you want peace, prepare for war" (Publius Flavius Vegetius Renatus, Prologo, Lib. III, *De Re Militari*). [Ed.]

[5] Matt. 11:12.

[6] Matt. 11:23.

[7] Matt. 19:11.

8 Matt. 20:22.

9 A Christian ascetic, *cir.* 388-459, who is reputed to have spent 37 years living on a raised platform ("pillar") near Aleppo in Syria. [Ed.]

10 St. Thérèsa of Lisieux (1873-1897), whose collection of autobiographical sketches, published as *The Story of a Soul* the year after her death, is considered a classic of Christian spirituality. [Ed.]

11 St. Thomas à Becket, Archbishop of Canterbury, "the Holy Blissful Martyr" (1118-1170), whose martyrdom at the probably unintended instigation of Henry II Plantagenet for opposing the growth and expansion of State power into areas formerly reserved exclusively to the Church is today, along with that of St. Thomas More, seen as a symbol of resistance to government tyranny. The pilgrimage to Canterbury to visit his shrine (dismantled and the wealth resulting from centuries of votive offerings confiscated by Henry VIII Tudor, who convicted St. Thomas posthumously of high treason) was one of the four great pilgrimages of the Middle Ages, along with Rome, Jerusalem, and Santiago de Compostella. [Ed.]

12 Luke 9:23-24.

13 Aramaic for "Field of Blood," more usually Aceldama or Akeldama, the Potter's Field where Judas Iscariot hanged himself and was buried. Matt. 27:7. [Ed.]

14 Matt. 27:40-44; Mark 15:30; Luke 23:39.

13. Freedom and Religion

THERE ARE TWO KINDS OF FREEDOM: freedom of *choice* and
freedom of *perfection*. Freedom of choice is the power of
the will to elicit or suspend its act of volition after the intellect has presented it with a particular good. This kind
of freedom implies a choice between at least two things;
e.g., shall I take spinach or onions for dinner? Freedom of
choice is liberty and implies the absence of constraint and
the power of self-determination.

But over and above the hundreds of free choices made
by the human soul, there is a higher kind of freedom;
namely, freedom of *perfection*. Freedom of choice refers to
particular goods, *e.g.*, health, power, success, content-
ment, ease, earthly knowledge, or immediate pleasure.
Freedom of perfection refers to the *ultimate* good; namely,
the attainment of perfect Truth for our intellect, perfect
Love for our will, and perfect Life for our existence. The
human person has a goal transcendent to the myriad
goals presented to it during life; namely, the possession of
God by whom it was made and in whom its happiness
consists.

Happiness follows upon the attainment of purpose. If a
pencil were conscious, it would be happy when it writes; if
the sun were conscious, it would be happy when it shines.
Now man, *as man* was made to know, love, and serve God.
In just the proportion that he attains that end, which is
his perfection, is he happy. Freedom of choice then is the
means to the end which is freedom of perfection. By making right choices we develop our personality in this world
and finally perfect it in the next world with God. Our personality is developed by the moral richness of our deliberate acts of choice and finally brought to its perfection the
moment it achieves union with its supreme Purpose. We
must not think of God as something wholly extrinsic to

our personality and think of obeying His law to please
Him as we might obey the law of a king or a president.
God is *our perfection*. What blooming is to a flower, that a
Godlike life is to our personality — the beginning of its
perfection. Freedom of choice is the *bridge*; Freedom of
perfection is the heavenly City. Freedom of choice implies
freedom *from* something *for* something. Freedom of choice
is not an end in itself, but only a means to an end, the last
of which is the relative perfection of man in the absolute
perfection of God.

In the light of the foregoing, it is easy to see the falsity
of the two liberties with which we began this book; namely, Liberty of Indifference and Liberty of Necessity. Liberalism, or Liberty of Indifference, insisted on freedom of
choice and forgot freedom of perfection. Totalitarianism
placed freedom of perfection not in God but in an earthly
dictator set up as God, and thus destroyed freedom of
choice. Liberalism was right in insisting on the right of
choice but wrong in forgetting why it wanted to be free.
Totalitarianism is right in insisting on purpose, but
wrong in making that purpose production as in Russia,
race consciousness as in Germany, and national consciousness as in Italy, instead of making it the complete
perfection of each man in God. Liberalism killed the end
of living; Totalitarianism killed both the end and the
means to it. Liberalism thwarted personality by restrict-
ing the development of man to individual acts of choice,
by making each man a law unto himself. Totalitarianism
frustrates personality by incarnating the end of man in
the will of a dictator and identifying the perfection of each
man with obedience to that arbitrary will. Liberalism forgot God; Totalitarianism forgets freedom and makes Caesar a God. Liberalism forgot freedom of perfection; Totalitarianism forgets both freedom of perfection and freedom
of choice, and by ignoring choice ignores the right of each
man to perfect himself as something beyond the race, the
nation, and the class.

Why is the Church opposed to both Liberalism and Totalitarianism? Because both distort the true nature of
man, and because both separate that which should not be

separated; namely, free choice as a means to the end which is self-perfection. Freedom is both a proving ground and a goal. God joined choice and perfection together; to tear them asunder is to do just as much violence to man as to separate his eye from color or his ear from sound. We were not sent into this world to choose in order to choose again and then to die without ever having made a supreme choice. To make freedom consist only in choice is to put man at the meeting place of a hundred roads, none of which go anywhere. Unless the road leads somewhere, there is no reason for taking it. If a city lies a thousand miles away then a hundred different roads to that city become meaningful. Courtship looks to marriage and choice looks to goals, purposes, and perfection, all of which liberalism forgot.

Neither were we sent into this world to have a Dictator stand at the crossroads of civilization and say, "you shall take this road and this road only, which leads to the increase of my authority and force; to choose any other road than the one I dictate means the surrender of life." Such a philosophy of life makes perfection of man reside in the totality of the race or the class instead of in himself, and it is man who must be free, not the herd.

The reason for so much unhappiness in the world today is the substitution of purposes instead of a purpose; petty, trifling goals instead of the eternal goal. Men were made to fly to the heavens but they clip their wings and grovel in the dust. There arises a tremendous disproportion between the Life, Truth, and Love for which they were made, and the fleeting pleasures, half-truths, and satieties with which they are momentarily satisfied. Modern man lives in a two-dimensional universe of length and breadth whereas he was meant to grow upward to the Divine in the three-dimensional universe of the spirit. Instead of unifying all his energies, political, social, intellectual, emotional, spiritual, and physical under one command and for one purpose, he allows each of them to run pell-mell in any direction, disrupting the unity of his being, and creating a state of civil war within his own heart making it as complex as the devil, who when asked his name replied: his name was "legion."[1]

Riot, confusion worse confounded, and total absence of peace make a soul like a planet which, when it runs out of its orbit, burns itself out in space. Man's only temporary escape is to drown himself in excitement and noise, for he cannot bear to be alone with himself and his conscience which carries on an unbearable repartee. He refuses to admit he has not finished the pattern of life. If he would only be strong enough to see his failures he could still be a freeman for there is one thing in the world worse than a sin, and that is a man who refuses to believe he is a sinner. There is hope for the man who has lost his way and wants to find it, but there is none for the blind who never want to see, nor the slave who wills never to be free.

Consider now the man who unfailingly chooses from the quiver of his life those good arrows which can be shot to the target of everlasting union with God. Will a time ever come when that man will no longer have freedom of choice and yet be free? Yes, when he attains the purpose of life in heaven. Once we perfect our personality by union with God we will no longer be free to choose because there will be nothing left to choose. There will be nothing left to desire for the Perfect leaves nothing to be desired. We cannot remain indifferent to the perfect; in the sight of it we become its slave; it is not the slavery of domination but the sweet slavery of love.

In this world we remain indifferent to the thousand and one good things presented to our choice, because none of them possess a perfection which can command our will. They leave us "cold" because they are not perfectly good. The piece of steel has affinity for the magnet and the weak magnet has attraction for the piece of steel, but the "pull" of the magnet is not strong enough, and the piece of steel remains indifferent to its attraction. So in life. The good things of life have some affinity for us inasmuch as they participate in goodness, truth, and love and life, but they have such a small fraction of these perfections that they do not compel us to choose them. But once we are brought into contact with the magnetic field of perfect Life and Truth and Love which is God, we fly to it as the bar of steel to the electric magnet, and in union with it do we find the satisfaction of our soul's desire and the fullness of our personality. It was God that we always wanted.

Take another example. A human heart is free to set its choice upon any other human heart as the object of its enduring affection. It is not forced to choose this person rather than that. But once the choice is freely made, it no longer wants to be free to choose. It spurns indifference and rejects the possibility that there might be any other. The perfection of choice to such a heart consists in lifelong companionship with the object of affection, and it considers its greatest freedom to be the slave of that person for life. To a higher degree, when the soul by right moral choice attains the Goodness which is God, it cannot not love. There is nothing left to be desired. It becomes the "slave" of Divine Love and yet is perfectly free because one with Him who can do all things. Thus does freedom of choice end in the freedom of perfection of our personality in God. Thus do we leave behind the false freedom to disobey His law, for though it is a mark of freedom to be able to sin, it is still greater freedom to be able not to sin, but only to love.

The freedom man craves is neither in the indefinite choice of indifferent goals, nor in the surrender of choice to the kingdom of earth. He seeks to make a choice which will dispense him from the necessity of choosing again. He wants a freedom which will give escape from the paradox of the chase and the capture.

Here in this life we are pulled between the two. We cannot have both together. There is joy in the chase for with it comes the prospect of a future good; there is joy in the capture for with it comes the possession of that good. But the capture takes away the thrill of the chase and the chase is maddening if it never ends in capture. Courtship ends in marriage and marriage ends courtship. The bagging of the game ends the hunt. No one is ever thirsty at the border of the well.

The incompatibility of chase and capture in this world manifests itself in the disillusionment which comes with the realization of our earthly desires. A material desire, once it is realized to some extent is destroyed. We look forward to some position or office or state of life and somehow or other it does not quite come up to our expectation. The reason is our desires borrow infinity from the soul, *e.g.*, I can imagine a mountain of gold, but I will never see one. When realized the desire is concrete, cribbed, materialized. Then arises the sense of disproportion between the ideal we conceived and the ideal we realized. Such is the reason for disappointment. To realize on this earth all we ever hoped for is indeed to mark us as failures, for we set our hopes too low and made our ideals too base. We are victims of disenchantment because broken with satiety and disgusted with what we have while still hankering for what we have not. Our ennui is really our unsatisfied hunger. The pessimist is one who is full of satiety of his own desire. He renounces food because stones do not satisfy; renounces thirst because he is still thirsty after salt.

True happiness is in the combination of both chase and capture. But how combine the chase and capture so that the chase will end in the capture but the capture will never mean the end of the chase? This is possible only to those souls who have lived for and found God. Once we attain the rapture of God we capture something so infinite that it will take an eternity of chase to sound the depths of its Life and Truth and Love and in that union of both capture and chase will be our happiness.

It was to give us this noble concept of freedom that the Son of God descended into our historical order and said to us: "If you continue steadfast in My Word, you shall be really My disciples, and shall know the truth, and the truth shall make us free. . . . If the Son sets you free, you shall be free indeed."[2] The knowledge of this truth is the knowledge of the purpose of living, for unless we know why we are living, there is no use in living. With that right knowledge of man comes the means to attain that end; namely, grace of that same Christ who gave us His Body and Blood that we might have life abundantly. The center of our being then is not in ourselves, but in God;

the secret of our freedom then is not in choice but in Goodness!

The greatest obstacle to the attainment of freedom in our civilization is a want of the sense of guilt. We all feel injured; but few of us ever feel guilty. The modern world always puts the blame on someone else, never on to its abuse of choice which is the foundation of guilt. In more Christian language we are not humble. Humility is dependence — dependence on God, just as Pride is independence of God. Humility is the cure of our self-love because it is the Truth of our worthlessness, of and by ourselves apart from God. Humility is not submission to the world nor passive resignation to its violence. On the contrary it is the refusal to submit to the world; it is the keeping ourselves spiritually free on the inside by consciousness of the goal of life, even though a thousand bars wall our body in. Freedom is in the spirit; not in matter. It is lost by a descent to the earth. That is why they who crucified our Lord asked Him to come down from the cross. No word in all the world signifies slavery better than the word *down*. Down to earth! down to kingdoms of Satan! down to security; down to Caesar; down to hate.

While they were shouting "down," there was ringing out over Calvary's hills the echo of another word He had spoken in anticipation of His Cross. "If I be lifted *up*, I will draw all things to Myself." In these two words "down" and "up" is hidden the problem of freedom. The loss of freedom is always a downward movement — down to earth with its choices. True liberty consists not in what we demand of God; namely, that He come down, but what God demands of us; namely, that we come up. The purchase of freedom is always an upward movement — up to Truth! up to the Goal of Life! up to Perfection! up to the flowering of personality! up to the freedom of the Spirit! even when hanging on a cross. Up! Up! Up! to God!

Endnotes

---

[1] Mark 5:9.
[2] John 8:31, 32, 36.

Selected Bibliography

Papal Encyclicals

Leo XIII, *Humanum Genus* ("On Freemasonry"), 1884.

Leo XIII, *Immortale Dei* ("On the Christian Constitution of States"), 1885.

Leo XIII, *Libertas Praestantissimum* ("On the Nature of Human Liberty"), 1888.

Leo XIII, *Rerum Novarum* ("On Capital and Labor"), 1891.

Leo XIII, *Graves de Communi Re* ("On Christian Democracy"), 1901.

Pius XI, *Quadragesimo Anno* ("On the Restructuring of the Social Order"), 1931.

Pius XI, *Divini Redemptoris* ("On Atheistic Communism"), 1937.

John XXIII, *Mater et Magistra* ("On Christianity and Social Progress"), 1961.

John Paul II, *Centesimus Annus* ("On the Hundredth Anniversary of *Rerum Novarum*"), 1991.

Books

Agar, Herbert, *Land of the Free*. New York: Houghton Mifflin Co., 1935.

Ashford, Robert H. A., *Binary Economics: The New Paradigm*. Lanham, Maryland: University Press of America, 1999.

Bales, Kevin, *Disposable People: New Slavery in the Global Economy*. Berkley, California: University of California Press, 2004.

Bellarmine, Robert, *De Laicis, or, The Treatise on Civil Government*. New York: Fordham University Press, 1928.

Belloc, Hilaire, *An Essay on the Restoration of Property*. New York: Sheed and Ward, 1936.

Belloc, Hilaire, *The Great Heresies*. New York: Sheed and Ward, 1937.

Berle, Adolf A., and Means, Gardiner C., *The Modern Corporation and Private Property*. New York: Macmillan and Co., 1940.

Black's Law Dictionary. St. Paul, Minnesota: West Publishing Company, 1951.

Borne, Étienne and Henry, François, *Le Travail et L'Homme*. Paris: Desclée de Brouwer, 1937; translated as *A Philosophy of Work*. New York: Sheed and Ward, 1938.

Briefs, Goetz, *The Proletariat: A Challenge to Western Civilization*. New York: McGraw-Hill Book Company, Inc., 1937.

Cahill, Rev. E., *The Framework of the Christian State*. Dublin, Éire: M. H. Gill and Son, 1932.

Chesterton, Gilbert Keith, *The Well and the Shallows*. New York: Sheed and Ward, 1935.

Cobbett, William, *A History of the Protestant Reformation in England and Ireland* (1827). Rockford, Illinois: TAN Books and Publishers, Inc., 1988.

Crook, J. A., *Law and Life of Rome, 90 B.C. - A.D. 212*. Ithaca, New York: Cornell University Press, 1967.

Crosskey, William W., *Politics and the Constitution in the History of the United States*. Chicago, Illinois: University of Chicago Press, 1953.

Dimitrov, Georgi, *The Working Class Against Fascism*. London: Modern Books, Ltd., 1935.

Fanfani, Amintore, *Catechism of Catholic Social Teaching*. Westminster, Maryland: The Newman Press, 1960.

Fanfani, Amintore, *Catholicism, Protestantism, and Capitalism.* New York: Sheed and Ward, 1939.

Ferree, Rev. William J., S.M., Ph.D., *Introduction to Social Justice.* New York: Paulist Press, 1948.

George, Henry, *Progress and Poverty.* New York: The Schalkenbach Foundation, 1935.

Greaney, Michael D., *The Restoration of Property: A Reexamination of a Natural Right.* Arlington, Virginia: Economic Justice Media, 2012.

Hoffman, Ross, *Tradition and Progress.* Milwaukee, Wisconsin: Bruce Publishing Company, 1938.

Jerrold, Douglas, *The Future of Freedom.* London: Sheed and Ward, 1938.

Kelso, Louis O. and Adler, Mortimer J., *The Capitalist Manifesto.* New York: Random House, 1958.

Kelso, Louis O. and Adler, Mortimer J., *The New Capitalists: A Proposal to Free Economic Growth from the Slavery of Savings.* New York: Random House, 1961.

Keynes, John Maynard, *A Treatise on Money, Volume I: The Pure Theory of Money.* New York: Harcourt, Brace and Company, 1930.

Kurland, Norman G., Brohawn, Dawn K., and Greaney, Michael D., *Capital Homesteading for Every Citizen: A Just Free Market Solution for Saving Social Security.* Arlington, Virginia: Economic Justice Media, 2004.

Lippmann, Walter, *The Good Society.* Boston: Little, Brown and Co., 1937.

Locke, John, *Two Treatises of Government.* Cambridge, UK: Cambridge University Press, 1988.

Madariaga, Salvador de, *Anarchy or Hierarchy.* New York: Macmillan, 1937.

Hamilton, Alexander, Madison, James, Jay, John, *The Federalist Papers* (1787). New York: Penguin Books (Signet Classics), 2003.

Mark, Karl and Engels, Friedrich, *The Communist Manifesto.* London: Penguin Books, 1967.

Moulton, Harold G., *The Formation of Capital*. Washington, DC: The Brookings Institution, 1935.

Moulton, Harold G., *The New Philosophy of Public Debt*. Washington, DC: The Brookings Institution, 1943.

O'Brien, George, *An Essay on Medieval Economic Teaching*. London: Longmans, Green and Co., 1920.

Rager, Rev. John Clement, S.T.D., *The Political Philosophy of Blessed Robert Bellarmine*. Washington, DC: Catholic University of America Press, 1926.

Rommen, Heinrich A., *The Natural Law*. Indianapolis, Indiana: Liberty Fund, Inc., 1998.

Rommen, Heinrich A., *The State in Catholic Thought*. St. Louis, Missouri: B. Herder Book Company, 1947.

Roosevelt, Nicholas, *A New Birth of Freedom*. New York: Charles Scribner's Sons, 1938.

Ryan, John A., *A Living Wage: Its Ethical and Economic Aspects*. New York: Grosset and Dunlap, Publishers, 1906.

Sheen, Fulton J., *The Cross and the Crisis*. Milwaukee, Wisconsin: Bruce Publishing Company, 1938.

Spencer, Herbert, *Social Statics, or, The Conditions Essential to Human Happiness Specified and the First of Them Developed*. New York: D. Appleton and Co., 1870.

Strachey, John, *The Theory and Practice of Socialism*. New York: Random House, 1936.

Tawney, R. H., *Equality* (1929). New York: Rowman and Littlefield, 1964.

Thurman, W. Arnold, *The Folklore of Capitalism*. New Haven, Conn.: Yale University Press, 1937.

Index

227

Other Books from Economic Justice Media

The Emigrant's Guide (1829). William Cobbett. A unique look at economic justice in early 19th century America through democratic access to capital ownership. xliv, 210 pp., ISBN 978-0-944-997-01-7, $20.00.

A Plea for Peasant Proprietors (1848, 1874). William Thomas Thornton. The classic and financially feasible plan to end the Great Famine in Ireland (1846-1852). xxii, 332 pp,, ISBN 978-0-944997-10-9, $25.00.

The Formation of Capital (1935). Harold G. Moulton. A counter proposal to the debt-backed Keynesian financing of the New Deal. This book laid the groundwork for the financing proposals in Louis Kelso's and Mortimer Adler's *The Capitalist Manifesto* (1958) and *The New Capitalists* (1961). xix, 208 pp., ISBN 978-0-944997-08-6, $20.00.

Capital Homesteading for Every Citizen (2004). Norman G. Kurland, *et al.* A blueprint for change presenting a policy manual for implementing the Just Third Way above and beyond both capitalism and socialism. xxiv, 331 pp., ISBN 978-0-944997-00-0, $18.00.

In Defense of Human Dignity (2008). Michael D. Greaney. A collection of essays first published in *Social Justice Review*, the official journal of the Central Bureau of the Catholic Central Union of America in St. Louis, Missouri. x, 303 pp., ISBN 978-0-944997-02-4, $20.00.

Supporting Life: The Case for a Pro-Life Economic Agenda (2010). Michael D. Greaney. Presents a common sense case that removing any economic incentive for abortion would greatly strengthen the Pro-Life movement. iii, 112, ISBN 978-0-944997-05-5, $10.00.

The Restoration of Property: A Reexamination of a Natural Right (2012). Michael D. Greaney. Why it is unnecessary either to confine capital ownership to a private sector elite or to a government bureaucracy, and how widespread capital ownership can be attained by shifting the financing of new capital formation from past to future savings. 127 pp., ISBN 978-0-944997-07-9, $10.00.

The Center for Economic and Social Justice

The Center for Economic and Social Justice (CESJ), a think tank established in 1984, promotes a free enterprise approach to global economic and social justice based on the natural law common to all faiths and philosophies through expanded capital ownership. CESJ is a non-profit, non-partisan, interfaith, all-volunteer organization with an educational and research mission.

CESJ's global membership shares a common set of moral values and works together toward a common purpose, transforming good ideas into effective action.

Building upon the ideals of the American Revolution — which was really a "New World" revolution to spread political democracy globally — CESJ focuses on extending economic empowerment to all. Going beyond the mere rhetoric of empowerment, CESJ has developed a common-sense, comprehensive proposal — the Capital Homestead Act — to liberate every person economically. To build equity with efficiency at the workplace, CESJ has developed a management system for corporations of the 21st Century known as "Justice-Based Management" and "Justice-Based Leadership."

CESJ's macro- and micro-economic concepts and applications are derived from the economic theories and principles of economic justice developed by the late lawyer-economist Louis Kelso and the Aristotelian philosopher Mortimer Adler. Combined with the ideas of Social Justice developed by Pius XI and refined by one of CESJ's founders, the late philosopher Rev. William Ferree, these ideas offer a new paradigm for the world of the 21st Century. We call this new paradigm — which transcends the power- and ownership-concentrating wage systems of traditional capitalism and traditional socialism — "the Just Third Way." For membership information and a list of free publications in electronic format (including the best-selling *Curing World Poverty* from 1994), visit:

http://www.cesj.org